BATMAN BEGINS

also by Christopher Nolan

MEMENTO & FOLLOWING

of related interest

THE MAKING OF MEMENTO
by James Mottram

BATMAN BEGINS

screenplay by
CHRISTOPHER NOLAN
and
DAVIS S. GOYER

story by
DAVIS S. GOYER

Batman created by
BOB KANE

faber and faber

First published in 2005
by Faber and Faber Limited
3 Queen Square London WC1N 3AU
Published in the United States by Faber and Faber Inc.
an affiliate of Farrar, Straus and Giroux LLC, New York

Typeset by Country Setting, Kingsdown, Kent CT14 8ES
Printed in England by Mackays of Chatham plc, Chatham, Kent

The rights of Christopher Nolan and David S. Goyer
to be identified as authors of this work
have been asserted in accordance with Section 77
of the Copyright, Designs and Patents Act 1988

Storyboards drawn by Martin Asbury and James Cornish

A CIP record for this book
is available from the British Library

ISBN 0-571-22994-8

2 4 6 8 10 9 7 5 3 1

Contents

Introduction

JAMES MOTTRAM

Should I bury the past out there with my parents, Alfred?
(Bruce Wayne)

Like Bruce Wayne's return to Gotham City, constructing his crime-fighting alter ego Batman from the ashes of his past, to the casual observer Christopher Nolan's *Batman Begins* appears to be a process of reinvention. After the no-budget entrapment tale *Following* (1998), the mind-bending meta-*noir Memento* (2000) and the remake of the Norwegian police procedural *Insomnia* (2002), Nolan's decision to resurrect Warner Bros. Pictures' most lucrative franchise initially seemed to be a departure from the films with which he has made his name. To borrow the words of Henri Ducard, Wayne's mentor during his seven-year absence from Gotham: 'You have become truly lost.'

The end result proves that he has done anything but succumb to the formulaic fare studios are often guilty of making. Aware that the vast playground a $100 million-plus movie offers is simply a larger canvas to paint on, Nolan – not unlike when Bryan Singer adapted Marvel Comics' *X-Men* for the big-screen – uses the blockbuster framework to further his own thematic obsessions. Just as billionaire Bruce Wayne is haunted by the past, following the murder of his parents in front of him as a child, so Nolan finds ghosts from his first three films returning for his fourth.

With the screenplay co-written by David S. Goyer, in retrospect a character like Bruce Wayne is tailor-made for Nolan's interests. As with *Memento*'s Leonard, events have trapped Wayne into a cycle of violence and vengeance. Both are emotionally hollow characters, though single-minded in their pursuit of justice. Compare Wayne also to Will Dormer, the detective at the heart of *Insomnia*, who likewise treads a delicate moral line between right and wrong. Nolan remains fascinated by the negative psychological effects of upholding law and order; and, as Wayne says, 'My anger outweighs my guilt.'

Once more, Nolan centres on the notion of identity. Just as we are forced to reconsider the memory-addled Leonard in *Memento* with the revelation that he's a relentless killer, *Batman Begins* asks us to reassess Wayne in light of his actions as a vigilante. 'As a symbol I can be incorruptible,' Wayne tells his faithful butler Alfred. Yet, as demonstrated when Batman ties Gotham crime-lord Carmine Falcone to a spotlight to first project the image of a bat into the night-sky, sometimes a symbol is not what it seems.

Earlier, he tells childhood friend Rachel, 'I'm not one of your good people,' after he sets out to kill the man who murdered his parents. Driven to overcome his fears, his subsequent odyssey sees him travel the world to understand the criminal mind. If he seeks 'the means to fight injustice', as taught him by Ducard and Rā's al Ghūl (the mysterious leader of a Ninja cult known as the League of Shadows), the residue of his flirtation with felons lives on. Like the criminals he fights in Gotham, Wayne's Batman guise must live outside the law, with only Sergeant Gordon acting as an ally on the inside. 'It's what you do that defines you,' Rachel tells him; by the conclusion, he will understand what she means.

As far back as *Following*, Nolan – via the figure of burglar Cobb – has shown us characters that excel in disguising their true intentions. Wayne, with his playboy exterior as much a disguise as his cape and costume, is not the only character who isn't what he seems. Ducard, as we discover, has another identity, revealed in the third act. Like Wayne, Falcone operative Dr. Jonathan Crane dons a mask to change his persona to Scarecrow.

Just as *Batman Begins* bears the thematic hallmarks of a Nolan film, so there are other links. Bit roles for *Following*'s Lucy Russell and Jeremy Theobald are complemented by significant supporting roles for *Memento*'s Mark Boone Jr, as Gordon's corrupt partner, and Larry Holden, as District Attorney Carlton Finch. Meanwhile, Nolan's wife Emma Thomas returns as his producer. Reuniting with Wally Pfister, his cinematographer on *Memento* and *Insomnia*, Nolan's production designer on the latter, Nathan Crowley, is also once again called upon.

More in line with the work of Frank Miller, whose graphic novels took the original Batman character into bleaker territory, Nolan's reworking of Batman is more like a complete overhaul. He eschews the high-camp theatrics particularly prevalent in the ABC 1960s TV series starring Adam West and the four preceding feature films – Tim Burton's *Batman* (1989) and *Batman Returns* (1992), and Joel Schumacher's *Batman Forever* (1995) and *Batman & Robin* (1997). Respecting, though not in awe, of the Batman mythology, Nolan does not veer so far from the traits of the character that he becomes unrecognizable. If the Batmobile, Batcave and Batsuit are all grounded in a reality distinct from what Burton and Schumacher gave us, Nolan still hits expected marks. Only this time, a signature line like 'I'm Batman' – used so sparingly, it's only heard once – has a potency its predecessors squandered.

As he notes below, in an interview I conducted with him at Pinewood Studios, two months before its June 2005 release, he expands the scale of the film in the final act. From the burning of Wayne's mansion to multiple police cars pursuing the Batmobile to the subway-bound finale, Nolan's *Batman Begins* delivers spectacle in spades, though never at the expense of story. With the reappearance of Rā's al Ghūl, whose organization has always burned civilizations to the ground when they become too decadent, Gotham City is threatened with being overcome after the water system is poisoned with a fear toxin.

If there is an element of James Bond gadgetry to the weapon needed to vaporize the water supply and induce the poison into the lungs of Gotham inhabitants, it's not to the detriment of the end result. Rather, it ties into the overriding theme of fear that is in the opening sequence and runs through every frame of the film. As the city descends into chaos, with the public experiencing horrific hallucinations courtesy of the toxin, Nolan allows the good people of Gotham literally to confront their fears – as Bruce Wayne has done all along. If the Batman legend has it that he must save the day, Nolan ensures the conclusion is as unsettling and downbeat as it can be. For a comic book film, *Batman Begins* is anything but two-dimensional.

London, May 2005

Christopher Nolan

INTERVIEWED BY JAMES MOTTRAM

JAMES MOTTRAM What's your own interest in Batman? Were you a comic-book fan?

CHRIS NOLAN Well, first and foremost I know Batman from the TV show, from when I was four or five years old. At that age, you don't realize how tongue-in-cheek and camp it all is. You take it seriously – and I loved the character. It says quite a lot about the elemental nature of the character that it can reach you through different interpretations, like the TV show – even though it was so kitsch and silly in a way. There's still something about that character, something about who he is and what he does, that comes through. It's part of everybody's up-bringing – I was watching it ten years after it had gone off air.

Were you aware of Frank Miller's work, such as Batman: Year One *and* The Dark Knight Returns, *that took the character into a much darker arena?*

Yeah, very much. I've always been more of a movie person than a comic person. But, at the same time, I had read the Batman comics and read them a lot. And in the 1980s I had read some of the key graphic novels coming out like *The Dark Knight Returns* and *Batman: Year One*. In terms of tone, and in terms of the notion that you could recreate for yourself a serious interpretation of the character . . . [it was] like the way you felt about the character when you were five years old. Frank Miller was doing it for grown-ups, really. That was quite exciting, it put you back into that childlike appreciation of the magic of character. Certainly, his work was a big influence on the tone of the film.

What did you make of the preceding films, notably by Tim Burton?

I think the first film has its place in film history; what Tim Burton did could certainly be considered visionary – but it didn't speak to me personally. It's not a great favourite of mine. It wasn't my Batman. It didn't speak to me on that level, even though I appreciated all the skill and artistry of it. It wasn't the Batman film I'd wanted to see, in terms of a film that showed his origin story. I felt like there was a version of *Batman* that never got made in 1979 – ten years before. When Dick Donner made *Superman* in 1978, it seems odd that they didn't do *Batman* in that same way – with that same epic sensibility.

You must have read Miller's books around the time of the 1989 Batman, *and already been thinking in the opposite direction to Burton . . .*

Yeah, it was right around that time. The thing with Burton is that he had the challenge of convincing a cinema audience that you could have a 'cool' Batman film. Convincing an audience who remembers that the TV show was ridiculous. And he did it, he succeeded. The way he did it was to make the entire world that he lives in – Gotham – as peculiar and extraordinary as Batman is. So he fits in with that hyper-real, hyper-stylized universe on its own terms. That then convinced everybody that you could have a 'cool' Batman film. So that isn't a hurdle that we have to get over with this film and, because of that, we are more free to treat the world around him as more ordinary and so allow his extra-ordinary nature to stand out. For me, it was very important that the audience watching the film would feel for people in Gotham – Batman is as extraordinary a figure for them as he is for us in the audience.

You're not giving us a gothic Gotham here . . .

It's gritty. It's not glamorous. In so far as it has a *noir*-ish quality to it, it's not a caricatured version of that. We just tried to shoot it in the same way you'd shoot any contemporary thriller. We don't stylize it to the point where the audience is noticing it – but you want a certain amount of mood in it. That was the guiding principle that Wally [Pfister, cinematographer] was following.

The redesign of the Batmobile is your most radical re-imagining. How do you explain that?

For me, even before we first wrote the script, we designed the Bat-mobile because I wanted to show that to the studio. I felt that would immediately explain to everybody the differences between approaches in the past and what we were doing. The Batmobile – even in the comics, but especially in the movies . . . well, it got frozen in time in the 1960s, I think. The car they adapted into the Batmobile for the TV show was a cutting-edge state-of-the-art car for that time – all cars had fins then and it became this retro look. So every Batmobile you've ever seen since then has had this styling of an older car. But if you look at the older comics, it was a contemporary vehicle but more extraordinary and more heightened. That's what the Batmobile should be. It should be a contemporary vehicle. It doesn't make any sense in the real world for Batman to stick goofy fins on his car. I firmly believe that our vehicle is the equivalent of what the Batmobile was in the late 1950s. It needed to be moved on.

Was that the same for the costume?

Yes. Though that required far less shifting. What they did with the costume in the 1980s was actually very contemporary and hi-tech, and had a huge influence on costume design in films from then on. So we just advanced from there. The only big change we've made is the use of the cape, as it features in the graphic novels. We came up with special fabric to do that and blow it around. It's a nightmare to try and get it to move the way it does in the comics, but we felt very strongly that we wanted it to do that. So our costume is matt black, and the cape is matt black and it's long and it flows.

Compared to, say, Sam Raimi's Spider-Man, *where he sketches out his costume, almost as a joke, your Batman builds his outfit very methodically . . .*

When you're telling the origin story of the character, if you're going to do it in a realistic fashion you have to take on that challenge and it's incredibly different. I really enjoyed the first forty-five minutes of *Spider-Man*, and it got to the bit with the costume and I just thought it was a complete sidestep. They knew they didn't want to have Aunt May sewing it, as she did in the comics, but they didn't have an alternative. They just took the leap into the fully-fledged costume. I felt that because we were determined to tell the story in a realistic way we had to bite the bullet. We got everything in place and the one thing I couldn't figure out was the mask; then I suddenly thought – you pull it apart and you have the ears separate from the head shape and you order it through different companies. [My co-writer] David Goyer came up with this idea about ordering the boots through this company in Malaysia – though I said you'd have to order tons of them. I've never seen that done before, explaining the origins of the costume. They make a joke about it in one of the Batman films where someone says, 'I like your tailor,' implying that Alfred has made the costume. And it's this latex thing and that's ludicrous. It was not good enough.

How did your collaboration with David S. Goyer come about?

How it worked was I'd gone to the studio and said what I'd wanted to do with the film and the basic idea of the story, which was drawn from what I knew of the origin stories from the comics – and I was certainly no expert. So I had the basic idea of dealing with the origin story and the seven years where Bruce goes around the world. I was looking for a writer to do a first draft, one who was very knowledgeable about comics, more than I was. I felt that the first draft needed to set us on the right track, in terms of the myth of Batman, the mythic quality and the iconography, and with all of the things we needed in there. David Goyer had some great initial thoughts on who the villain would be, how the villain could relate to the origin story – so I got very excited about working with him. He was about to direct *Blade: Trinity*, so he had a very small window of time. We met for a couple of months and talked through the story and he came up with a story outline based on us thrashing around ideas and me saying what I wanted in the film. Then, he – within seven or eight weeks – provided a first draft, gave that to me and then had to go off and do his thing. So I took it from that point and did another eight drafts.

Did he come back and work with you again?

No, he was actually busy the whole time. But I would call him up and talk to him from time to time about things that I was changing, ask his advice on certain things where I was departing from the first draft, in terms of how it related to the comic mythology. He was always a good sounding board but it had to be long-distance.

So it was different from the way you worked with Hillary on Insomnia?

It was similar at the beginning in that when David was doing his draft, he would show me things and we would talk about things. So we had quite a collaborative period there – but then he had to go off. So it wasn't until we'd already shot most of the film that he was able to come back.

So it was David who suggested the villains?

Yes. Rā's al Ghūl was not a villain I was familiar with. As soon as he mentioned him, I went back and researched him and read a lot of the 1970s comics he appears in, in the Neal Adams/Dennis O'Neil period. That's a period of comic-book lore that draws very much from the James Bond films of the time. So Rā's al Ghūl has a lot of similarities / affinities with the Bond villains of the 1970s – such as Hugo Drax from *Moonraker*.

In the comics, he revitalizes himself regularly to increase his life expectancy . . .

He does, but it's sort of cloaked in pseudo-science in the comics. So even with that, he's still a pretty grounded character. He seemed perfect for me. You're looking for a Bond villain in a sense because you're looking for a villain who is colourful and interesting, and has a degree of threat to him that relates to the real world. So you're looking for a villain who can be threatening but doesn't overshadow the hero. And I think the best of the Bond movies have done that really well. They've given you these memorable villains, but Bond is always the centre of the movie. That's never been in dispute.

You don't, however, use Scarecrow as a 'sidekick', a Jaws to Rā's al Ghūl's Drax. Rather there seems a hierarchy we must progress through to reach the real villain . . .

We wanted to have an escalation of threat. I think Scarecrow, in a sense, performs the function of a henchman, but because Rā's al Ghūl is off-screen he seems like the central threat. We always thought it was very important that we have a second-act villain who would be seen as the main villain so that we could bring back our first-act mentor as a third-act villain. The central difficulty David was facing was my demand to relate the first act to the third act. What you have is Bruce Wayne leaving Gotham; he's not Batman yet. He goes on this journey which could be a detour – and something the audience wants to get past to get to Batman. The challenge in the screenplay when we were first working out the story was, 'How does that pay off at the end of the film? How does that relate to what happens?' So we decided pretty early on that the mentor of the first act should be the super-villain of the third act.

The Scarecrow's use of hallucinogens seems to relate to the main theme of fear . . .

Yes. We figured out a way to relate his fear toxin to Rā's al Ghūl, the training and the blue poppy. I liked the idea of a nemesis for Batman, who is all about the use of fear to control others, which is Batman's symbolism; so Scarecrow being somebody who uses fear to manipulate others . . . it's a nice balance.

Is this your one departure from a more grounded Gotham?

The hallucinogenic aspect is rooted in science enough so that it allows us a segue into the more theatrical and elaborate hallucinogenic effects. The idea of fogging in the island, getting a bit more gothic with things – we felt we needed to offer the audience a stylistic explanation of how you can relate this film to other more exotic Batman material.

So the specifics of the plot aren't taken from any of the comics, then?

Not that I know of; there is no definitive account in the comics of the origin story. What you get are these flashbacks and glimpses. Over the period of the history of the comics there have been some quite interesting things that have arisen. The studio sent me a Batman story early on called *The Man Who Falls*. It's a DC Comics story from the 1970s. It's not even a whole comic. I think it appeared in an anthology. It was a very good jumping-off point. It suggested the idea of travelling around the world, meeting criminals and flirting with the criminal life and learning about them that way. Then, in the forest, he goes to a martial arts teacher. It had a great feel to it. It's very short, only a few pages. That was very important. So there are those kinds of influences. Then, looking at the middle act of *Batman Begins*, it draws a lot from *Batman: Year One*, with Bruce Wayne becoming Batman. But then with all of the stuff in between, what we would call 'mileposts', we were free to figure out what we wanted to do.

Were you privy to any of the other recent scripts written – notably Darren Aronofsky's take on Batman: Year One?

No, this was always a new thing. I was aware of the fact that Aronofsky and Frank Miller had collaborated on a script, and I gather it was a pretty faithful adaptation of *Batman: Year One*. But with what we were doing, the area that *Batman: Year One* deals with was only ever going to be the middle of the story. *Batman: Year One* ends in a pretty grounded

Gotham, where he's dealing with organized crime. I always wanted this film to go much bigger by the end. I felt that Batman deserves a film of enormous scope. We needed a super-villain and a very grand design of destroying the city.

Christian Bale has said the closest character he's played to Bruce Wayne is Patrick Bateman from American Psycho. *Do you see that?*

The similarity is very interesting to me. What's darkest about Bruce Wayne is not that he's utterly enraged. Or at least it's not just that. He is driven by rage; very primal and negative impulses. But it's also that there is this hollow quality to him. He's damaged goods. You experience that trauma at the beginning. For my money, having Christian do this part . . . I think it relates a lot to Patrick Bateman. When Rachel touches his face at the end and says 'This is your mask,' you kind of believe that. Christian manages to make him funny and charming, and there is a good sense of humour there, but you never forget what happened to him as a child. It hangs in everything he does. There's a burnt-out quality, in moral terms, that does relate to Patrick Bateman.

Was it Bale's ability to commit so fully to roles like American Psycho *that made you want to cast him?*

I think that was a big part of it. I felt that you would be able to look into Christian's eyes and believe he had the determination and self-discipline to recreate himself as a super hero, which is what Bruce Wayne does. I mean, Bruce Wayne is just a guy who does a lot of push-ups really! But that's a hell of a leap into being Batman, so whoever was going to play him, you'd have to be able to look into his eyes and see that fire. And Christian has that in real life and he can apply that intensity to his roles.

Did you consider many others or was he the first choice?

There were a lot of young actors interested in doing it. Christian was the first I met with. We'd barely started writing the script when I met him. I called the studio right away and said, 'You really should take a look at this guy because I think he's a very strong contender.' So I got in there early. It was very clear to me that he fitted the role. Then other actors we would look at, it would be a question of different interpretations. That is the interesting thing about casting. It takes the character in a very different way if you cast it in a particular way. With

Bruce Wayne, there are a lot of different ways he could've been played. But to me Christian was the way we were writing the character. He was what we saw before we thought about who would play the character and that's a very rare thing to find. Normally, when you're casting, you've already written the script and you've written it without an actor in mind. Then that actor comes along and takes it in a different direction, which can be wonderful. In my experience, it's always worked well for me. For example, when I wrote *Memento*, I certainly didn't have anyone in mind in the role. When I first met Guy Pearce, he didn't seem like the character as written on the page. But in talking to him I realized how much he'd related to the script. He took the character in a different direction that became definitive. The difference is that when you're sitting down to write Bruce Wayne, that character already exists in the comics, so you know what his essence is. So when we set out to cast the film, we were looking for that essence. So when we found it, as we did with Christian, it fits and it's necessary.

The acting style of all the performers is diametrically opposed to the larger-than-life turns seen in the four preceding films. Did you have any guidelines for the actors?

The philosophy behind everything, from design to photography to acting, was grounding it in reality. With great actors, that naturally manifests itself in a more realistic, naturalistic and low-key style.

Do you have any particular approach to drawing out performances from actors?

You just cast it right. With Liam Neeson, for example, the danger was he'd played this mentor figure in his other movies. When I met Liam, we threw around this notion of does this help us or hurt us? In the end, we decided, because of who he really turns out to be, it works for us. My younger brother consulted on the script, and we'd talk a lot about ideas, and one of the things he said to me early on – and it was something that I ended up sticking to – was that everything Rā's al Ghūl says, with one exception, should be true. And everything he says in the film is true. He doesn't ever cross that line to mad villain-speak. Everything he says as a mentor applies to his motivations behind doing everything he does at the end. It's just about perception, about degree, about tone of voice, about how we view that character. When we meet him with Bruce at the beginning, he seems to offer answers. We like the sound of what he has to say and we trust him. The baggage Liam carries from other movies is part of us trusting him just like that. Which for me, makes it very interesting when he comes back. He's saying the same stuff, but we've changed with Bruce. Our perception of what this guy is all about has changed utterly. Therefore, to me he becomes a more threatening villain. He's logical, he isn't wrong; he's just too extreme.

Do you see this as a continuation of your interest with identity and the way we perceive characters?

Yeah, in a way. Now that I've finished it, I look back and it relates quite strongly to things we looked at in *Insomnia*, in terms of ends justifying means and the conflict between pragmatism and idealism. The idea of what is OK to do, how far can you go and still be on the right side of things. That was very much what Al Pacino's character in *Insomnia* is wrestling with. I think it's actually the essence of Batman as a figure. He is on the edge. He's on that line between right and wrong. He stays on the right side of the line – not being a vigilante, a vengeful figure who isn't morally correct. For us, the process of making the film was dealing with that discrepancy, saying, 'What distinguishes him from Charles Bronson in *Death Wish*? What is it that makes him OK?' There isn't a simple answer to that, but I think the film makes you see that.

Both Bruce Wayne and Leonard, from Memento, *are haunted by their pasts. Was that going through your mind when writing?*

Actually, at that stage, I don't think it was. Now that I look at it I think they are very similar characters, with this hollow, burned-out quality very present in both characters. I was thinking more about Howard Hughes, as I had been working on a script about him. The thing about Howard Hughes as a young man that Bruce Wayne recalls is that Hughes was orphaned as a young man and given the keys to the kingdom and billions of dollars to play with. Essentially, he was given complete freedom to do whatever he wanted to do, in practical terms. For me it was fascinating to see where that would lead. It's something we all think we want, but when you look at a story like Hughes's or, in fictional terms, Bruce Wayne's, you wouldn't want to be in their shoes.

Did you find it psychologically demanding, stepping up to the challenge of making a blockbuster?

Each film I've done has got exponentially bigger – though I think with this we've peaked in terms of size! This film was a lot bigger and it meant a lot more careful planning and a certain restriction in terms of spontaneity. We had to be a little more rigid in certain sequences because of the practical considerations. But in shooting we managed to keep a pretty high degree of flexibility. We didn't use any Second Unit; we shot everything ourselves. Which, I gather, is very unusual for a film of this size. Certainly, people were a little bit wary of this at first, when I said I didn't want a Second Unit director. They were a little bit shocked by that, but we showed them how it would work.

Did that make the process longer?

No, not really. The thing with Second Unit is that it's actually pretty time-consuming. You set up a smaller unit that's cheaper to run. They run in parallel to you, but their hit rate of shots is pretty low, as they're shooting on your behalf. In my case, I was very particular about how I wanted the action to be shot. Our main unit shoot was a little bit longer, I suppose, than some of these films are.

How did you find shooting big action set-pieces for the first time?

I actually found it really enjoyable, to be honest, with very few exceptions. We had such good special effects guys. By special effects, I mean the floor effects, the guys doing things on-set, as opposed to the visual effects guys in post-production. They're great too – but in relevance to the action, the special effects guys, the stunt guys and the riggers were so good that I was really able to work in the way I'm used to working, which was very fast and very efficiently, and getting a lot of stuff done. Working with Wally Pfister for a third time . . . he knows the way I like to work and was able to figure out ways of accommodating that. So we managed to get a lot of stuff done in a short space of time and have a lot of fun doing it. I can only remember a couple of occasions where we really got bogged down in the scale of things, and generally it had more to do with the sets or the lighting: just doing big, big shots. That just takes time. Once you've set the arena of it . . . like with the car chase: we would find ways to do multiple runs and go up and down a stretch of road and shoot in both directions and get a library of footage together very quickly.

How rigorously did you work with storyboards and adhere to them?

I worked with the artist pretty closely for a few months in pre-production to try and nail down certain sequences so that people could figure out how to do them, and then I never looked at them again. To me, it's a slightly false way of working. The storyboards are very important at the beginning, in pre-production. To me, they seemed vital in the process. I suddenly realized I had a lot of very nervous people around me needing information. So, however much I could explain things verbally, until they had pictures in front of them that expressed how I intended to shoot things, they couldn't really do their job properly. It was a blueprint for me to communicate. We had a couple of very good storyboard artists who were able to actually put my intentions onto paper quite closely. I then didn't tend to consult them – certainly not when I was shooting. Once everyone calms down and gets the stuff built, they don't need to look at them too much either. We had the storyboards there on the set for reference, but tended not to use them. I think what's funny about that is, if you compare the finished film to the storyboards, they're actually pretty close. They're probably as close as they would've been if we had been studying them shot for shot. But I think that's mostly a function of how good the storyboard artists are in interpreting my intentions.

Was it important for you to have Wally and your production designer, Nathan Crowley, who worked with you on Insomnia, *on board?*

It was very, very important. With people who know you, and know the way you work, the ease of communication is just a huge asset, particularly when you're taking on such a big project. It was also a lot of fun for me to have guys I'd worked with who had never done a film as big as this. The first time we walked around the set, half-built, in Cardington, and saw what is, I think, the biggest set ever built, we were able to laugh with each other and go, 'How the hell are we going to do this?' That was a pretty extreme moment. Then once we'd been in there a couple of days, it was like any other shoot.

Were you ever concerned about working on a billion-dollar franchise?

I always think very carefully about who I'm getting into business with. My belief is that, as a responsible filmmaker, once you're in there, it's their money, so you're going to have to work with them. There's no way round that, so you're going to have to think very carefully about your situation. But in the case of this film, Warner Bros. were very,

very firmly convinced that they needed a fresh approach. And that's a unique opportunity, where you have this franchise and you have this very valuable character and iconic figure – but they're saying you've got to do something new with it. You don't have to do all the stuff that came before. It was all about: 'What are you going to do to make it different?' It was actually a very exciting position to be in. The more I spoke to Jeff Robinov and Alan Horn at Warner Bros., and pitched them my vision of the thing, as David was writing, they really got it. It was very clear to me that they understood what I was saying I was going to make. My thing with filmmaking, the claim I would make for myself as a filmmaker, is that I do make the film that I say I'm going to make. However much it might feel like we're meandering along the way and being spontaneous, I think with all of my films I've looked back and thought, 'That's pretty close to what I've said I'm going to do.' Part of that is a function of writing, or co-writing, my own scripts. I've worked it out pretty thoroughly before we were going to actually film it. I felt good about the relationship with the studio, as I felt good that they understood what I was going to do. Then the real question – which I was nervous about – was: 'When they start seeing it, will they acknowledge the fact that this is what I said I was going to do?' The truth is, they've been absolutely marvellous. They got it, looked at the dailies and said: 'This is the film you said you were going to make.'

Have Warner Bros. held back on tie-in toys and games, etc?

They're doing some pretty great merchandizing things, but they're a lot more restrained than they have been in the past. I think what they know with this film is it can't be cart before horse. They got in trouble with that last time. With this film, there's an acknowledgement that the film has to come first and people have to be convinced by the film. So there's a great toy Batmobile, for example, but people are going to have to see it in the film and like what it does – and then they'll get excited about the toy. It can't be the other way round, because it is a fresh start.

What's the deal with the title? It was known as 'Intimidation Game' for a while . . .

It was always just a code name. It was always going to be called *Batman Begins*. With a film like this, which has all the interest on it, to protect the script and the cans of film we had to give it a code. 'The Intimidation

Game' was my take on what might sound like a big Warner Bros. action movie! Unfortunately, I was a little too close, as people started believing it as a title. We've changed it now to 'Flora's Wedding', which sounds like a romantic comedy!

With the scene at the end that shows us the Joker as a potential villain, are you signed on for a sequel or even interested in doing another one?

I really don't know. I've tried to put everything into this film. Everything that I wanted to see Batman do, I've tried to put into this film. The truth is, in leaving it open-ended – which we always wanted to do – it wasn't about sequel-baiting. It's much more about sending the audience away with all these characters living on in their minds and spreading outwards and upwards. So that's why that's there. But that immediately does start you thinking that they are great characters. So I don't know. I would never say 'never'. Actors sign on for multiple movies but that doesn't tend to happen with directors – they're more replaceable! I certainly want to do something smaller next.

David S. Goyer

INTERVIEWED BY JAMES MOTTRAM

A comic book devotee ever since his Michigan childhood, David S. Goyer has carved an entire career out of adapting the medium for the big screen. He came to prominence in 1996, penning *The Crow: City of Angels*, the sequel to the 1994 film that took its inspiration from the James O'Barr-created comics. In 1998, Goyer was co-writer on Alex Proyas's *noir*-inflected *Dark City*. At the same time, he adapted *Blade*, the Marvel Comics story of the eponymous vampire-hunter. He went on to write the sequels *Blade II* (2002) and *Blade: Trinity* (2004), which he also directed. This marked his second outing as director, having made his 2002 debut with the robbery tale *ZigZag*. Between the two, he collaborated with Christopher Nolan on the screenplay for *Batman Begins*.

JAMES MOTTRAM *Were you a fan of the Batman comic books rather than the television shows?*

DAVID S. GOYER I was a huge comic book reader. Between my brother and myself, we had thousands and thousands of comic books in our collection. Obviously, I watched the TV show as a little kid, but my biggest exposure to Batman was in the comic books. Primarily, the DC Comics during the seventies and then later, in the eighties, the Frank Miller stuff.

How did you relate to the portrayal of Batman in the films compared to the comic books?

Well, I liked the way he was portrayed in the comic books much more than he was in the films. I liked the first of the previous films [Tim Burton's 1989 *Batman*]. But I felt the later films became more akin to the TV show and were somewhat out of synch with the way that Batman was currently being depicted in the comic books.

What was it you liked about him as a character?

What I like about Batman is that he is the most realistic of the super heroes. There is a grittiness and grimness to him. People sometimes draw distinctions between the Marvel super heroes and the DC super heroes. There's Spider-Man, who has all this self-doubt, and the Fantastic Four, who are always bickering, and then the Hulk, who obviously has a lot of problems. The Marvel heroes are more conflicted. In the pantheon of DC Comics heroes, Batman is the only one who's really conflicted. Superman and Wonder Woman are effectively gods. Green Lantern isn't tortured or tormented, and nor is the Flash. But Batman is. Conflicted heroes are more interesting to watch because they're more human – we can relate to them.

When Chris Nolan first came to you, did he immediately say he wanted his Batman to be a tortured soul?

I'm pretty sure we both thought that, inherently. Given our backgrounds, I don't think either of us would ever consider anything but that. I know that we were as interested in depicting Bruce Wayne as we were Batman.

In previous outings, there hasn't been much to Bruce Wayne as a character . . .

In the movies and the television show, he was boring. But for us, we thought he was the most interesting character. I always got the sense with the other movies that, whenever we were with Bruce Wayne, the audience was marking time until Batman would put on the cape and cowl again. We were interested in getting the audience so invested in Bruce Wayne that they wouldn't care whether he was in the costume. So that was our primary goal in doing this film.

What did you specifically want to highlight about Wayne?

Obviously he's conflicted and tormented, but as a kid he was very lonely and isolated. We treated him like this Prince Regent whose parents had died. He was kept away from the masses and the public by all the people of Wayne Enterprises and Wayne Manor because he's the heir to the throne and this impossibly huge fortune. So we used to refer to the young Bruce Wayne as the 'loneliest boy in the world' – we had this image of him being a young prince as a prisoner in this castle. He would look down at the rest of the world and never get to walk amongst us. It was one of the reasons why Bruce, when he leaves Gotham, was so anxious to shed his identity and be able to travel without people realizing he is Bruce Wayne.

The fact that there is no definitive origin story, did that give you free rein to experiment?

It did, because it was an enormous blank space in terms of the Batman mythology. Prior to Frank Miller's *Batman: Year One*, all you ever really saw was Bruce's parents being killed. Then you flashed forward to Bruce at twenty-seven in his study, and a bat crashes through the window. Then in the next panel, he's Batman on the rooftop – and that was it! There was no time given to how or where he learnt all of these skills, or even who taught him. Even *Batman: Year One* starts with Bruce returning to Gotham after having been gone for seven years. It doesn't get into where he was, or who he studied with, and that's a huge portion of our film.

Was there much difference between adapting Batman and adapting Blade?

Enormous differences. *Blade* is as comic book as you can get. There's nothing realistic about *Blade*. The film vernacular is much more extreme in *Blade* – speed-ups and things like that. It's also very different because Batman is so well known. Blade was completely unknown and I had much more latitude in changing the Blade mythology than I did with *Batman*. I mean, even my grandmother knows Batman is Bruce Wayne.

Did that make it harder adapting Batman?

Yes. It was a thin edge that we had to walk on. We had to appease the comic book fans but also the mainstream audience. And also Warner Bros. It was an interesting balancing act.

Based on your own experiences with studios, were you surprised that Chris got the freedom he did to completely overhaul the Batman franchise?

Absolutely. Going into the project, I had some trepidation about whether they would give Chris the latitude to do this. But the people at Warner Bros. really stood by their word. They allowed Chris to make the movie that he pitched them. The final film and the final script are remarkably similar to the things that Chris and I discussed in the first few conversations we had, when we were working out the story.

Has that been your experience before, on other films you've worked on?

Usually not. This was a unique experience, and all the more unique because it was such a massive project and there was so much riding on it.

How did it work, given that you were directing Blade: Trinity *some of the time Chris was writing?*

I did a couple of drafts, then Chris started writing, and he would call me on the phone and we would throw ideas back and forth. It was very smooth. Chris and I worked incredibly well together. We saw eye-to-eye virtually all the time. It was a really great collaboration. Most of the things he ended up tweaking were those he and I had already been discussing. There's very little that's in the final script that didn't exist in our initial conversations when we were working out the story.

What made you choose Scarecrow and Rā's al Ghūl as the chief villains?

Chris wasn't familiar with the Rogues Gallery and he knew that I was. So we had a lot of discussions about who was out there. We quickly decided that we didn't want to use anyone that had been done in the films before, because we felt that they were somewhat tainted. So I took him by the hand and led him through the other remaining major players in Batman's Rogues Gallery. I immediately knew that I wanted to use Scarecrow and Rā's al Ghūl. Having said that, I did the due diligence and said, 'Let's talk about Clayface, Killer Croc, the Ventriloquist and the Calendar Man' – some of the other lesser-known Batman villains.

Would you say your portrayal of Scarecrow differs from the comic books?

Our film is a bit more realistic than the previous Batman films, so our Scarecrow is not quite as extreme a portrayal as the comics. The other addition was having Jonathan Crane be the head of Arkham Asylum, which he is not in the comic books. But, primarily, he's the same character.

Did you struggle in linking the first act to the third act?

Absolutely. We had to have the character of Rā's al Ghūl be in the beginning and be in the end, but we had to make it feel organic. We had to reveal at the end that Rā's al Ghūl/Ducard was this grand master behind everything, including Scarecrow. We had to make his ultimate reveal feel *inevitable*. It was Chris's idea that Ducard should exist; that the characters of Batman's mentor and his prime adversary be the same two people. I think the audience is genuinely surprised when Ducard/Rā's al Ghūl shows up because you don't expect to see him and it's a revelation that they're one and the same. Rā's has an important line when he says, 'I was the one that taught you to use an alias. What makes you think I wouldn't use an alias?' That was the thorniest issue we grappled with; not making it seem like they were two separate movies. We'd already done a draft or so before that happened.

Much of what Rā's says in the film makes a certain sense.

He's not crazy in the same way as the Joker or the Riddler. Many of his aims and goals are something that you can, in the abstract, at least sympathize and identify with. The world is being despoiled and civilization is screwing things up. I think that makes him a much more compelling villain and more well-rounded than some of the traditional *Batman* villains. His aims are not just, 'I want to build a giant house of cards in Gotham City and give everyone a joker smile' – his aims are much larger and wider-reaching than that. He's got this whole history – an organization behind him that's been in existence for thousands of years.

One thing you don't focus on is Rā's al Ghūl's ability to regenerate, which is in the comic books. Was that because Chris wanted to keep it grounded in reality?

Yeah. We talked about it, but there's nothing we did that disputes that. As you know, in comic books, if you don't see a body, someone isn't necessarily dead. So we don't absolutely rule out the fact that Rā's al Ghūl could return. But we felt that the main challenge of this film was keeping everything grounded and believable. By hitting the Lazarus Pit head on, it would break that. It's still possible that Rā's al Ghūl could do that, and does that, but you could view it either way.

Has there ever been any reference to Bruce Wayne being trained by Rā's al Ghūl?

No. That was the biggest piece of the mythology that we added and tinkered with. In the comic books, he meets Rā's al Ghūl well after he's already Batman. Rā's al Ghūl serves the same paternal function, to an extent. They always had that kind of relationship, but we decided to backdate that meeting so that Bruce meets Rā's al Ghūl well before he's Batman. Fortunately, the people at DC Comics thought that was a nice twist to the Batman legend.

Did you have to run all your ideas past DC Comics?

Absolutely. We met with them for a number of days in New York and presented our ideas. We wanted their stamp of approval and to know if there was anything we were doing that was dramatically altering the canon. Rā's al Ghūl as Batman's mentor was one of the biggest issues that we hoped they would approve of. We also wanted to burn Wayne Manor to the ground and I was worried they wouldn't let us do it. My point was, it could always be rebuilt exactly the way it was. I just thought that would be really important for Bruce's character in this film literally to be responsible for destroying the house that Wayne built. He lives in the shadow not of only his father but also all the Waynes who have come before him. At that point in the film, he very much feels like a failure for having put that all in jeopardy. Again, the people at DC felt that was a great addition.

The theme of fear spreads from Bruce Wayne to the whole city. Was that always in there from the beginning?

Pretty much. We wanted Bruce to have this horrific experience with bats when he was a child that became this formative phobia that he had to grapple with. It just seemed like a natural way to go. Scarecrow traffics in fear. Batman puts on this monstrous costume in order to instil fear in people's hearts. Then he has to grapple with his own fear. It seemed like a logical way to go. We folded Rā's al Ghūl's methodology into that. The secondary theme is Bruce being in the shadow of his father and feeling that he wants to do the memory of his father justice.

You only once use the phrase: 'I'm Batman.' Were you trying to be cautious with such moments, so as not to turn it into a cartoon version of the character?

Absolutely. The watchword was realism. Keep it real, as much as possible. It's funny. The source material is obviously comic books but the movie does not feel like a comic book movie. There are huge stretches of the film where you feel you could be watching a David Lean or John Huston film.

Did Chris ever ask your opinions on casting?

Yes, he did. We'd have conversations about casting all the time. Pretty much everyone we got was someone we discussed from the very beginning. He and I had always talked about Christian Bale. Michael Caine was always our first choice for Alfred. As soon as I mentioned incorporating Lucius Fox into the movie, we talked about Morgan Freeman. One time he did call me, he said he was down to Liam Neeson and one other actor. We had a long conversation about it. Ultimately, he went the way I thought he would go. We had been talking about using a younger actor, but I felt that Ducard needed to have a paternal relationship with Bruce rather than a fraternal relationship. Ducard needed to be older.

Once Bale was cast, were you able to tailor your writing to his talents?

A little bit. We thought Bale was uniquely suited to playing the three different personalities that comprise Batman. There's Batman, which is one personality. Then there's the public Bruce Wayne, which is as much a secret identity as Batman is – this billionaire playboy persona is really a front to distract people from Batman. Then there's the private Bruce Wayne who, in a sense, is the darkest Bruce Wayne of all. He's even more tormented than Batman. Chris had to find someone who could play all of those roles.

What are you working on next?

I'm writing *The Flash* for me to direct at Warner Bros. That'll be my last comic book adaptation! He's the opposite of Batman. He loves being the Flash because he doesn't even have a secret identity. He's not a vigilante. The world loves him. He's a media star. He's somebody the best day of whose life was when he became the Flash. He loves everything about it.

Batman Begins

THE SCREENPLAY

Black. A low keening which becomes screeching that builds and builds until –

Red flickers through black as the screen bursts into life.

Clouds of reeling bats silhouetted against a blood-red sky, bolting away from camera, massing in the sky . . . forming a density the shape of an enormous bat-like symbol.

More bats mass, swamping the symbol, darkening the screen to –

Black. Distant children's laughter which comes closer as –

SUNLIGHT FLICKERS THROUGH BLACK. SUNLIGHT THROUGH TREES

1

Running through a summer garden.

A boy (Bruce Wayne, aged eight) chasing a girl (Rachel Dawes, also eight).

YOUNG BRUCE
Rachel! Let me see!

They reach a Victorian greenhouse. Rachel runs inside.

EXT. GARDENS, WAYNE MANOR – DAY   2

Young Bruce peers down rows of plants on long trestle tables. Rachel grabs him, pulling him under a table.

YOUNG BRUCE
Can I see?

RACHEL
Finders keepers – I found it.

YOUNG BRUCE
In *my* garden.

3

Rachel considers this. Then opens her hand to reveal a flint arrowhead. Young Bruce stares. She smiles. Young Bruce grabs the arrowhead. Sprints for the back door, laughing.

Finders keepers!

EXT. DISUSED KITCHEN GARDEN, WAYNE MANOR – CONTINUOUS 3
Young Bruce races through the garden, Rachel behind – scrambles over a crumbled wall into the mouth of a disused well . . . the boards across the well give way – he plummets into . . .

INT. OLD WELL – CONTINUOUS   4
Young Bruce drops thirty feet – lands painfully on the rubble-strewn bottom of the shaft.

EXT. KITCHEN GARDEN, WAYNE MANOR – CONTINUOUS   5
Rachel runs to the well.

                              RACHEL
    BRUCE?!

INT. OLD WELL – CONTINUOUS   6
Young Bruce lifts his head from damp dirt and rocks, groaning.

EXT. KITCHEN GARDEN, WAYNE MANOR – CONTINUOUS   7
Rachel sprints towards the house.

                              RACHEL
    MOM!! MISTER ALFRED!!

INT. OLD WELL – CONTINUOUS   8

Young Bruce, in shock, groans. He hears squealing – freezes, peering into the darkness of an opening between rocks . . .

Bats explode from the darkness, filling the air. He screams – curls against their flapping, squawking, fluttering blackness.

A jolt: older green eyes flick open, waking . . . in darkness. Filthy, sweating darkness . . . and we are –

4

The eyes belong to a bearded, weathered, young man's face. Bruce Wayne, aged twenty-eight. An Old Asian Man sits staring at him. Their cell is a metal cage. Shouts echo along brick passages.

Wayne and the Old Man line up for gruel. Prisoners are scattered in small groups. All eyes on Wayne.

                    OLD MAN
They are going to fight you.

                    WAYNE
Again?

                    OLD MAN
Until they kill you.

Wayne holds out his plate. Watches gruel get dribbled onto it.

                    WAYNE
Can't they kill me *before* breakfast?

Wayne turns from the table. His path is blocked by an Enormous Man, backed by five aggressive prisoners. The Enormous Man smashes his plate away.

                 ENORMOUS MAN
                 (*broken English*)
You are in hell, little man . . .

He punches Wayne – Wayne goes down hard.

. . . and I am the devil.

Wayne picks himself up. Dusts himself off.

                    WAYNE
You're not the devil . . .

The Enormous Man swings again – Wayne catches his fist, kicks the big man's knee out and, as he goes down, boots his face.

. . . you're practice.

Six Prisoners rush Wayne all at once . . . Wayne fights skillfully and hard, flipping one prisoner into another, kicking as his arms are held,

*not before several prisoners have hit the deck. Gunfire – two Guards
break it up, shooting into the air . . . they grab Wayne.*

> GUARD

Solitary!

> WAYNE
> (*indignant*)

Why?

> GUARD

For protection.

> WAYNE

I don't need protection.

The Guard points angrily at the unconscious Prisoners.

> GUARD

Protection for *them*.

INT. SOLITARY, BHUTANESE JAIL – MOMENTS LATER   II

Wayne is tossed into the dank cell. The door slams.

> VOICE
> (*out of shot*)

Are you so desperate to fight criminals that you lock yourself
in to take them on one at a time?

*The voice is mellifluous. European. Wayne turns to the shadows.
Touches his split lip. Sardonic.*

> WAYNE

Actually, there were seven of them.

*A man steps into the light: powerfully built, distinguished, in a well-
cut suit and tie. He smiles.*

> DUCARD

I counted six, *Mr. Wayne.*

> WAYNE

How do you know my name?

> DUCARD

The world is too small for someone like Bruce Wayne to

disappear . . . (*Gestures around them.*) No matter how deep
he chooses to sink.

WAYNE

Who are you?

DUCARD

My name is merely Ducard. But I speak for Rā's al Ghūl. A man
greatly feared by the criminal underworld. A man who can offer
you a path.

WAYNE

What makes you think I need a path?

Ducard looks around the cell.

DUCARD

Someone like you is only here by choice. You've been exploring
the criminal fraternity . . . But whatever your original intentions
. . . you've become truly *lost.*

Wayne stares at Ducard, struck by his words.

WAYNE

What path does Rā's al Ghūl offer?

DUCARD

The path of one who shares his hatred of evil and wishes to
serve true justice. The path of the League of Shadows.

WAYNE
(*dismissive*)

You're vigilantes.

DUCARD

A vigilante is just a man lost in the scramble for his own
gratification . . . He can be destroyed, or locked up . . .
(*Indicates cell.*) But if you make yourself more than just a
man . . . if you devote yourself to an ideal . . . if they can't
stop you . . . then you become something else entirely . . .

WAYNE

Which is?

Ducard moves to the door. Which opens to his touch.

7

DUCARD

A legend, Mr. Wayne.

A Guard steps aside to let Ducard pass.

Tomorrow you'll be released. If you're bored of brawling with thieves and want to *achieve* something, there's a rare flower – a blue poppy – that grows on the Eastern slopes. Pick one of these flowers. If you can carry it to the top of the mountain, you may find what you were looking for in the first place.

WAYNE

And what *was* I looking for?

Ducard looks at Wayne with a glint in his eye.

DUCARD

Only you can know that.

The door slams shut.

Wayne lies in the darkness of his cell, staring up . . .

Shadows of bats cross his face, his eyes close and we are –

INT. BOTTOM OF THE OLD WELL – DAY (WAYNE'S MEMORY)   12

The last of the bats flutter up the well shaft . . . Young Bruce lies there, exhausted, weeping softly.

MALE VOICE
(*out of shot*)

Bruce?

Young Bruce looks up: a figure, long coat billowing, lowered down the shaft . . . Thomas Wayne, Young Bruce's father.

EXT. GARDENS, WAYNE MANOR – MOMENTS LATER   13

Thomas carries his son towards the house. At his side, a fifty-year-old man in a somber suit calmly coils a rope: Alfred.

ALFRED

Will we be needing an ambulance, Master Wayne?

8

THOMAS
(*shakes head*)
I'll set the bone, then take him for X-rays later.

ALFRED
Very good, sir.

INT. HALL, WAYNE MANOR – CONTINUOUS   14

They pass a tearful Rachel standing with her mother, Mrs. Dawes, the housekeeper.

MRS DAWES
I'm very sorry, sir, I've told her –

Thomas nods at her, smiling. Bruce reaches out to Rachel as they pass. Hands her something. The arrowhead. She smiles.

Thomas carries Bruce up the main stairs. The house is vast and grand, but full of flowers and life.

INT. BRUCE'S BEDROOM, WAYNE MANOR – LATER   15

Alfred moves to the bedside. Looks down at Young Bruce.

ALFRED
Took quite a fall, didn't we?

Young Bruce looks up at Alfred. Manages a slight smile.

And why do we fall, Master Bruce?

Alfred reaches up to the curtains. Young Bruce says nothing.

(*Smiles gently.*) So that we might better learn to pick ourselves up.

Alfred closes the curtains.

Wayne tumbles through the dust, rolling, bumping and we are –

EXT. DUSTY PLAIN – DAY   16

Wayne rolls along – a Chinese army truck speeding off. A Soldier tosses Wayne's small pack after him. Wayne watches the truck speed off. Picks himself up. Grabs his pack. Turns to look across the plain to the distant foothills.

EXT. HIMALAYAN FOOTHILLS — DAY   17

*A field of exquisite blue poppies. Wayne approaches. Picks one.
Studies its brilliant blue in the cold sunshine.*

EXT. TINY HAMLET, HIMALAYAS — DAY   18

*Wayne, exhausted, freezing, hungry, wanders up the street. As locals
see him they head inside. Doors slammed, bolted.*

> CHILD
> (*out of shot*)

No one will help you.

*Wayne turns to find a Young Child staring at him. The Child points
at the blue flower pinned to Wayne's chest. An Old Man appears at
the Child's side.*

> WAYNE
> (*weak*)

I need food.

> OLD MAN

Then turn back.

Wayne looks at the Old Man. Then carries on up the mountain.

EXT. MOUNTAIN — DAY   19

Wayne struggles through driving snow up an icy ridge . . .

*He clears the ridge, flops down into the snow, painfully raises his
scarf-wrapped face to the cutting wind to see a monastery perched on
jagged rock.*

EXT. HIMALAYAN FORTIFIED MONASTERY — DAY   20

*Wayne climbs the steps to the vast doors of the monastery. Unwraps
a severely frostbitten fist. Pounds desperately against the ice-covered
wood, knocks echoing deep within.*

*A grinding noise from within. Wayne stops, straightens. The doors
swing open to darkness . . .*

Wayne shuffles forward into a low-ceilinged wooden hall lit by flickering lamps. Hands trembling, Wayne pulls at brittle scarves. He starts as the doors thud shut behind him.

At the far end, on a raised platform, sits a dark, robed figure: Rā's al Ghūl. Wayne moves unsteadily towards him.

> WAYNE
> (*hoarse*)

Rā's al Ghūl?

Armed warriors of various races emerge from the shadows, their dress a mixture of modern combat and ethnic dress.

> DUCARD
> (*out of shot*)

Wait.

The Warriors hold. Wayne looks at the source of the command: Ducard leans against a nearby pillar.

Wayne reaches into his layers of clothing. Pulls out the blue poppy. Holds it out, shaking.

Rā's al Ghūl starts to speak in Urdu. Ducard translates.

What are you seeking?

> WAYNE

I . . . I seek . . . the means to fight injustice. To turn fear against those who prey on the fearful . . .

Ducard takes the flower. Considers its delicate blue petals. Puts the flower into his buttonhole. Rā's al Ghūl speaks.

> DUCARD
> (*translating*)

To manipulate the fears of others you must first master your own. (*His own words.*) Are you ready to begin?

> WAYNE
> (*trembling with fatigue*)

I . . . I can barely –

Ducard kicks him – Wayne crashes to the floor.

DUCARD

Death does not wait for you to be ready . . .

Wayne crawls, gasping. Ducard strikes him in the ribs

Death is not considerate, or fair. And make no mistake – here, you face death . . .

Ducard turns – whips his leg in a fearsome roundhouse kick aimed straight at Wayne's neck – but Wayne blocks the kick with a lateral movement of his forearm. He stares at Ducard, eyes blazing. Ducard smiles.

Wayne rises. Assumes a martial stance. Ducard strikes – Wayne blocks and parries, driving his body through pain into a series of fluid, skilled moves . . .

Tiger Crane . . . Ju Jitsu . . . (*Smiles.*) Skilled. But this is not a dance –

Ducard's head smashes Wayne's cheek – Wayne falters – Ducard smashes him in the groin – slams Wayne's chin, sends him down hard.

And you are afraid . . .

Ducard crouches at Wayne's side. Looks into his glazed eyes.

(*Curious.*) But not of me.

Ducard pulls the flower from his lapel. Leans in close to replace it on Wayne's chest, his lips at Wayne's ear . . .

Tell us, Wayne . . .

Violent flapping, screeching black bats – swarming, chittering.

(*Voice-over, whispers.*) What *do* you fear?

Young Bruce's eyes open, and we are –

INT. BRUCE'S BEDROOM, WAYNE MANOR – DAWN (WAYNE'S MEMORY)   22

Young Bruce, breathing hard. Light cuts across the bedclothes. He looks to the door. Thomas is there.

THOMAS
(*gentle*)

The bats again?

Young Bruce nods. Thomas approaches. Sits on the bed.

You know why they attacked you? (*Off look.*) They were afraid of you.

YOUNG BRUCE

Afraid of me?

THOMAS

You're a lot bigger than a bat, aren't you? All creatures feel fear.

YOUNG BRUCE
(*smiles*)

Even the scary ones?

Thomas smiles back, reaches into his dressing-gown pocket.

THOMAS

Especially the scary ones. (*Thinks.*) Here, let me show you something – (*Freezes.*) But you can't tell anyone, right?

Young Bruce nods, eager. Thomas pulls out a long jewel case. He opens it: pearls glow in the half-light.

For your mother.

Young Bruce grins. Thomas winks at him, snaps the case shut –

INT. ELEVATED TRAIN (MONORAIL) – EVENING (WAYNE'S MEMORY)   23

Looking out to Gotham. Young Bruce, reflected in the glass, stares out in wonder at the city. His parents beside him, dressed up – Martha idly stroking her pearls.

The brand new train car is crowded with Gothamites.

YOUNG BRUCE

Did you build this train, Dad?

THOMAS
(*nods*)

Gotham's been good to our family . . . but now the city's suffering. People less fortunate than us are enduring very hard times. So . . .

Thomas draws a circle in the condensation on the window.

. . . we built a new, cheap public transportation system to unite the city . . .

Thomas draws spokes through the circle, creating a wheel. Thomas taps his diagram at the central hub of the wheel, then points through the glass to a tall 1930s skyscraper.

. . . and at the center . . . Wayne Tower.

> YOUNG BRUCE
> Is that where you work?

> THOMAS
> No, I work at the hospital. I leave the running of our company to better men.

> YOUNG BRUCE
> Better?

> THOMAS
> Well, more interested men.

> ANNOUNCER
> (*over loudspeaker*)
> Wayne Station. Wayne Station next.

EXT. GOTHAM – CONTINUOUS   24

The monorail train turns inwards on a 'spoke' . . . shooting towards the central station at the base of Wayne Tower.

EXT. WAYNE PLAZA – MOMENTS LATER   25

Young Bruce clings to his father's hand as they walk through the rush-hour crowds. Young Bruce stares up at the magnificent Wayne Tower, watching the setting sun set fire to the gold lettering of the WAYNE ENTERPRISES *name.*

Rich orchestral strings rise, and we are –

INT. GOTHAM OPERA HOUSE – LATER   26

A gilded house packed to the rafters for Boito's Mefistofle. Young Bruce seated between his parents. On stage: witch-like creatures cavort. Dark birds on wires descend, flapping.

Young Bruce stares, uneasy, at their violent motions.

Insert cut: bats explode from a dark crevice.

Young Bruce starts breathing faster, staring fixedly.

Screeching, flapping black bats swarm all around . . .

*Young Bruce, gulping panic breaths, looks around for an exit –
they're in the middle of a row. He grabs his dad's arm.*

> YOUNG BRUCE
> (*desperate whisper*)
>
> Can we go?!

*Thomas stares at his son, confused. Martha looks over. Young Bruce
looks at his father, pleading. Thomas nods. They make their way
along the row, Thomas nodding apologies . . .*

EXT. SIDE ALLEY, GOTHAM OPERA HOUSE – CONTINUOUS   27

*The Waynes emerge from a side exit. Martha crouches before Bruce,
tries to meet his eyes. He stares down, ashamed.*

> MARTHA
>
> Bruce, what's wrong?

> THOMAS
>
> He's fine.

Martha looks up. Thomas gives her a conspiratorial look.

> I just needed a bit of air. Bit of opera goes a long way, right,
> Bruce?

*Young Bruce looks up at his dad, who winks. Young Bruce smiles
gratefully.*

> Come on.

*Thomas, coat over his arm, ushers his family down the dark alley,
heading for the welcoming glow of the main boulevard.*

*A figure emerges from the shadows in front of them. A Man. With a
gun. Shifting uneasily. Skinny. Hungry. Desperate.*

> MAN
>
> Wallet, jewelry! Fast!

THOMAS
(*calm tone*)
That's fine, just take it easy.

Thomas hands Young Bruce his coat, then reaches for his wallet. The Man jerks the gun at Thomas, eyes darting. Young Bruce stares up at the gun trembling in the Man's hand.

Here you go.

The Man grabs at the wallet but fumbles it. It falls. The Man glances down at the wallet, then back to Thomas, scared.

(*Reassuring tone.*) It's fine, it's fine . . .

The Man crouches for the wallet, eyes on Thomas.

. . . just take it and go.

The Man feels for the wallet, looks at Martha. Her pearls.

MAN
I said jewelry!!

She starts pulling off her rings. The Man jerks the gun at her neck. Thomas steps protectively in front of his wife.

THOMAS
Hey, just –

Boom. Young Bruce flinches. Thomas looks down at his bleeding chest. Then back to the Man, saddened.

Thomas crumples. Martha screams. The Man reaches for Martha's pearls – but she scrambles desperately for Thomas.

MARTHA
THOMAS!! THOMAS!!

MAN
Gimme the damn . . .

But Martha flails, trying to grab her fallen husband.

The Man shoots her. Then yanks at her necklace, which breaks. Spilling pearls all over the asphalt.

The Man stands. Turns to Young Bruce. Who stares at him. Uncomprehending. The Man cannot bear the boy's gaze . . .

16

And then he runs. Young Bruce looks at the bodies of his parents, drops to his knees, head down: pearls dot the asphalt beneath him. Some of them are bloody.

Young Bruce starts to shiver.

INT. POLICE STATION – NIGHT   28

Chaos: Reporters and Cops vying for a piece of the crime of the decade. In the Captain's office, Young Bruce. Bewildered, forgotten. Still clutching his father's overcoat.

> MALE VOICE
> (*out of shot*)

Is that your father's?

Young Bruce looks up: a young beat cop stands over him – Jim Gordon (twenty-nine). Gordon crouches, reaches for the coat. Young Bruce huddles over it, protective.

> GORDON
> (*reassuring*)

It's OK.

Gordon's tone prompts Young Bruce to trust him. Gordon takes the coat, drapes it gently across Young Bruce's shoulders.

> MALE VOICE
> (*out of shot*)

GORDON! You gotta stick your nose into everything?!

Gordon turns to Captain Loeb, who glares at him.

> CAPTAIN LOEB

Outta my sight.

Gordon nods at Young Bruce, whose eyes wish Gordon would stay. Gordon leaves. Loeb turns to Young Bruce.

Good news . . . we got him, son.

Young Bruce looks up at him, dazed. Uncertain.

EXT. GROUNDS, WAYNE MANOR – DAY   29

Two open graves. Mourners disperse, guided by Security Guards. Alfred stands with Young Bruce. A man approaches, Earle (forty-seven). He nods at Alfred, crouching.

EARLE
(*indicates Alfred*)
You're in excellent hands, Bruce. And we're minding the empire.
When you're all grown up, it'll be waiting.

EXT. WAYNE MANOR – LATER   30

Mourners file towards the gates. Rachel walks with her mother.
Looks up at Bruce's high window. Sees him watching. Waves. Young
Bruce pauses, then returns the wave.

INT. BRUCE'S BEDROOM – CONTINUOUS   31

Alfred enters. Looks tenderly at Young Bruce's back.

ALFRED
I thought I'd prepare a little supper.

No response. Alfred turns.

Very well.

YOUNG BRUCE
(*out of shot*)
Alfred?

Alfred turns back. Young Bruce is looking at him with tears pouring
down his cheeks. Alfred tilts his head.

ALFRED
(*voice catching*)
Master Bruce?

YOUNG BRUCE
It was my fault, Alfred.

Alfred's mouth opens.

I made them leave the theater –

ALFRED
Oh, no, no, no –

Alfred moves to Young Bruce, taking the boy in his arms.

YOUNG BRUCE
If I hadn't got scared –

18

ALFRED

No, no, Master Bruce. Nothing you did. Nothing anyone ever
did can excuse that man.

Alfred holds Young Bruce away to look directly into his eyes.

It's his, and his alone. Do you understand?

Young Bruce nods. Then buries his face in Alfred's chest, sobbing.

YOUNG BRUCE

I miss them, Alfred. I miss them so much.

ALFRED
(*whispering*)

So do I, Master Bruce. So do I.

Tears well in Alfred's eyes as he holds the boy.

DUCARD
(*voice-over*)

And do you still feel responsible?

EXT. BALCONY, MONASTERY – DAY   32

Ducard and Wayne stand overlooking the glacier.

WAYNE

My anger outweighs my guilt.

Ducard nods. Understanding. Then leads Wayne into –

INT. MAIN CHAMBER, MONASTERY – DAY   33

*Warriors spar in various groupings around the different levels.
Wayne watches Ninjas hanging upside down on pillars. Ducard
shows him hand-spikes.*

DUCARD

The Ninja is thought invisible. But invisibility is largely a matter
of patience.

*A mezzanine level stacked with boxes and bottles. Ninjas pour
powders into packets, mixing compounds. Ducard takes a pinch of
a powder – throws it down – bang! Wayne flinches – Ducard smiles.*

Ninjitsu employs explosive powders.

WAYNE

As weapons?

Ducard hands Wayne a pinch of the powder.

DUCARD

Or distractions. Theatricality and deception are powerful
agents. You must become more than just a man in the mind of
your opponent.

Wayne tosses the powder – on the small explosion we cut –

EXT. FROZEN LAKE, HIMALAYAS – DAY   34

*Wayne and Ducard circle each other on the ice, swords poised to
strike. Dark figures in the white and blue landscape.*

*Ducard nods. Then strikes at Wayne, who deflects the blow using a
silver gauntlet with three scallops (thick, hooklike projections).
Ducard skids left, breath steaming . . .*

*Wayne steps sideways on the ice, his foot landing on a thin patch
which creaks, water bubbling underneath.*

DUCARD

Mind your surroundings. Always.

*Wayne strikes – Ducard blocks with his own bronze gauntlet. Wayne
slips right and flies in with a short thrust – Ducard's arm flips down
in a backhand move.*

Ducard catches Wayne's sword in one of his scallops.

Your parents' death was not your fault . . .

*Ducard rotates his arm, wrenching Wayne's sword from his grasp – it
skids along the ice. Ducard looks at Wayne.*

. . . it was your father's.

*Wayne, enraged, dives at Ducard, swinging at him with the scallops,
furious, reckless. Ducard parries with his sword, they lock – noses
inches apart, Wayne breathing . . . angry . . .*

Anger will not change the fact that your father failed to act.

WAYNE

The man had a gun!

DUCARD

Would that stop you?

WAYNE

I've had training.

DUCARD

The training is nothing. The will is everything. The will to act –

Wayne pushes Ducard back – Ducard strikes down at Wayne with his sword . . . Wayne blocks the strike with forearms crossed, slides between Ducard's legs across the ice to where his sword lies. Grasping his sword he spins, sweeping at Ducard's feet. Ducard leaps – Wayne catches his foot, brings him down onto the ice. Wayne thrusts his sword at Ducard's throat –

Stops inches from Ducard's bare neck. Ducard freezes, arms at his sides. Wayne looks down at Ducard in triumph.

WAYNE

Yield.

Ducard shakes his head.

DUCARD

You haven't beaten me. You've sacrificed sure footing for a killing stroke.

Ducard taps the ice beneath Wayne's feet with his sword – the ice gives way, plunging Wayne through the surface.

EXT. SHORE, FROZEN LAKE – EVENING   35

Ducard feeds a small fire. Wayne rubs his arms, shivering violently against hypothermia. Ducard looks at Wayne.

DUCARD

Rub your chest. Your arms will take care of themselves.

Wayne rubs his torso.

You're stronger than your father.

WAYNE
(*eyes blazing*)

You didn't know my father.

But I know the rage that drives you . . . that impossible anger
strangling the grief until your loved one's memory is just poison
in your veins . . . (*Distant.*) And one day you catch yourself
wishing the person you loved had never existed so you'd be
spared your pain . . .

Wayne looks up at Ducard, struck by his words.

I wasn't always here in the mountains. Once I had a wife. My
great love. (*Looks into fire.*) She was taken from me. Like you,
I was forced to learn that there are those without decency. Who
must be fought without hesitation or pity. (*Looks at Wayne.*)
Your anger gives you great power, but if you let it, it will
destroy you. As it almost did me.

                    WAYNE

What stopped it?

                    DUCARD

Vengeance.

Wayne nods. Bitter.

                    WAYNE

That's no help to me.

                    DUCARD

Why . . . ?

INT. MONORAIL TRAIN – DAY (WAYNE'S MEMORY)   36

*Looking out to Gotham. Bruce, now twenty-two, reflected in the
glass, stares sadly out at the city.*

                    DUCARD
                  (*voice-over*)
Why could you not avenge your parents?

The train is now filthy and covered in graffiti.

                    ANNOUNCER
                (*over loudspeaker*)
Wayne Station. Wayne Station next.

A yellow cab sits at the end of the drive.

Bruce stares at the imposing house.

> CABBIE
> You wanna pull up?

Alfred emerges from the house, peering at the cab. Bruce smiles sadly at the sight of his old friend.

Alfred leads Bruce through the main hall and up the main staircase. The house is now dark and empty. Dustcloths cover much of the furniture.

> ALFRED
> Will you be heading back to Princeton after the hearing,
> or could I persuade you to spend an extra night or two?

> BRUCE
> I'm not heading back at all.

> ALFRED
> Don't you like it there?

> BRUCE
> I like it fine . . . they just don't feel the same way.

Alfred glances back at Bruce. Irritated.

> ALFRED
> (*turns up the stairs*)
> I've prepared the master bedroom.

> BRUCE
> My old room will be fine.

> ALFRED
> With all due respect, sir, Wayne Manor is your house.

BRUCE
(*irritated*)
No, Alfred, it's my father's.

ALFRED
Your father is dead, Master Wayne.

BRUCE
(*gestures*)
And this is a mausoleum. When I have my way I'll pull the
damn thing down brick by brick.

Alfred turns on Bruce, angry.

ALFRED
This house, *Master Wayne*, has sheltered six generations of the
Wayne family.

BRUCE
Why do you give a damn? It's not *your* family, Alfred.

Alfred looks away. Bruce immediately regrets his words.

ALFRED
(*quiet*)
I give a damn, sir, because a good man once made me responsible
for what was most precious to him in the whole world.

Bruce looks at Alfred. Nods. Alfred opens the door.

Miss Dawes offered to drive you to the hearing.

BRUCE
Rachel? Why?

ALFRED
She probably hopes to talk you out of going.

BRUCE
Should I just bury the past out there with my parents, Alfred?

ALFRED
I don't presume to tell you what to do with your past, sir. Just
know that there are those of us who care what you do with
your future.

                              BRUCE
Haven't given up on me, yet?

                              ALFRED
                          (*conviction*)
Never.

INT. MASTER BEDROOM – CONTINUOUS   40

*Bruce puts his bag on the bed. Looks around the room. Uncomfortable.
The room is full of his parents.*

*At the mantel, Bruce stares at a framed photograph of his parents:
He wipes dust from it. Smiles at it. He turns to look at a case on the
table. Inside it is his father's stethoscope.*

*Insert cut: Young Bruce wearing the stethoscope, pressing it against
Thomas's chest, listening . . . Thomas shifts the position of the
diaphragm – Young Bruce smiles as he hears the beating.*

Bruce moves to the bed. Opens his case: inside it is a gun.

INT. MAIN HALL, WAYNE MANOR – LATER   41

Bruce walks through the hall to the kitchens.

INT. KITCHENS, WAYNE MANOR – CONTINUOUS   42

*Bruce stops at the open pantry door to stare at Rachel, now a
beautiful young woman of twenty-two. She runs her fingers over
the shelves of cans and boxes, a sad smile on her face .*

                              WAYNE
Alfred still keeps the condensed milk on the top shelf.

Rachel looks up, smiling at the tins of the sweet liquid.

                              RACHEL
Hasn't he noticed that you're tall enough to reach, now?

                              WAYNE
Old habits die hard, I guess.

She turns to face Bruce.

                                25

RACHEL

Never used to stop us, anyway.

WAYNE
(*smiles at the memory*)
No. No, it didn't.

RACHEL

So, you still trying to get kicked out of the entire Ivy League?

BRUCE
(*shakes head, smiling*)
Turns out you don't actually need a degree to do the international playboy thing. But you. . . . intern at the DA's office . . . quite the over-achiever.

Rachel shrugs modestly. Looks around.

RACHEL

I miss this place.

Wayne shakes his head, sadly.

WAYNE

This place is nothing without the people who made it what it was. Now there's only Alfred.

Rachel looks at Wayne significantly.

RACHEL

And you.

Wayne looks into her eyes. Sees the hope. Shifts.

WAYNE

I'm not staying, Rachel.

Rachel takes this in, hiding disappointment. Awkward.

RACHEL

Oh. I thought maybe this time . . . but you're just back for the hearing?

Bruce nods. Rachel looks down. Then back to Bruce.

Bruce, I don't suppose there's any way I can convince you not to come?

BRUCE

Someone at this *proceeding* should stand for my parents.

RACHEL

We all loved your parents. What Chill did is unforgivable.

BRUCE

Then why's your boss letting him go?

RACHEL

In prison he shared a cell with Carmine Falcone. He learned
things and he'll testify in exchange for early parole.

BRUCE

Rachel, this man killed my parents. I cannot let that pass. I need
you to understand.

Rachel looks at Bruce. Gently nods.

EXT. COURTHOUSE – DAY   43

Moving in on an imposing building surrounded by skyscrapers.

INT. COURTHOUSE – DAY   44

*A small bureaucratic proceeding. A five-person panel chaired by
Judge Faden. Bruce sits amongst the observers. Watching the back of
Chill's head. Rachel's boss, Finch, is speaking.*

FINCH

The depression hit working people like Mr. Chill hardest of all.
His crime was appalling, but it was motivated not by greed but
by desperation. Given the fourteen years already served and his
extraordinary level of cooperation with one of this office's most
important investigations . . . we strongly endorse his petition for
early release.

FADEN

Mr. Chill?

*Chill glances around nervously. Rises. The years have not been kind.
He clears his throat.*

CHILL

Your honor, not a day's gone by when I didn't wish I could take back what I did. Sure, I was desperate, like a lot of people back then. But that doesn't change what I did.

Chill sits. Judge Faden nods, consults his paperwork.

FADEN

I gather a member of the Wayne family is here today . . .

Chill reacts, turning. Bruce studies his weathered face.

CHAIRMAN

Does he have anything to say?

Chill spots Wayne's cold eyes. Has to look away. Bruce rises, walks out, all eyes on him. Including Rachel's.

EXT. PARKING LOT, COURTHOUSE – MOMENTS LATER   45

Bruce moves to Rachel's car. Crouches beside the front tire, picks up his gun, stuffs it up the sleeve of his overcoat.

The side exit opens and two Cops come out. A shout goes up from the pressmen around the front of the courthouse.

REPORTERS

They're taking him out the side!!

Reporters swarm around the building as Chill emerges.

REPORTER 1

Chill, any words for the Wayne family?!

Chill, head down, presses on. Bruce straightens. Breathes. Starts walking towards Chill. A Reporter spots him.

REPORTER 2

It's Bruce Wayne!

The Reporters clear a path, eager for a confrontation.

BLONDE FEMALE REPORTER

Joe! Hey Joe!!

This one catches Chill's eye – blonde, local TV type.

Bruce's hand drops to his side as he moves . . . he's breathing hard . . . thinking . . . deciding . . .

Falcone says hi!!

She thrusts a gun at Chill's chest and fires. Chill drops.

Bruce stops in his tracks. Reporters dive for cover – Cops jump on the Blonde Reporter, pinning her . . .

Bruce. Fifteen feet away. Loaded gun up his sleeve. Face as uncomprehending as the night Chill killed his parents. Rachel moves to Bruce, pulling him away from the chaos.

> RACHEL
> Come on, Bruce. Come on, we don't need to see this.

Bruce yanks his arm away.

> BRUCE
> I do.

INT. RACHEL'S CAR – EVENING   46

Rachel drives. Bruce sits there, hands in his lap. Staring.

> RACHEL
> The DA couldn't understand why Judge Faden insisted on making the hearing public. Falcone paid him off to get Chill out in the open.

> BRUCE
> Maybe I should be thanking them.

Rachel turns to Bruce, appalled.

> RACHEL
> You don't mean that.

> BRUCE
> What if I do, Rachel? My parents deserved justice.

> RACHEL
> You're not talking about justice, you're talking about revenge.

> BRUCE
> Sometimes they're the same.

RACHEL

They're *never* the same, Bruce. Justice is about harmony . . .
revenge is about you making yourself feel better. That's why we
have an impartial system –

BRUCE

Well, your *system* is broken.

RACHEL

Don't you tell me the system's broken, Bruce! I'm busting my
ass in school so that I can do something to fix it. You care about
justice . . . ?

Rachel yanks the wheel.

EXT. FREEWAY, GOTHAM – CONTINUOUS   47

Rachel's car screeches across two lanes, onto an exit ramp.

INT./EXT. RACHEL'S CAR ON SURFACE STREETS – CONTINUOUS
                                                              48

The streets below are dark, crowded and threatening.

RACHEL

Look beyond your own pain, Bruce.

*Rachel gestures at the filthy streets. Down dark alleys, shadowy
figures conduct business.*

This city is rotting. They talk about the depression as if it's history,
but it's not – things are worse than ever down here. Falcone
floods our streets with crime and drugs, preying on the desperate,
creating new Joe Chills every day. Falcone may not have killed
your parents, Bruce, but he's destroying everything they stood for.

They pull up in front of a basement club.

You want to thank him for that, here you go. We all know
where to find him . . . (*Gestures at club.*) But as long as he
keeps the bad people rich and the good people scared no one
will touch him. Good people like your parents who'll stand
against injustice are gone, Bruce. And what chance does
Gotham have when the good people do nothing?

She pokes him in the chest. Bruce looks down at her finger.

> BRUCE
> I'm not one of your 'good people', Rachel.

> RACHEL
> What do you mean?

> BRUCE
> All these years I wanted to kill him . . . (*Pulls up sleeve.*) . . . now I can't.

Turns his hand over. Rachel stares at the gun in his hand. She looks at Bruce. Shocked. Realizing.

> RACHEL
> You were going to kill him yourself.

She slaps him. Bruce does nothing. Rachel slaps him again and again. Nothing. She stops. Tears flowing.

> Just another coward with a gun. No better than Chill.

Rachel looks into Bruce's eyes.

> Your father would be ashamed of you.

Bruce stares at Rachel. Opens his door.

EXT. DOCK AREA, GOTHAM – CONTINUOUS   49

Bruce makes his way to the water. Takes out his gun. Turns it, studies the light off its metal.

Insert cut: the trembling barrel of Chill's gun.

Bruce, with contempt, flings his gun into the black water.

EXT. BASEMENT CLUB, FACING DOCKS – LATER   50

Bruce strides towards the entrance.

INT. BASEMENT CLUB – CONTINUOUS   51

Bruce enters the crowded club. He spots a figure holding court at a corner table. Falcone. Bruce pushes through the crowd, attracting curious stares. Falcone looks up.

FALCONE

You're taller than you look in the tabloids, Mr. Wayne.

A Thug appears at Bruce's side. Pats him down.

No gun? I'm insulted.

BRUCE

Only a coward needs a gun.

Falcone shrugs. Motions him to sit.

FALCONE

Coulda just sent a thank you note.

BRUCE

I didn't come here to thank you. I came here to show you that not everyone in Gotham is afraid of you.

FALCONE
(*laughs*)

Just those that know me, kid. Look around – you'll see two councilmen, a union official, a couple off-duty cops, a judge . . .

Judge Faden sits at a nearby table, eyeing Bruce nervously. Falcone pulls a gun from under the table. Holds it to Bruce's forehead. People stop their conversations, staring.

I don't have a second's hesitation blowing your head off in front of them . . . that's power you can't buy. The power of fear.

BRUCE
(*smiles*)

I'm not afraid of you.

FALCONE

Because you think you've got nothing to lose. But you haven't thought it through – you haven't thought about your lady friend from the DA's . . . or that old butler of yours . . .

Bruce tries to hide his reaction. Falcone lowers his gun.

People from your world always have so much to lose. That's why they keep me in business – I stop the desperate heading uptown the way Joe Chill did. You think because your mommy and daddy got shot you know the ugly side of life, but you don't. You've never tasted desperation – you're Bruce Wayne,

32

Prince of Gotham – you'd have to go a thousand miles to meet someone who didn't know your name. So don't come down here with all your anger . . . trying to prove something to yourself – this is a world you'll never understand. And you'll always fear what you don't understand.

Falcone nods – a Thug punches Bruce's side, Bruce turns – is grabbed by two Thugs – he fights back, but is overwhelmed.

You got spirit, kid, I'll give you that. More than your old man, anyway.

Bruce looks at Falcone. Blood on his face. Surprised.

In the joint Chill told me about the night he killed your parents . . . said your dad begged for mercy. *Begged.* Like a dog.

Bruce stares back at Falcone.

EXT. FALCONE'S BASEMENT CLUB, DOCK AREA – MOMENTS LATER   52

Two Bouncers toss Bruce into the street – he hits the deck, rolling across the asphalt. A Homeless Man, warming at a flaming oil drum, watches Bruce struggle to his feet.

MALE VOICE
Shoulda tipped better.

Bruce turns. Walks over to the Man, wiping the blood off his face. The Homeless Man looks him up and down.

Bruce stares at the Man. Thinking. Takes out his wallet. Removes the money. Hands it to the Homeless Man.

HOMELESS MAN
For what?

BRUCE
Your jacket.

Bruce drops his wallet into the fire. The Homeless Man laughs. Bruce pulls off his tie, throws it into the fire. He pulls off his overcoat, bundles it up ready to –

HOMELESS MAN
Lemme have it, that's a good coat.

33

Bruce looks at the Homeless Man, who has removed his own. They exchange clothing.

> BRUCE
>
> Be careful who sees you with that. (*Off look.*) They're gonna come looking for me.

> HOMELESS MAN
>
> Who?

> BRUCE
>
> Everyone.

Bruce, less incongruous in his 'new' coat, wanders the stacks. A horn sounds. Bruce's eyes lock on to the ship preparing to leave. Bruce runs towards it through the shadows . . .

INT. WALKWAY, MONASTERY – DAY (PRESENT)   53

Ducard watches Wayne face off against a shaven-headed warrior.

As they spar, shouting from across the monastery distracts Wayne and he gets put down. Ducard shakes his head.

> DUCARD
>
> Childish, Wayne.

Wayne sits there, looking over as two Warriors drag a screaming man towards a cage . . .

> WAYNE
>
> Who is he?

> DUCARD
>
> He was a farmer. Then he tried to take his neighbor's land and became a murderer . . .

Wayne watches them lock the Murderer into the cage . . .

> Now he's a prisoner.

The cage is winched ten feet off the ground. The Murderer's arms hang through the cage. He is whimpering.

> WAYNE
>
> What will happen to him?

DUCARD

Justice. Crime cannot be tolerated – criminals thrive on the indulgence of society's 'understanding'. You know this.

Wayne nods, staring at the Murderer in the cage, troubled. Ducard watches Wayne.

Or when you lived among the criminals . . . did you make the same mistake as your father? Did you start to *pity* them?

Wayne looks at Ducard, thinking . . . shrugs.

WAYNE

The first time you steal . . . so that you don't starve . . . you lose many assumptions about the simple nature of right and wrong.

EXT. CROWDED MARKET, AFRICAN PORT TOWN – EVENING
(MEMORY)   54

Bruce picks up a mango from a stack to examine it.

WAYNE
(*voice-over*)
. . . so that you don't starve . . .

He uses his lower hand to slip a plum into his pocket.

EXT. ALLEY, AFRICAN PORT TOWN – LATER   55

Bruce squats in a doorway. Bites hungrily into his plum. He looks up. A Child in rags sits in the next doorway, staring. Bruce stares back, juice dripping.

WAYNE
(*voice-over*)
. . . you lose many assumptions about the simple nature of right and wrong.

Bruce hands the Child the plum. Licks his fingers. Hard.

EXT. CAR PARK, LONDON – DAY   56

Bruce watches an Old Man slim-jim a sports car's window.

                    WAYNE
                  (*voice-over*)
     As I traveled, I learned . . .

EXT. BUILDING, SHANGHAI – DAY   57

Wayne and Stocky Chinese Man sit in a car, watching a truck being loaded.

                    WAYNE
                  (*voice-over*)
     I felt the fear before a crime . . .

INT. WAREHOUSE, SHANGHAI – DAY   58

The truck races in – two Criminals yank the doors shut after.

                    WAYNE
                  (*voice-over*)
     . . . and the thrill of success . . .

Bruce and Stocky jump down from the cab, laughing.

                    BRUCE
     Where's your friend?

                   STOCKY
                  (*shrugs*)
     Not friend. Friend of friend.

Bruce stops laughing. Looks at Stocky with contempt. The doors explode – Cops burst in, shouting in Mandarin.

INT. SAME – LATER   59

The back of the truck is opened – Cops inventory piles of boxes pulled out of the back.

                    WAYNE
                  (*voice-over*)
     . . . without becoming one of them.

Bruce sits in a line of criminals, hands cuffed behind back. A Cop yanks him to his feet, hauling him over to an Officer.

COP
(*in Mandarin*)
He refuses to give his name.

OFFICER
(*to Bruce*)
Fool, what the hell do I care what your name is? You're a criminal.

BRUCE
(*in fluent Mandarin*)
I'm not a criminal.

OFFICER
Tell that to the guy who owned these!

He kicks a box: close on the Wayne Enterprises logo.

INT. PRISON COURTYARD – DAY   60

Wayne is led across the courtyard. The Prisoners stare.

DUCARD
(*voice-over*)
You travelled the world to understand the criminal mind and conquer your fear . . .

INT. THRONE ROOM – NIGHT   61

Close on Wayne's blue poppy – now shriveled dry – on the altar. Wayne, clad in black Ninja uniform, watches as Ducard, also in black, picks it up, takes a pestle and mortar, drops in the dried flower, and grinds it to dust.

DUCARD
But a criminal isn't complicated, and what you really fear is inside yourself. You fear your own power. Your own anger. The drive to do great or terrible things . . . you must journey inwards . . .

Ducard pours the dust into a small brazier. Lights it. Motions to Wayne.

Drink in your fears. Face them. You are ready.

37

Wayne breathes the smoke. He shakes his head. Reacting to the effects of the smoke, his mind is plagued by images: Chill's trembling gun – Young Bruce falling – Thomas staggering.

Ducard puts on his Ninja mask. Motions Wayne to do the same. Wayne struggles to think through the effects of the smoke . . .

Dozens of identical Ninjas step forward from the shadows: Ducard has melted into the crowd. Wayne raises his guard . . .

> To conquer fear, you must become fear . . . you must bask in the fear of other men . . . and men fear most what they cannot *see* –

Ducard strikes at Wayne – Wayne spins, parries – but Ducard has gone. The Ninjas move in unison, forming walls . . .

> It is not enough to be a man . . . you have to become an idea . . . a terrible thought . . . a *wraith* . . .

The Ninja nearest Wayne turns and slashes – it is Ducard. Wayne leaps sideways, rolling through the wall of Ninjas. He looks at his arm – it has been slashed, the uniform torn – a dead giveaway. Wayne looks around, crouched, ready . . .

One wall of Ninjas parts, revealing a wooden box. Wayne stares at it, mind spinning from the smoke.

> Embrace your worst fear . . .

Wayne cautiously approaches the box. Carefully lifts the lid. Peers inside . . .

Bats explode from the box, filling the air – Wayne dives away from the box, staring up at the squawking bats – flinching . . .

Ducard leaps at Wayne, who rolls sideways, blocking. Wayne turns to face Ducard, but he is lost in the Ninjas, bats filling the air, Wayne flinching with their attacks . . .

Wayne stays low. Slashes the arm of the Ninja nearest him – the man does not move. Wayne turns. Fighting to think.

A Ninja paces softly through the crowd. As he speaks, we can tell this is Ducard . . .

> Become one with the darkness . . .

Ducard falls in behind a Ninja with a slashed sleeve . . . He knocks him to his knees, sword against throat –

> You cannot leave any sign . . .

Ducard pulls off his own mask. Disappointed.

> WAYNE
> (*out of shot*)

I haven't.

A sword is at Ducard's neck – Wayne is behind him, pulling off his mask. Ducard looks around . . . several of the Ninjas around them have slashed sleeves. Ducard smiles. From across the chamber . . . clapping. Rā's al Ghūl sits, watching.

> RĀ'S AL GHŪL

Impressive.

The Ninjas turn, in unison, and sit. Wayne releases Ducard. Ducard leads Wayne in front of Rā's. Rā's leads them to a brazier, with a branding iron sticking out over the rim. Rā's al Ghūl begins speaking in Urdu.

> DUCARD
> (*translating*)

We have purged your fear. You are ready to lead these men. You are ready to become a member of the League of Shadows.

Rā's al Ghūl indicates the Murderer kneeling before them.

(*continues translating*) First you must demonstrate your commitment to justice.

Ducard hands Wayne his sword. Wayne looks at the Murderer, who looks back with pleading eyes.

> WAYNE

No. I'm no executioner.

> DUCARD

Your compassion is a weakness your enemies won't share.

> WAYNE

That's why it's so important. It separates me from them.

> DUCARD

You want to fight criminals. This man is a murderer.

> WAYNE

This man should be tried.

DUCARD

By whom? Corrupt bureaucrats? Criminals mock society's laws.
You know this better than most.

Rā's al Ghūl steps forward, eyes burning. Starts speaking . . .

RĀ'S AL GHŪL
(*accented English*)

You cannot lead these men unless you are prepared to do what
is necessary to defeat evil.

WAYNE

Where would I be leading these men?

RĀ'S AL GHŪL

Gotham. As Gotham's favored son you will be ideally placed to
strike at the heart of criminality.

WAYNE

How?

RĀ'S AL GHŪL
(*accented English*)

Gotham's time has come. Like Constantinople or Rome before
it . . . the city has become a breeding ground for suffering and
injustice . . . it is beyond saving and must be allowed to die.
This is the most important function of the League of Shadows.
It is one we have performed for centuries. Gotham must be
destroyed.

Wayne turns to Ducard.

WAYNE

You can't believe in this.

Ducard looks at Wayne, then looks down, troubled.

DUCARD

Rā's al Ghūl rescued us from the darkest corners of our own
hearts . . . what he asks in return is the courage to do what is
necessary.

WAYNE

I'll go back to Gotham. And I'll fight men like this. But I won't
be an executioner.

40

Wayne looks at the Murderer kneeling next to the brazier.

DUCARD
(*low, emphatic*)
Wayne, please, for your own sake . . . there is no turning
back . . .

*Wayne looks at Ducard. Then raises his sword, preparing to strike.
The Murderer's head is bowed, trembling.*

*Wayne strikes down with his sword, missing the Murderer's neck by
inches, striking the white-hot branding iron, flipping it off the brazier
and through the air into the mezzanine where the explosives are
stored.*

What are you doing?

WAYNE
What's necessary.

Wayne strikes Ducard in the head with the flat of his sword . . .

*Rā's strikes at Wayne – Wayne parries – explosions roar from the
balcony, shooting flame across the ceiling. Rā's and Wayne fight as
explosions surround them . . .*

*Wayne leaps clear as flaming debris collapses onto Rā's, crushing
him . . . the flames are rising, Ninja bodies are strewn around, fresh
explosions rip across the hall as Ninjas flee, and Wayne spots Ducard
lying unconscious.*

*Wayne picks up Ducard, hauls him out of the throne room into a
passage, smashing through an ornate screen . . .*

EXT. MOUNTAINS – CONTINUOUS   62

*Wayne and Ducard crash down onto a steep slope of ice and rock,
the monastery exploding above them . . . Wayne rolls over, grabs
a rock, looks across to see –*

*Ducard, unconscious, sliding down the icy slope. His limp form
rotates, spinning as his body gathers momentum, rushing towards the
edge of the cliff . . .*

*Wayne dives after him, sliding headfirst down the ice . . . the cliff
closer and closer, as Wayne races after Ducard . . .*

Mere feet from the cliff edge, Wayne grabs Ducard – raises his free gauntlet-clad arm, and smashes at the ice, digging in with the bronze scallops . . . stopping on the edge. Ducard hangs limply over a tremendous drop – Wayne struggles with the dead weight. Wayne pulls Ducard up onto the ice. Breathing.

EXT. TINY HAMLET, HIMALAYAS – DAY   63

Wayne carries Ducard down the road.

INT. SHERPA'S HUT – MOMENTS LATER   64

Wayne kicks the door open. The Old Man he saw on his way up the mountain stares back at him. Then motions Wayne to put Ducard down onto some mats. The Old Man wipes blood from Ducard's temple. Looks at Wayne, who is moving to the door . . .

> OLD MAN
> I will tell him you saved his life.

Wayne stops. Turns. Looks back at Ducard.

> WAYNE
> Tell him . . . I have an ailing ancestor who needs me.

Wayne puts his hands together in formal salute. Bows.

EXT. LANDING STRIP, KHATMANDU – EVENING   65

A gleaming G5 sits on the runway. Wayne, ragged, filthy, approaches the plane. The door opens: Alfred stands there in the doorway. Wayne pauses at the foot of the steps.

> ALFRED
> Master Wayne. It's been some time.

> WAYNE
> (smiles)
> Yes. Yes, it has.

Alfred looks him over.

> ALFRED
> You look rather fashionable. Apart from the dried blood.

Wayne sits, drink in hand, ragged against rich leather.

> ALFRED
>
> Are you coming back to Gotham for long, sir?

> WAYNE
>
> As long as it takes.

Alfred looks at Wayne, curious.

> I'm going to show the people of Gotham that the city doesn't belong to the criminals and the corrupt.

Alfred looks at Wayne, thinking.

> ALFRED
>
> During the depression your father nearly bankrupted Wayne Enterprises combating poverty . . . he believed that his example would inspire the wealthy of Gotham to save their city . . .

> WAYNE
>
> Did it?

> ALFRED
> *(nods sadly)*
>
> In a way . . . their murder shocked the wealthy and powerful into action.

> WAYNE
> *(nods, bitter)*
>
> People need dramatic examples to shake them out of apathy. I can't do this as Bruce Wayne. A man is just flesh and blood, and can be ignored or destroyed. But a *symbol* . . . as a symbol I can be incorruptible, everlasting . . .

> ALFRED
>
> What symbol?

> WAYNE
>
> I'm not sure, yet. Something elemental. Something terrifying.

> ALFRED
>
> I assume, sir, that since you're taking on the underworld, this 'symbol' is a persona to protect those you care about from reprisals?

WAYNE
(*nods*)
You're thinking about Rachel?

ALFRED
Actually, sir, I was thinking of myself.

WAYNE
Have you told anyone I'm coming back?

ALFRED
I haven't figured out the legal ramifications of raising you from
the dead.

WAYNE
Dead?

ALFRED
It's been seven years.

WAYNE
You had me declared dead?

ALFRED
Actually, it was Mr. Earle. He wanted to liquidate your majority
shareholding. He's taking the company public. Your shares
brought in an enormous amount of capital.

WAYNE
Good thing I left everything to you, then.

ALFRED
Quite so, sir. (*Closes his eyes.*) You're welcome to borrow the
Rolls, by the way. Just bring it back with a full tank.

EXT. GOTHAM – SUNRISE   67

Moving over spires of the city, catching gold of first light.

INT. UNMARKED POLICE SEDAN – EVENING   68

*Gordon, now forty-six and a Detective, in the passenger seat. Worn
eyes watching his partner, Flass, forty-two, glad-hand the owner of
the liquor store they are parked outside. Flass squeezes into the
driving seat holding a wad of cash.*

44

Don't s'pose you want a taste?

Gordon looks at Flass, cold. Flass shrugs. Counts his money.

I keep offering 'cause who knows, maybe one day you'll get wise.

GORDON

Nothing wise in what you do, Flass.

FLASS

Yeah? Well, Jimbo, you don't take your taste – makes us guys nervous you might decide to roll over –

GORDON
(*irritated*)

I'm no rat, Flass. (*Calmer.*) In a town this bent, who's there to rat to, anyway?

Flass laughs at this, hits the gas.

EXT. POLICE STATION – NIGHT   69

Gordon slams the car door. Watches Flass pull away. Weary. Someone watches him from a doorway. It is Wayne.

INT. FALCONE'S CLUB – NIGHT   70

Judge Faden sits sandwiched between two Girls, drink and cigar in hand. Falcone gets up from the table.

FADEN

Carmine! Where are you going?

FALCONE

Duty calls. You have yourself a good time, Judge.

Falcone leans in to the Club Manager.

If he's too cheap to get a hotel, at least make him take his car around to the alley. (*Shakes his head.*) No class.

Falcone heads into his back office.

Judge Faden exits the club, a Girl on his arm. Faden guides her into a waiting limo. A Street Person comes over to the rear windows of the car, knocking. The Driver gets out.

> DRIVER
>
> Get lost!

The Driver kicks the Street Person away from the limo. A Homeless Man warming by a fire starts shouting. It is the Homeless Man that Bruce gave his coat to years before. The coat is worn but recognizable.

> HOMELESS MAN
>
> Leave him alone! Let him be!

The limo moves off. Close on the Street Person watching it leave. It is Bruce. He glances down at a tiny camera in his lap. Smiles at the screen: Faden and the Girl.

INT. GOTHAM COURTHOUSE – DAY 72

Rachel sits at the lawyer's table watching, appalled, as a thin, bespectacled man testifies. This is Doctor Crane. He clears his throat, nervous. Leans in to the microphone.

> CRANE
>
> In my opinion Mr. Zsaz is as much a danger to himself as to others . . .

A shaven-headed prisoner sits in the dock. Victor Zsaz.

> . . . and prison is probably not the best environment for his rehabilitation.

INT. STAIRCASE, DISTRICT ATTORNEY'S OFFICE – DAY 73

Rachel hurries down the marble stairs after Crane.

> RACHEL
>
> Dr. Crane!

> CRANE
> (*guarded*)
>
> Yes, Miss Dawes?

                                    RACHEL
        You seriously think that Victor Zsaz shouldn't be in jail –?

Crane looks at her, bewildered.

                                    CRANE
        I would hardly have testified to that otherwise, would I, Miss
        Dawes?

They pass through the doors into the portico.

                                    RACHEL
        This is the third of Carmine Falcone's thugs that you've seen fit
        to have declared insane and moved into your asylum . . .

                                    CRANE
        Well, the work offered by organized crime has an attraction to
        the insane.

                                    RACHEL
        Or the corrupt.

Crane turns to Rachel. Stares. Then speaks over her shoulder.

                                    CRANE
        Mr. Finch, I think you should check with Miss Dawes here just
        what implications your office has authorized her to make. If
        any.

Crane walks off. Finch comes over, takes Rachel's arm.

                                    FINCH
        What're you doing, Rachel?

                                    RACHEL
                                   (*annoyed*)
        What are you doing, Carl?

Finch takes her elbow and guides her into a doorway.

                                    FINCH
        Looking out for you. (*Glances around.*) Rachel, Falcone's got
        half the city bought and paid for . . . drop it.

                                    RACHEL
        How can you say that?

FINCH
Because much as I care about getting Falcone . . . I care more
about you.

Rachel looks at Finch. Smiles sadly.

RACHEL
That's sweet, Carl. But we've been through all this . . .

*Across the car park, sitting in a doorway. A Street Person watches
Rachel kiss Finch on the cheek. Moving closer, we see that the Street
Person is Wayne. He watches them for a beat, then moves along.*

INT. LIBRARY, WAYNE MANOR – NIGHT   74

*Wayne, cross-legged on the floor, studies papers and photos: Gordon,
Rachel . . . Wayne picks up Rachel's picture: a long-lens candid photo
of her leaving work.*

Wayne hears a chittering. He rises, moving out into the main hall . . .

INT. MAIN HALL, WAYNE MANOR – CONTINUOUS   75

Wayne stares: a small shadow flutters around the ceiling.

ALFRED
(*out of shot*)
A blessed bat again, sir.

Wayne turns to find Alfred standing there with a tea service.

They nest somewhere on the grounds.

Wayne watches the dark shape flicker around the ceiling.

EXT. GROUNDS, WAYNE MANOR – DAY   76

*Wayne walks across the gardens to the greenhouse. He wears a long
overcoat, a coil of rope over one arm.*

INT. GREENHOUSE – CONTINUOUS   77

*Now derelict. Glass cracked or missing, paint peeled from wrought
iron. Wayne stands in the entrance, remembering –*

Insert cut: Rachel, laughing, sprinting between the tables.

Darkness, punctured by light as boards are yanked, splintering from the mouth of the well, high above.

Wayne lowers himself down the shaft, overcoat billowing. He undoes his rope at the bottom. Turns, finding –

The dark crevice between the rocks. Wayne crouches, pushing into the blackness, crawling through into –

INT. CAVERNS – CONTINUOUS 79

Wayne climbs down a jagged rock crevice. Air blows in his face. The crevice widens into a low-ceilinged chamber. Wayne hears the rush of water. He crouches, advances through the low chamber. It turns downwards, steeper – Wayne carefully slides on his back, lowering himself into –

Limitless black. Wayne stands. A roar of water now. He reaches into his coat, pulls out a chemical torch. Cracks it, throwing light into –

A vast cavern. An underground river, a jagged ceiling, far above, which, as Wayne peers, starts to move –

Bats explode from the ceiling. Thousands descend, screeching, attracted to the light. Wayne instinctively crouches. But as they swarm around him terrifyingly –

Wayne rises to his feet amidst a cyclone of bats, watching the fluttering blackness with a profound calm.

And he knows the symbol he must use.

INT. FALCONE'S BASEMENT CLUB, BACK OFFICE – NIGHT 80

Falcone slides a drink across his desk to Crane.

> CRANE
> No more favors. Someone's sniffing around.

> FALCONE
> I scratch your back, you scratch mine, Doc. I'm bringing in your shipments.

> CRANE
> We're paying you for that.

Maybe money isn't as interesting to me as favors.

Crane leans forward. Icy calm.

CRANE

I'm aware that you're not intimidated by me, Mr. Falcone. But you know who I'm working for. . . and when he gets here –

FALCONE

He's coming to Gotham?

CRANE

And he's not going to want to hear that you've endangered our operation just to get your thugs out of jailtime.

Falcone considers this. Nods.

FALCONE

Who's bothering you?

CRANE

There's a girl in the DA's office . . .

FALCONE
(*shrugs*)

We'll buy her off.

CRANE

Not this one.

FALCONE

Idealist, huh? Well, there's an answer for that, too.

CRANE

I don't want to know.

Falcone looks at Crane with thinly disguised contempt.

FALCONE

Yes, you do.

INT. BOARD ROOM, WAYNE TOWER – DAY   81

A board meeting in full swing. Earle presiding.

EXECUTIVE

... but we're showing *very* healthy growth in these sectors –

FREDERICKS

I don't think that Thomas Wayne would have viewed heavy arms manufacture as a suitable cornerstone of our business –

EARLE
(*irritated*)

I think, Fredericks, that after twenty years, we ought to be at a point where we stop asking ourselves what Thomas Wayne would have done . . .

INT. OUTER OFFICE, WAYNE TOWER – CONTINUOUS 82

A young, beautiful Assistant at her desk, head down.

WAYNE
(*out of shot*)

Good morning, I'm here to see Mr. Earle.

The Assistant reaches for a list. Impatient.

ASSISTANT

Name?

WAYNE

Bruce Wayne.

The Assistant starts looking for the name. Then realizes. She looks up. Staring. Wayne, immaculately turned out (suit, tie, perfect hair). He smiles. She smiles back.

INT. BOARD ROOM, WAYNE TOWER – CONTINUOUS 83

Earle looks at Fredericks, annoyed.

EARLE

Thomas Wayne wouldn't have wanted to take the company public, either, but that's what, as responsible managers, we're going to do . . .

Earle hits the intercom.

Jessica, get me that prospectus.

Silence.

Jessica . . . ?

INT. RECEPTION AREA – CONTINUOUS 84

Earle whips open the door. Wayne, his back to Earle, has his arms wrapped around Jessica's hips, showing her a golf putt along the carpet . . .

> EARLE
>
> Jessica, who's answering the phones?!

> WAYNE
>
> It's Wayne Enterprises, Mr. Earle – (*Turns to Earle.*) I'm sure they'll call back.

Earle stares. Dumbstruck. Wayne smiles.

> EARLE
>
> Bruce?

Board members lean over, staring through the door.

We thought . . . you were dead.

> WAYNE
> (*smiles*)
>
> Sorry to disappoint.

Fredericks smiles. Wayne hands Earle his putter.

INT. EARLE'S OFFICE, WAYNE ENTERPRISES – LATER 85

Earle pours Wayne a cup of coffee. Cautious.

> EARLE
>
> You realize, Bruce, that it's too late to stop the public offering . . .

Wayne takes the coffee. Smiling reassuringly.

> WAYNE
>
> I understand. I'll be handsomely rewarded for my shares. I'm not here to interfere – I'm looking for a job. (*Off look.*) I just want to get to know the company that my family built.

                              EARLE
Any idea where you'd start?

                              WAYNE
Applied Sciences caught my eye.

                              EARLE
                            (*surprised*)
Mr. Fox's department? (*Shrugs.*) Perfect. I'll make a call.

Wayne nods. Rises.

Oh, and Bruce? Some of the secretaries and so on . . . because
of your name they may assume . . .

                              WAYNE
I'll be absolutely clear with everyone that I'm just another
humble employee.

INT. FINCH'S OFFICE – DAY   86

Rachel hands Finch paperwork. He studies her.

                              FINCH
Have you seen him yet?

                              RACHEL
Who?

                              FINCH
Wayne.

                              RACHEL
                            (*confused*)
Bruce? What do you mean?

                              FINCH
You haven't heard? It's been all over the news today. He's back.

Rachel stares. Taking it in.

INT. APPLIED SCIENCES DIVISION – DAY   87

*Lucius Fox, an African-American man (fifty-two) reclines at a desk in
a darkened room. He looks at Wayne over his glasses.*

                              FOX
Environmental applications, defense projects, consumer
products . . . all prototypes, none in production at any level
whatsoever.

                             WAYNE
None?

Fox pauses, turns to Wayne, a wicked gleam in his eye.

                              FOX
What did they tell you this place was?

                             WAYNE
They didn't tell me anything.

                              FOX
Earle told me *exactly* what it was when he sent me here . . .

*Fox throws a switch – lights flicker on, revealing a massive warehouse,
stacked with shapes under dust covers, tools, lab equipment . . .*

        . . . a dead end where I couldn't cause any more trouble for the
rest of the board.

Fox leads Wayne through the stacks.

                             WAYNE
You were on the board?

                              FOX
Back when your father ran things.

                             WAYNE
You knew my father?

                              FOX
Sure. Helped him build his train.

Fox leads Wayne to an area stacked with harnesses.

        Here we are.

Fox pulls out a box. Inside: a grappling gun and harness.

        Pneumatic. Magnetic grapple. Monofilament tested to 350
pounds.

Wayne feels the weight. It is light. Strong. He picks up the harness that goes with it. Shoulder straps with a wide, hi-tech belt. Wayne shoves the back end of the gun into the belt buckle – it clicks into place.

INT. SAME – MOMENTS LATER   88

Fox leads Wayne through some tall crates.

> FOX
>
> Beautiful project, your dad's train – routed right into Wayne Tower, along with the water and power utilities. Made Wayne Tower the unofficial heart of Gotham. Course Earle's left it to rot . . .

Fox stops at a tall crate. Checks paperwork. Opens the crate: a bodysuit – clear silicone over jointed armor.

> Here it is: the nomex survival suit for advanced infantry. Kevlar bi-weave, reinforced joints . . .

Wayne feels the fabric of the suit.

> WAYNE
>
> Tear-resistant?

Fox hacks at the suit with his pen – it doesn't even mark.

> FOX
>
> This sucker'll stop a *knife*.

> WAYNE
>
> Bullet-proof?

> FOX
>
> Anything but a straight shot.

> WAYNE
>
> Why didn't they put it into production?

> FOX
>
> The bean-counters figured a soldier's life wasn't worth the three hundred grand.

Fox looks at Wayne. Suspicious.

> So what do you want with it, Mr. Wayne?

WAYNE

I want to borrow it. For spelunking. (*Off look.*) You know,
cave-diving.

Fox shrugs. Puts the lid back on the crate.

FOX

You get a lot of gunfire down in those caves?

WAYNE
(*smiles*)
Listen, I'd rather Mr. Earle didn't know about me borrowing.

FOX

Mr. Wayne, the way *I* see it . . .

Fox waves his arm, taking in the enormous facility.

All this stuff is yours, anyway.

INT. CAVERNS BENEATH WAYNE MANOR – DAY   89

*Wayne, high on the cavern wall, in climbing harness, hammers a
bracket into the rock securing a line of industrial lamps.*

WAYNE

OK! Give it a try.

*Alfred throws a switch on a portable generator: the lamps flicker on,
dimly lighting the length of one wall. Alfred peers at the damp, dingy
surroundings.*

ALFRED

Oh, *charming.*

Alfred sees the bats covering the entire ceiling.

At least you'll have company.

*Wayne rappels to the cave floor, looks up to a high corner: crumbling
brickwork. Alfred follows his gaze.*

Must be the lowest foundations of the south-east wing.

*Wayne climbs up, poking through the rock ceiling: the bottom of
a wrought-iron spiral staircase. In the center of the spiral: a dumb-
waiter lift, fallen off its track. Wayne grabs the chains of the lift,
rattles them – sending a wave echoing up into the darkness.*

During the Civil War your great-grandfather was involved with the underground railroad. Secretly transporting freed slaves to the North. I suspect these caverns came in handy.

Wayne jumps down. Moves to the small river. Follows it to where it disappears under rocks. Steps over. Alfred follows. The roar of water gets louder and the light gets brighter as Wayne follows the tunnel around a dog leg, emerging.

Behind the face of a waterfall. Wayne grins, hops across slick rocks right up to the beautiful curtain of water.

> WAYNE
> (*awe*)

Alfred, come up here.

Alfred is twenty feet behind on the dry rocks.

> ALFRED

I can see it very well from here, thank you, sir.

Wayne, mesmerized, reaches for water that is liquid light.

INT. BATCAVE – DAY   90

Wayne places two bronze gauntlets on a trestle table. Fires up a paint sprayer. Coats them matt black. Wayne moves onto the body-suit. Starts coating it black.

INT. SAME – LATER   91

Wayne is showing Alfred diagrams. We catch only glimpses.

> ALFRED

If we order the main part of this . . . (*Points.*) . . . *cowl* from Singapore

> WAYNE

Via a shell corporation.

> ALFRED

Indeed. Then, quite separately, place an order through a Chinese manufacturer for *these* –

Alfred points at a diagram which looks like a pair of horns.

                         WAYNE
                        (*nods*)
Put it together ourselves.

                         ALFRED
Precisely. Of course, they'll have to be large orders to avoid
suspicion.

                         WAYNE
How large?

                         ALFRED
Say, ten thousand.

                         WAYNE
                        (*smiles*)
Least we'll have spares.

INT. FALCONE'S CLUB – NIGHT   92

Flass approaches Falcone's table. Sits.

                         FALCONE
I need you at the docks tomorrow.
                         FLASS
Problem?

                         FALCONE
Insurance. I don't want any problems on this last shipment.
Flass shrugs.

                         FLASS
Sure. Word on the street is you got a beef with someone in the
DA's . . .

                         FALCONE
Is that right?

                         FLASS
And that you've offered a price on doing something about it.

                         FALCONE
What's your point, Flass?

FLASS

You seen this girl? Cute little assistant DA . . . that's a lot of heat to bring down, even in this town.

FALCONE

Never underestimate Gotham. Besides, people get mugged on the way home from work every day . . .

EXT. FALCONE'S BASEMENT CLUB, DOCK AREA – NIGHT   93

Wayne, opposite the club, has his hand under his hood, adjusting a directional microphone hooked over his ear.

FLASS
(*over mike*)

Sometimes it goes bad.

EXT. ROOFTOPS, GOTHAM – NIGHT   94

Moving in on a rooftop balustrade to discover Wayne, in black body-suit and gauntlets, crouched, watching the police station across the street. He pulls on a black balaclava. Climbs through the shadows using Ninja spikes on his hands and feet.

INT. BULLPEN – CONTINUOUS   95

Gordon walks through the bullpen, pulling off his coat.

INT. GORDON'S OFFICE – CONTINUOUS   96

Gordon slumps into his chair, back to the window. Reaches for the phone – the light goes out.

WAYNE
(*out of shot*)

Don't turn around.

Gordon freezes – Wayne is behind him, pressing a stapler between Gordon's shoulder blades as if it were a gun.

GORDON

What do you want?

WAYNE

You're a good cop. One of the few.

Gordon narrows his eyes, puzzled.

Carmine Falcone brings in shipments of drugs every week, nobody takes him down. Why?

GORDON

He's paid up with the right people.

WAYNE

What would it take to bring him down?

GORDON

Leverage on Judge Faden. And a DA brave enough to prosecute.

WAYNE

Rachel Dawes in the DA's office.

GORDON

Who are you?

WAYNE

Watch for my sign.

GORDON

You're just one man?

WAYNE

Now we are two.

GORDON

We?

No response. Gordon turns around. No one. He jumps to the window – looks down, looks up: a shadow slips onto the roof –

INT. BULLPEN – CONTINUOUS   97

Gordon races across the bullpen, drawing his gun, hits the stairwell – two uniforms see him go, run after him.

EXT. ROOFTOP – CONTINUOUS   98

Wayne moves to the edge of the roof – the gap is too big. He turns back – the door smashes open. Gordon gun is raised.

GORDON

FREEZE!

Wayne races for the gap – leaps . . . drops fast . . . misses the top storey – grabs the balcony below . . . it breaks away – drops him onto the one below. Winded, Wayne climbs onto the wall.

From the other roof, Gordon watches Wayne melt into the shadows. The Uniforms arrive either side.

UNIFORM I

The hell was that?!

GORDON
(*dismissive*)

Some nut.

But Gordon's expression is less certain.

INT. APPLIED SCIENCES DIVISION – MORNING   99

Fox watches Wayne approaching with a slight limp.

FOX
(*smiles*)

What's it today? More 'spalunking'?

WAYNE

Spe-lunking. And no, today it's base-jumping.

FOX

Base-jumping? What, like parachuting?

WAYNE

Kind of. Do you have any lightweight fabrics?

Fox looks at Wayne over his glasses. Smiles.

FOX

Oh, yeah.

INT. SAME – MOMENTS LATER   100

Fox hands Wayne a sheet of black fabric.

FOX

Notice anything?

Wayne examines it, shrugs. Fox puts on a glove.

Memory fabric – flexible ordinarily, but put a current through it . . .

Fox grabs the fabric – which instantly pops into the rigid shape of a small one-man tent. Wayne raises his eyebrows.

. . . the molecules align and become rigid.

Wayne pushes on the tent, feeling its strength, fascinated.

> WAYNE
> What kind of shapes can you make?

Fox releases the tent, which instantly collapses.

> FOX
> It could be tailored to any structure based on a rigid skeleton.

Wayne lifts the black fabric, flicking it in a whipping motion. Thinking.

> WAYNE
> Too expensive for the army?

Fox takes it back from Wayne. Sardonic.

> FOX
> Guess they never thought about marketing to the billionaire base-jumping, spelunking market.

> WAYNE
> Look, Mr. Fox, if you're uncomfortable –

> FOX
> Mr. Wayne, if you don't tell me what you're really doing, then when I get asked . . . I don't have to lie. But don't treat me like an idiot.

> WAYNE
> (*nods*)

Fair enough.

Wayne sees something behind Fox: a vehicle, covered by a tarp. Huge tires visible.

What's that?

Fox, a twinkle in his eye, rolls up the memory fabric.

> FOX
> The Tumbler? Oh, you wouldn't be interested in that.

Wayne shoots Fox a look, and we are –

P.O.V.: RACING ALONG, INCHES ABOVE A TEST TRACK   101

INT. TUMBLER ON TEST TRACK – MOMENTS LATER   102

Wayne pilots using aircraft-like control sticks. Fox, in the passenger seat, hangs on as Wayne pushes the vehicle.

The Tumbler shoots past: low and wide, a cross between a Lamborghini Countach and a Humvee. Sandy camouflage, stealth-angled panelling and variable-angle flaps across the back.

Fox shouts over the noise of the engine.

> FOX
> She was built as a bridging vehicle! You hit that button –

Wayne reaches.

> NO, NOT NOW!!

Wayne recoils.

> It boosts her into a rampless jump! In combat, two of them jump a river towing cables, then you run a bailey bridge across! Damn bridge never worked – but this baby works fine!

Wayne inspects the cockpit: a forward-slung 'gunner's' driving position between their legs, video screens, electronic controls, windows with heads-up display. Wayne accelerates . . .

The tumbler tears down the straightaway, skids to a halt.

INT. TUMBLER – CONTINUOUS   103

Fox jolts with the stop. Turns to Wayne, a little green.

> FOX
> What do you think?

Wayne turns to Fox with a slight smile.

WAYNE

Does it come in black?

INT. BATCAVE – DAY   104

Close on: the cowl. Black, with a slight graphite sheen. Dramatic, iconic even without its ears.

A baseball bat smashes into the crown, cracking it in two. Alfred picks the pieces off the table, frowning.

ALFRED

Problems with the graphite mixture, apparently. The next ten thousand will be up to specifications.

Wayne looks up from adjusting a servo-mounted microphone.

WAYNE

At least they gave us a discount.

ALFRED

Quite. In the meantime, might I suggest, sir, that you try to avoid landing on your head?

Wayne shoots Alfred a look. Then fits the microphone into the horn-shaped 'ear' from the cowl.

INT. BATCAVE – DAY   105

Wayne takes the hi-tech harness for the grapple and cuts off the shoulder straps, leaving a belt with sliding attachments.

INT. SAME – LATER   106

Wayne lifts a gloved hand, metal contacts on the fingertips. With his other hand, he picks up a fabric glove, ribbons dangling from each finger. He thrusts the gloved hand into the fabric glove – the ribbons shoot out – rigid finger-extensions like the skeleton of a bat's wing. Wayne fans the projections, testing.

INT. SAME – LATER   107

Wayne grinds metal at a lathe. Alfred approaches with a thermos. Wayne stops grinding, blows on his handiwork . . . Alfred looks at the steel carved into a bat's wing.

64

                              ALFRED
Why the bat, Master Wayne?

                              WAYNE
Bats frighten me. (*Slight smile.*) And it's time my enemies shared
my dread.

*Wayne tilts the crude Batarang, watching light dance across the
brushed steel. He throws it whistling into darkness . . .*

EXT. DOCKS – NIGHT   108

*Down in the stacks, Thugs unload boxes from an open container.
Headlights light them up – everyone freezes. A sedan pulls up. Flass
emerges. Approaches one of the Thugs holding a box. Opens it,
yanks out a stuffed toy. A bear.*

                              FLASS
Cute.

Flass rips open the toy, pulls a plastic package from inside.

(*Mock surprise.*) Oh? What have we here?

*Nobody reacts. Flass hands the toy back to the Thug. Who tosses it
onto a pile of bears. Next to it is a pile of rabbits.*

Flass heads over to a limousine. Gets in.

INT. LIMO – CONTINUOUS   109

Falcone sits, looking at a stuffed rabbit. Flass gets in.

                              FLASS
Looks fine out there. (*Looks at rabbit.*) So the bears go straight
to the dealers?

                              FALCONE
And the rabbits go to our man in the Narrows . . .

Flass looks at the rabbit.

                              FLASS
What's the difference?

Falcone looks at Flass.

FALCONE

Ignorance is bliss, my friend. Don't burden yourself with the
secrets of scary people.

FLASS

Scarier than you?

FALCONE
(smiles)
Considerably scarier than me.

EXT. THE STACKS – CONTINUOUS   110

*A Thug hands a box to a Second Thug, who walks away along the
corridor of containers. The First Thug turns back to the darkness of
the open container, reaches in –*

He is yanked into the darkness with an echoing cry.

*Second Thug turns, stares uneasily down the deserted corridor to the
black mouth of the open container . . .*

SECOND THUG

Steiss?

*No reply. He puts down his box. Draws his gun. A Third Thug
comes around the corner.*

THIRD THUG

Come on, we gotta –

*He sees the Second Thug's gun. Draws his own. They move
cautiously towards the open container . . .*

*The Thugs peer into the blackness of the open container. Behind
them, a lamp hanging above the corridor shatters – the Thugs turn,
startled, to see another lamp go dark – then another and another,
darkness advancing towards them.*

*As the closest lamp shatters, a glint of metal drops to the ground . . .
the Second Thug bends, picks it up, staring –*

*A bat-shaped, brushed-steel plate. The Second Thug looks up,
confused, but the Third Thug is staring above him.*

SECOND THUG

What?

The Second Thug looks up himself: a dark shape hanging from a crane directly above him . . .

A giant Bat, wings folded, head pointed towards the ground.

What the hell –?

The Bat drops – wings whip out, rigid – catch the air – flipping the shape downwards – enveloping the Second Thug in darkness. The Third Thug bolts, racing between containers, arms pumping.

He sprints headlong down the narrow corridor, skids around a corner, races towards –

Blackness sideswipes the Third Thug, spinning him off his feet, whipping him into darkness with a piercing scream . . .

EXT. TRUCK OUTSIDE THE STACKS – CONTINUOUS   111

Other Thugs react to the scream . . .

INT. LIMO, DOCKS – CONTINUOUS   112

Falcone and Flass hear the scream. Flass jumps out.

EXT. THE STACKS – CONTINUOUS   113

Thugs, guns drawn, advance into the stacks . . .

EXT. THE STACKS – CONTINUOUS   114

A Fourth Thug whips around a corner to see a Jumpy Thug covering the other end of the corridor . . .

The Fourth Thug nods, steps backwards. Movement in the shadow behind him . . . Batman is already in frame – his arm flashes forward with his cloak, wraps the Thug's neck, yanks him backwards into the shadows . . .

Jumpy Thug opens fire, strobing the stacks, revealing indistinct glimpses of movement.

Elsewhere in the stacks, Thugs react to the gunfire . . .

Jumpy Thug fires blindly at strobing shadows – glimpses of –

A dark, cloaked figure moving from shadow to shadow. Jumpy Thug empties the clip. Fumbles for another . . .

JUMPY THUG

WHERE ARE YOU?!

A whispered word at his ear:

BATMAN

Here.

Batman's face, upside down, at the Thug's shoulder – Jumpy Thug screams as he is enfolded by darkness.

Flass stands outside the stacks, gun drawn, listening. He moves back to the limo.

INT. LIMO – CONTINUOUS   115

Flass pokes his head in.

FALCONE

What the hell's going on?!

FLASS

You've got a *problem* out there. Bail.

Falcone reaches for the floor, pulls out a shotgun.

EXT. OUTSIDE THE STACKS – CONTINUOUS   116

Flass pauses, listening to the shouts and gunfire. Then moves off into the night.

EXT. THE STACKS – CONTINUOUS   117

Falcone advances through the stacks, shotgun in hand . . . he rounds a corner to see:

Five Thugs, various weapons in hand, in a loose defensive ring, peering out into the darkness . . .

A shadow drops into the center of their ring –

Thugs fly backwards – Falcone glimpses a dark shape spinning in the middle, taking them out one by one . . . Falcone bolts –

Falcone jumps in, clutching his shotgun. Taps it against the partition.

FALCONE
Let's go.

Nothing. He lowers the partition: the Driver is unconscious.

A thump jolts the limo – Falcone flinches – his head whips around looking through the windows as thumps pound the car . . .

Falcone whips the shotgun from side to side, aiming at shadows – some real, most imagined. The thumps stop. He is breathing now . . . scared . . . eyes darting . . .

(*Under his breath.*) What the hell are you?

Silence . . .

Smash!! Glass shatters – black-clad arms shoot down through the sun-roof – grab Falcone by the lapels and yank him up through the opening – bringing him nose-to-nose with . . .

The Batman. Crouched, panther-like on the roof of the limo, magnificent cloak billowing around . . . Falcone's terrified eyes gaze at the eyes staring from the black cowl . . .

BATMAN
I'm Batman.

Falcone screams . . .

EXT. ALLEY – MOMENTS LATER   119

The scream echoes down the alley. The Homeless Man looks up from his brazier, curious. He moves to the corner, peering around to see –

Batman standing, iconic, on the roof of the limo, cloak billowing . . . the Homeless Man's eyes go wide. Batman turns his head towards the Homeless Man –

BATMAN
Nice coat.

– and flies up from the limo, disappearing into the shadows high above . . .

The Homeless Man looks down at his coat, then back up to the shadows . . .

                         HOMELESS MAN
                            (quiet)
        Thanks.

INT. MONORAIL TRAIN – NIGHT   120

Rachel stares out at the lights of Gotham. The car is filthy, covered in graffiti. A Thin Man sits at one end. Talking on his phone. The train pulls into a station. Rachel rises.

EXT. STAIRS DOWN TO THE CAR PARK – CONTINUOUS   121

As Rachel makes her way down the dimly lit stairs, she becomes aware of the Thin Man walking behind her and instinctively pulls her bag close.

A Hefty Man appears at the bottom of the stairs. He lingers, half-blocking the exit. Rachel slips her hand into her purse as the Thin Man accelerates behind her.

Near the bottom, Rachel bolts – Hefty grabs her arm, spinning her back, tossing her up the steps towards the Thin Man.

Rachel smacks the Thin Man in the head with her purse – Hefty grabs her ankle – Rachel spins around, yanking her hand out of her purse holding a tazer . . .

                           RACHEL
        Hold it!

Behind her: a black shape whips around the Thin Man, tearing him sideways off his feet in a spasm of shadow . . .

Hefty's eyes go wide as, behind Rachel, he sees a black demon-like shape with what look like horns envelope his partner . . . He bolts, racing off down the street . . . Rachel looks at her tazer with surprised satisfaction, then back at Hefty's fleeing form.

        That's right! You better run!

Rachel turns to look up the stairs and screams –

Crouched on the railings behind her, dark cloak blowing, the black demon-like shape . . .

70

Rachel fires the tazer – the projectiles shoot into the dark shape, trailing wires, lodging in the shape's chest where they spark, providing flickering illumination of a masked face . . .

Batman.

He calmly yanks on the wires, pulling the tazer from Rachel's grasp. She stares at Batman, disbelieving, as he pulls the projectiles from his chest and coils the wires.

BATMAN

Try mace.

He tosses the tazer back to Rachel and nods at the Thin Man, lying unconscious beneath him.

Falcone sent them to kill you.

RACHEL

Why?

BATMAN

You rattled his cage.

Rachel peers at the silhouette, trying to see more. Batman tosses some photos onto the floor in front of her: Judge Faden and the Girls.

RACHEL

What's this?

BATMAN

Leverage.

RACHEL

For what?

BATMAN

To get things moving.

RACHEL

Who are you?

BATMAN

Someone like you. Someone who'll rattle the cages.

A train shoots overhead, strobing light onto the walkway, obscuring Rachel's view . . . when it clears, Batman is gone.

MALE VOICE
(*out of shot*)
Ma'am? Is everything OK?

Rachel tears her eyes from the empty spot on the railing. A Transit Cop is at the foot of the stairs.

EXT. DOCKS – CONTINUOUS   122

Gordon approaches, coffee in hand: tied-up Thugs sit against the container full of drugs. Uniforms hold back a line of Press, who snap away at the surreal scene. Gordon crouches to look at the Thugs, curious.

UNIFORMED COP
(*out of shot*)
Falcone's men?

GORDON
(*shrugs*)
Does it matter? We'll never tie him to it, anyway.

UNIFORMED COP
(*out of shot*)
I wouldn't be too sure of that.

Gordon looks up. The Uniformed Cop is pointing. At a harbor light trained on the heavens. Gordon rises, walks towards it. Two Cops stand there, staring.

Falcone is strapped to the light, unconscious, arms spread. Coat ripped, hanging from his arms in a strange pattern.

COP 1
The hell is that? Looks like . . .

Gordon follows their gaze up to where the beam of light casts Falcone's shadow onto the clouds.

COP 2
Like a *bat*.

Gordon stares at the projection. It is a bat-symbol.

GORDON
Cut him down.

72

Gordon moves away, thinking. Something catches his eye. A block away. Halfway up a building. A black flag blowing in the wind . . . Not a flag . . . a dark figure, wearing a cape, sitting on a ledge . . . Batman. Watching.

INT. FINCH'S OFFICE – MORNING   123

Rachel tosses a newspaper onto Finch's desk, beaming. The front page: a huge photo of Falcone strapped to the light.

                          RACHEL
          No way to bury it now.

                          FINCH
          Maybe so, but there's Judge Faden –

                          RACHEL
          I've got Faden covered.

                          FINCH
          And this 'bat' they're babbling about.

                          RACHEL
          Even if these guys'll swear in court to being thrashed by a giant
          bat . . . we have Falcone at the scene– drugs, prints, cargo
          manifests – this bat character gave us everything.

Finch considers. Grins.

                          FINCH
          Damn right. Let's get frying.

INT. BULLPEN, POLICE HEADQUARTERS – MORNING   124

Loeb addresses Captains, Sergeants, Lieutenants. Gordon at the back. Loeb holds up the paper, smacks the front page.

                          LOEB
          Unacceptable. I don't care if it's rival gangs, Guardian Angels
          or the goddamn Salvation Army – get them off the street, and
          off the front page.

                    CAPTAIN SIMONSON
          They say it was one guy . . . or thing.

LOEB

Dipping into their own supply – it was some asshole in a costume.

Gordon raises his hand. Loeb nods, cautious.

GORDON

This guy did deliver us one of the city's biggest crime lords.

LOEB
(*glares*)

No one takes the law into their own hands in *my* city, understand?

INT. MASTER BEDROOM, WAYNE MANOR – DAY   125

Alfred opens the curtains. Wayne wakes, squinting.

WAYNE
(*groggy*)

Bats are nocturnal.

ALFRED

Bats, maybe . . . but even for billionaire playboys, three o'clock is pushing it. The price of leading a double life, I fear.

Alfred puts down a tray: water, fruit, newspaper.

Your theatrics made an impression.

WAYNE

Theatricality and deception are powerful weapons, Alfred. It's a start.

Wayne glances at the paper. Gets out of bed, bare-chested. Alfred sees bruises across his torso and arms.

ALFRED

If those are to be the first of many injuries . . . it would be wise to find a suitable excuse. Polo, for instance.

Wayne throws Alfred a look.

WAYNE

I'm not learning polo, Alfred.

ALFRED

Strange injuries, a non-existent social life . . . these things beg
the question of what, *exactly*, Bruce Wayne does with his time.
And his money.

Wayne considers this.

WAYNE

What *does* someone like me do?

ALFRED
(*shrugs*)

Drive sports cars, date movie stars . . . Buy things that aren't for
sale.

*Wayne looks at Alfred. Nods. Downs the water, stands straight, feet
together – falls forward to the floor – into his dizzyingly fast push-
ups. Alfred watches. Concerned.*

Who knows, Master Wayne – if you start *pretending* to have
fun, you might even have a little by accident.

INT. BOARDROOM, WAYNE ENTERPRISES – AFTERNOON   126

Earle, alone at the table. An Executive walks in, troubled.

EXECUTIVE

We have a situation.

EARLE

What kind of situation?

EXECUTIVE

Coastguard picked up one of our cargo ships last night. Heavily
damaged. Crew missing, probably dead.

EARLE

What happened?

EXECUTIVE

Ship was carrying a prototype weapon. A microwave emitter . . .

EXT. CARGO SHIP AT SEA – DAY (FLASHBACK)   127

Establishing.

An industrial machine the size of a small van sits in a cargo bay,
watched by a Security Guard.

> EXECUTIVE
> (*voice-over*)
> It's designed for desert warfare – it uses focused microwaves to
> vaporize the enemy's water supply . . .

The Security Guard is grabbed from behind, neck snapped. Two men
approach the machine. Start switching it on . . .

INT. EARLE'S OFFICE, WAYNE ENTERPRISES – CONTINUOUS   129

> EXECUTIVE
> Looks like someone fired it up . . .

> EARLE
> (*voice-over*)
> What caused the damage?

INT. CARGO BAY – NIGHT (FLASHBACK)   130

The two Men brace themselves against the machine as it shudders,
emitting energy in a wave –

> EXECUTIVE
> (*voice-over*)
> The expansion of water into steam creates an enormous
> pressure wave . . .

Pipes explode, belching steam . . . all over the ship, sailors are tossed
around by exploding pipes and drains . . .

INT. EARLE'S OFFICE, WAYNE ENTERPRISES – DAY   131

> EARLE
> Where's the weapon?

The Executive shifts, uneasy.

> EXECUTIVE
> It's missing.

EXT. HOTEL RESTAURANT, DOWNTOWN GOTHAM – EVENING 132

A Bugati Veyron pulls up to the valet station. Wayne emerges.

> VALET
> Nice car.

> WAYNE
> You should see my other one

Valets scramble to the passenger side. Open the door to find two Blondes, one on the other's lap.

INT. HOTEL RESTAURANT – MOMENTS LATER   133

Floor-to-ceiling glass overlooking Gotham. A terrace with a decorative fountain. Earle and his Guests at a table. Earle sees Wayne enter with the Blondes. He sighs. Then waves.

EXT. SAME – LATER   134

The table is littered with bottles and empty plates.

> FEMALE GUEST
> At least he's getting something done.

> MALE GUEST
> Bruce, help me out here.

Wayne turns from the Blondes. They stand up and walk over to the pool. Wayne smiles, turns to the Female Guest.

> WAYNE
> A guy who dresses up like a bat clearly has *issues*.

> FEMALE GUEST
> But he put Falcone behind bars.

Wayne watches as, behind them, one of the Blondes slips off her dress and lowers herself into the pool . . . the other one, giggling, follows her lead.

> MALE GUEST
> And now the cops are trying to bring *him* in, so what does that tell you?

They're jealous?

Wayne nods, considering. The Maitre D' sidles up, annoyed.

MAITRE D'
Sir, the pool is for decoration, and your friends do not have
swimwear.

WAYNE
Well, they're European.

MAITRE D'
I'm going to have to ask you to leave.

Wayne takes out his checkbook. Starts writing.

(*Contemptuous.*) It's not a question of money.

WAYNE
(*looks up, smiling*)
I'm buying this hotel. And making some new rules for the pool
area.

*The Maitre D' stares at Wayne. Dumbstruck. The Blondes beckon
Wayne. He walks to the edge of the pool. Earle turns away, shaking
his head. Behind him, out of focus, Wayne is pulled into the pool.*

EXT. HOTEL — LATER   135

*Wayne and the Blondes, wet hair, in white hotel robes, waiting. The
Valet pulls up in the Bugati. The Blondes climb in. Wayne turns to
the valet station.*

RACHEL
(*out of shot*)
Bruce?

Wayne turns. Rachel is there, dressed for dinner. Beautiful.

WAYNE
Rachel.

RACHEL
I'd heard you were back. (*Looks at robe.*) What are you doing?

WAYNE

Just . . . swimming. (*Changes subject.*) It's good to see you.

RACHEL

I missed you – you were gone a long time.

WAYNE

I know, did you . . . ? I mean, how are things . . . for you?

RACHEL

The same. The job's getting worse.

WAYNE

Can't change the world on your own.

RACHEL

What choice do I have? You're too busy . . . swimming.

Wayne stares at her.

WAYNE

Rachel, all this . . . it's not all I am, inside I'm . . . *different.*

BLONDES
(*from car*)

Come on, Bruce! We have some more hotels we want you to buy!

Rachel glances at the Blondes. Then back to Wayne.

RACHEL

Bruce, deep down, you may be the same great little kid you used to be . . . but it's not who you are underneath . . . (*Pokes his chest.*) It's what you *do* that defines you.

Rachel moves past him. Wayne stands there, eyes burning.

INT. COUNTY JAIL, RECEIVING – DAY   136

Crane, briefcase in hand, is buzzed through thick steel and glass doors and met inside by a Prison Official. They walk.

PRISON OFFICIAL

Dr. Crane, thanks for coming down . . .

CRANE

Not at all. So he cut his wrists?

PRISON OFFICIAL

Probably looking for an insanity plea, but if anything
happened . . .

CRANE

Of course, better safe than sorry.

INT. INTERVIEW ROOM, COUNTY JAIL – CONTINUOUS   137

*Crane enters. Falcone sits at a table, wrists bandaged. Crane places
his briefcase on the table. Falcone smiles.*

FALCONE

Dr. Crane, it's all too much, the walls are closing in, blah, blah,
blah. Couple more days of this food, it'll be true.

CRANE

What do you want?

FALCONE

I wanna know how you're gonna convince me to keep my
mouth shut.

CRANE

About what? You don't know anything.

FALCONE

I know you wouldn't want the cops taking a closer look at
the drugs they seized. I know about your experiments on the
inmates at your nuthouse . . . (*Off look.*) I don't get into
business with someone without finding out their dirty secrets.
Those goons you hired . . . I own the muscle in this town.

Falcone leans forward. Looks Crane in the eye.

I've been smuggling your stuff in for *months,* so whatever he's
got planned, it's big. And I want in.

Crane studies Falcone. Considering. Sighs.

CRANE

I already know what he'll say . . . that we should kill you.

Falcone leans forward, glaring at Crane with contempt.

FALCONE
Even *he* can't touch me in here. Not in my town.

Crane shrugs. Leans forward. Pops the locks on his briefcase. Smiles at Falcone.

Crane reaches into his briefcase. Inside is a breathing apparatus attached to a small burlap sack mask.

CRANE
Would you like to see my mask?

He pulls the mask out of the case. Holds it up.

I use it in my experiments. Probably not very frightening to a guy like you. But those crazies . . .

Falcone stares at Crane, uneasy. Crane puts on the mask. It is a sack with eye holes and twine stitching for a mouth.

. . . they can't stand it . . .

FALCONE
When did the *nut* take over the asylum –?

Whump – a cloud of white smoke shoots out of Crane' briefcase. Falcone pushes his chair back, coughing, surprised.

CRANE
They scream and cry . . .

Falcone looks up at Crane in his mask.

Through Falcone's eyes: tiny lizard tongues flick out of the holes in Crane's mask.

. . . much as you're doing now.

Crane towers over Falcone, flaming eyes and flaming mouth . . .

Falcone screams.

INT. CORRIDOR OUTSIDE INTERVIEW ROOM – MOMENTS LATER
138

Crane emerges with his briefcase. The Prison Official hovers outside. Screams echo from inside the room.

CRANE

Oh, he's not faking. Not that one.

The Prison Official nods gravely. Crane leans in.

I'll talk to the Judge, see if I can get him moved to the secure wing at Arkham. I can't treat him here.

EXT. BACK ALLEY, GORDON'S APARTMENT – CONTINUOUS 139

Through the window: Gordon's pregnant wife, Barbara tries to get their two-year-old to eat. Gordon kisses her, picks up the trash. Comes out into the dark. Thunder rolls around.

BATMAN
(*out of shot*)

Storm's coming.

Gordon looks up: Batman is crouched in the fire escape.

GORDON

The scum's getting jumpy because you stood up to Falcone.

BATMAN

It's a start. Your partner was at the docks with Falcone.

GORDON

He moonlights as a low-level enforcer.

BATMAN

They were splitting the shipment in two. Only half was going to the dealers.

GORDON
(*surprised*)

Why? What about the other half?

BATMAN

Flass knows.

GORDON

He won't talk.

BATMAN

He'll talk to me.

Gordon looks up. Close on Batman, in the shadows.

GORDON

Commissioner Loeb set up a massive task force to catch you.
He thinks you're dangerous.

BATMAN

What do you think?

Gordon gets to his feet, dusts off his pants.

GORDON

I think you're trying to help . . .

Gordon looks up. But Batman is gone.

. . . but I've been wrong before.

EXT. CARGO SHIP, DOCKS – NIGHT   140

*Three men walk through the canyons of shipping containers, checking
the tags with a flashlight. They stop at one.*

FINCH

This is the one I'm talking about.

DOCK EMPLOYEE 1

What's your problem with it?

FINCH

It shouldn't exist. This ship left Singapore with 246 containers
and arrived with 247. I'm guessing there's something I'm not
supposed to find in there.

Dock Employee 1 takes Finch by the arm, conspiratorial.

DOCK EMPLOYEE 1

Listen, counselor . . . we know the way things work in this
town. You and me . . . we don't want to know what's in Mr.
Falcone's crate.

Finch looks at Dock Employee 1. Smiles.

FINCH

Things are working different. Open it.

*Dock Employee 1 shrugs. Hauls the doors open. Finch looks inside:
the industrial machine the size of a small van.*

His torch picks out the Wayne Enterprises logo on the side.

What the hell is this thing?

Behind him: Dock Employee 2 raises a silenced gun – fires. Dock Employee 1 helps drag the body into the container.

EXT. FALAFEL STAND, SURFACE STREET – NIGHT   141

Raining. Flass stuffs falafel into his mouth. Grabs a banknote from the Vendor. Flass walks down a dark street.

Yanked from the pavement, he's pulled up between buildings, falafel falling, up and up until face-to-face with . . . The Batman. Rain pouring off his cowl. Holding Flass by his ankle. Flass is screaming.

> BATMAN
>
> Where were the other drugs going?

> FLASS
>
> I don't know, I swear to God

> BATMAN
>
> Swear to ME.

Batman drops Flass three flights down on the wire . . . pulls taut – whips him back up.

> FLASS
> (*terrified whispers*)
>
> I never knew . . . never . . . shipments went to some guy for a couple days before they went to the dealers

> BATMAN
>
> Why?

> FLASS
>
> There was something else in the drugs, something hidden –

> BATMAN
>
> What?

> FLASS
>
> I don't know – I never went to the drop-off. It's in the Narrows – cops only go there in force . . .

BATMAN
Do I look like a cop?

Batman drops Flass into a stack of garbage cans.

EXT. THE NARROWS – NIGHT   142

*An island in Gotham River connected by five bridges. At one end is
an insane asylum, the rest is a ramshackle labyrinth of crumbling
public housing, makeshift additions growing like fungus. A walled
city. Slick with rain.*

Batman crouches, watching. Drops from his perch . . .

EXT. HOUSING PROJECT, THE NARROWS – MOMENTS LATER   143

*Batman climbs silently along the wall, window to window. He stops
at one, pulls a small black optic from his utility belt, extends it into a
tiny periscope. Angles it to look in the window: in the darkened
apartment, the furniture is stacked up around the walls. In the center
is a large pile of stuffed rabbits.*

*The sound of a window opening, accompanied by noise: voices raised
in anger. Batman looks over to the next window – a Little Boy climbs
out onto the fire escape. He threads his legs through the railings,
staring out at the Narrows. Batman allows himself to make a noise.*

*The Little Boy looks up, sees Batman – his eyes go wide. Batman
puts his fingers to his lips.*

LITTLE BOY
It's *you*, isn't it? (*Looks next door.*) You're here to get that guy?
They already took him. To the hospital.

Little Boy points to the asylum looming over the Narrows.

FEMALE VOICE
(*from inside*)
Get your ass back in here!

The Little Boy reluctantly rises, opens the window. Stops.

LITTLE BOY
The other kids won't believe me.

85

Batman looks at the Little Boy. Hands him the optic. The Little Boy's eyes light up as he takes it and climbs inside. Batman opens his own window.

INT. APARTMENT, NARROWS – CONTINUOUS   144

Batman picks up one of the toys from the pile. It has been split open. Noise at the door prompts him to melt into shadow.

Crane and two Thugs enter. Crane indicates the toys.

CRANE

Get rid of all traces.

THUG 1

Better torch the whole place.

Crane nods. Notices rain spattering off the sill of the open window. The Thugs pulls out Molotov cocktails. Thug 1 pours gasoline onto the toys, then pours a trail into –

INT. BATHROOM – CONTINUOUS   145

Thug 1 sets the bottle on the toilet tank. Lifts the lid to pee . . . catches sight of something in the cracked mirror . . .

He opens his mouth to scream – Batman smashes him into the mirror.

INT. APARTMENT, NARROWS – CONTINUOUS   146

Thug 2 turns to the bathroom door, holding his lit Molotov cocktail.

A cord wraps around the bottle – yanks it into the shadows. Its fuse is extinguished. Thug 2 stares at the darkness.

Batman rips from the bathroom – Thug 2 tries to pull a gun – Batman smashes him to the ground.

Batman turns to Crane – now wearing his mask. Crane's hand flashes towards Batman, who dodges a small puff of smoke. Batman moves for Crane – coughs, chokes – losing balance – gasping . . . Batman looks at Crane, sees a monster: flaming eyes, elongated limbs, spinning like a dervish . . .

Batman reels, in the throws of a hallucination. Crane smashes the bottle over him, soaking him with gasoline . . . Batman lurches for the windows, images assaulting his mind –

Insert cut: bats explode from the dark crevice.

Batman turns to Crane. Who holds a flaming lighter.

CRANE

Need a light?

Crane tosses the lighter at Batman . . . who bursts into flames.

Insert cut: Rā's al Ghūl opens his box – bats burst forth.

Batman, in flames, spins – leaps desperately at the windows.

EXT. WAREHOUSE, THE NARROWS – CONTINUOUS   147

Batman smashes through the window, cloak ablaze . . . Falling . . .
Tries to activate his cloak – but only gets one side to pop open . . .
the deployed wing causes him to spiral.

Insert cut: Young Bruce falling, falling in the well shaft –

Batman plummets, trailing flame, unopened wing fluttering with the
violent flapping of –

Bats: screeching, flapping, fluttering darkness . . .

Batman's stiff wing hooks a railing – slows him with a jolt – rips –
dropping him to the ground with a crash . . .

Young Bruce hits the dirt at the bottom of the shaft –

– and a sizzle, as wet pavement damps the flames. Groaning, Batman
rolls his burning batsuit along the asphalt.

Two Men at a hole-in-the-wall store stare at Batman, astonished.

Batman, smoldering, looks up: the two Men loom, menacing.
Batman lurches into an alley . . . the two Men look at each other,
dumbfounded. Batman raises his grapnel gun, fires up at the enclosed
roof – rides up – punches his way through wire and metal, crawls
onto his back, staring up at the skyscrapers of Gotham. Rain
blurring his vision.

Insert cut: Young Bruce watches his father crumple.

Batman fumbles at his belt. Pulls out a tiny phone.

BATMAN
(hoarse)

Alfred?! Alfred?!

87

Alfred drives, looks through the rear-view mirror at Batman, who lies in the back, flinching at invisible antagonists.

> BATMAN
>
> BLOOD! Alfred?! Blood! A sample — take a sa — sample — poisoned . . .

To Batman — the car is filled with bats . . . Mefistofle rises . . .

Young Bruce in the throes of his panic attack gulps air — turns to his Father, looks him in the eye and condemns him.

> YOUNG BRUCE
> (*shouting*)
> We HAVE to go, NOW, Dad! !

Young Bruce drags his parents from their seats.

INT. MASTER BEDROOM, WAYNE MANOR — MORNING   149

Wayne awakes. Shivering. Red-eyed from crying. Alfred sits at his bedside, watching over him.

> WAYNE
> (*hoarse*)
> How long was I out?

> ALFRED
> Two days. It's your birthday.

> WAYNE
> (*remembering*)
> I've felt these effects before . . . but this was so potent. Some kind of weaponized hallucinogen, administered in aerosol form . . .

> FOX
> (*out of shot*)
> You are definitely hanging out at the wrong clubs, Mr. Wayne.

Wayne turns to see Fox sitting by the window.

> ALFRED
> I called Mr. Fox when your condition worsened after the first day.

FOX

I analyzed your blood, isolating the receptor compounds and
protein-based catalysts.

WAYNE

Am I meant to understand all that?

FOX

No. I just want you to know how hard it was. Bottom line,
I synthesized an antidote.

WAYNE

Could you make more?

FOX

Planning on gassing yourself again?

WAYNE

You know how it is, Mr. Fox . . . you're out on the town,
looking for kicks . . . someone's passing around the weaponized
hallucinogens.

Fox shakes his head at Wayne, getting up to leave.

FOX

I'll bring you what I have – but the antidote should serve as
inoculation for now. (*to Alfred*) Alfred, always a pleasure.

Alfred nods.

ALFRED

Lucius. (*to Wayne*) Get some more sleep.

INT. MAIN HALL, WAYNE MANOR – LATER   150

*Tables of food and decorations fill the hall. Alfred is talking to
Rachel at the front door.*

ALFRED

Are you sure you won't come in?

RACHEL

I have to get back. I just wanted to leave this . . .

Rachel is holding a small gift-wrapped package.

89

                              WAYNE
                          (*out of shot*)
      Rachel?

She looks up to see Wayne standing there in his dressing gown.
Alfred withdraws. Rachel looks at Wayne, his messed hair, red eyes.

                              RACHEL
      Looks like someone's been burning the candle at both ends.

Wayne doesn't know what to say. Rachel reaches up to touch a bruise
on his cheek.

      Must've been quite an occasion.

                              WAYNE
                           (*sheepish*)
      Well, it is my birthday . . .

                              RACHEL
      I know – I'm sorry, I can't come tonight. I was just dropping off
      your present.

Rachel's phone rings.

      Rachel Dawes. What?! Who authorized that?! Get Crane there
      right now – don't take no for an answer . . . and call Dr.
      Lehmann, we'll need our own assessment on the Judge's desk
      by morning.

Rachel hangs up. Wayne looks at her.

                              WAYNE
      What's wrong?

                              RACHEL
      It's Falcone. Dr. Crane moved him to Arkham Asylum on
      suicide watch.

                              WAYNE
      You're going to Arkham now? It's in the Narrows, Rachel.

Rachel gives him a look.

                              RACHEL
      You have yourself a great time – some of us have work to do.

She hurries past him. Stops. Turns. Looks at him, softer. Hands him his present.

Happy birthday, Bruce.

She races out the door. Wayne opens the present: a note saying 'Finders keepers.' And the arrowhead. Wayne watches her go, thinking.

INT. HALLWAY, WAYNE MANOR – LATER   151

Wayne hurries down the hallway. Alfred in pursuit.

                         ALFRED
But Master Wayne, the guests will be arriving

Wayne turns.

                         WAYNE
Keep them happy until I arrive. Tell them that joke you know.

Wayne hurries off. Alfred watches him go, exasperated.

INT. STUDY – CONTINUOUS   152

Wayne steps to the piano, hits four notes – a large, ornate mirror swings open. Wayne steps through.

INT. STONE STAIRCASE – CONTINUOUS   153

Wayne descends. Arrives at the top of the wrought-iron spiral staircase, steps onto the dumb waiter at its center.

Wayne pulls a lever, releasing the lift which plummets vertiginously down the center of the spiraling stair.

INT. BATCAVE – CONTINUOUS   154

The lift hits the bottom with a great rattle of chains. Wayne moves to a padlocked box. Opens it: the bat suit hangs there – a phantom, black eyes staring back at him.

He reaches for it.

Fox consults a mass spectrometer.

> EARLE
> (*out of shot*)

Having fun?

Fox swings around in his chair. Earle is standing there.

> FOX

Bill. What's a big shot like you doing in a place like this?

> EARLE

Has Wayne been around much?

> FOX

In and out. Nice kid.

> EARLE

Forget about kissing his ass to get back in, Lucius. Despite the name, he's only an employee.

> FOX

You came all the way down here to tell me that?

Earle shifts, uncomfortable.

> EARLE

Actually, I need information. The Wayne Enterprises 47-B, I-ME.

Fox turns to his computer. Starts typing.

> FOX

It's a microwave emitter . . . designed to vaporize an enemy's water supply . . .

> EARLE

I know all that. Any other applications?

Fox turns from his computer, thinking.

> FOX

Well, as I recall, rumor was, they tested dispersing water-based chemical agents into the air . . . (*Looks at Earle.*) But that would be illegal, wouldn't it?

EARLE

Cut the crap, Fox. I need everything on the project development up to my office right away.

Earle walks off.

FOX

What happened . . . you lose one?

EARLE
(*turns, cold*)

I'm merging Applied Sciences with Archiving. You're top of the early retirement list . . . (*Smiles at reaction.*) Didn't you get the memo?

EXT. ARKHAM ASYLUM, THE NARROWS – EVENING   156

Rachel's car crosses the bridge to the Narrows.

INT. CORRIDOR, ARKHAM ASYLUM – MOMENTS LATER   157

An Orderly talking to a Nurse at one end. Further along, Rachel stands looking through a wire-reinforced window: inside a cell, Falcone strapped to the bed, staring at the ceiling, mumbling.

FALCONE

Scarecrow . . . s-scarecrow . . . s-s . . .

Crane hurries along the corridor, heading for Rachel.

CRANE

Ms. Dawes, this is most irregular. I've nothing to add to the report I filed with the judge.

RACHEL

Well, I have questions about your report. (*Off look.*) Such as, isn't it *convenient* for a fifty-two-year-old man with no history of mental illness to have a complete psychotic break just when he's about to be indicted?

CRANE
(*motions*)

You can see for yourself, there's nothing convenient about his symptoms.

Rachel considers Falcone's terrified gaze.

RACHEL

What's 'scarecrow'?

CRANE

Patients suffering delusional episodes often focus their paranoia onto an external tormentor, usually one conforming to the Jungian archetypes. (*Shrugs.*) In this case, a scarecrow.

EXT. ARKHAM ASYLUM – CONTINUOUS   158

Batman, upside down, clings to the wall above the window at the end of the corridor. He racks audio-focus through the Orderly's conversation, settling on Crane's voice.

INT. CORRIDOR, ARKHAM ASYLUM – CONTINUOUS   159

Rachel looks at Falcone, mumbling, delusional.

RACHEL

He's drugged.

CRANE
(nods)

Psychopharmacology is my primary field – I'm a strong advocate.

Crane turns to Falcone. Staring.

Outside, he was a giant. In here, only the mind can grant you power.

RACHEL

You enjoy the reversal.

CRANE

I respect the mind's power over the body. It's why I do what I do – ultimately, I'm just trying to help.

RACHEL
(hard)

I do what *I* do to put scum like Falcone behind bars, not in therapy. I want my own psychiatric consultant to have full access to Falcone, including bloodwork to find out *exactly* what you have him on.

94

Crane stares at her. Shrugs.

INT. ELEVATOR – CONTINUOUS   160

Crane steps in, Rachel follows. He puts a key into the panel.

                         CRANE
     First thing tomorrow, then.

                         RACHEL
     Tonight. I've already paged Dr. Lehmann over at County General.

Crane turns the key.

                         CRANE
     As you wish.

The elevator descends. The doors open onto:

INT. DESERTED WING, SUB-LEVEL ARKHAM ASYLUM – CONTINUOUS
                                                              161

*A long, decrepit corridor. Water dripping, clearly disused. Crane
steps off the elevator. Rachel follows, perturbed.*

INT. ABANDONED HYDROTHERAPY ROOM – CONTINUOUS   162

Rachel follows Crane into a vast room.

*Tables stretch off into the room, covered in bags of powder, scales,
aluminum barrels and dozens of Inmates working the powder,
refining it. Two Inmates are pouring powder from one of the barrels
into a large hole in the floor. One of them looks up: Zsaz. Rachel
stares at his vacant eyes.*

                         CRANE
     This is where we make the medicine. Perhaps you should have
     some. Clear your head.

He turns, but Rachel is gone. Crane smiles . . .

INT. DERELICT CORRIDOR, DISUSED WING – CONTINUOUS   163

Rachel races into the elevator . . .

95

Rachel hits the second floor button. Nothing. She hits all the buttons, floors, the alarm . . . all dead without the key.

The door opens to Crane's masked face. He reaches out.

> CRANE
>
> Let me help you . . .

A small puff of gas sprays from his sleeve. Rachel recoils, coughing, choking. She looks up at Crane:

The eyeholes of the burlap mask are flaming.

Rachel screams.

INT. ABANDONED HYDROTHERAPY ROOM – CONTINUOUS   165

The Thugs drag Rachel into the room. Crane turns Rachel's face to look up at his mask. She gulps panic breaths.

> CRANE
>
> Who knows you're here?

Rachel shakes her head.

> WHO KNOWS?!!

Rachel pulls away, burying her head in her arms.

The lights go out.

The Thugs look around, unnerved. Crane pulls off his mask.

> (*Fascinated.*) He's here.

> FIRST THUG
>
> Who?

> CRANE
>
> The Batman.

The Thugs exchange nervous glances.

> FIRST THUG
>
> What do we do?

> CRANE
>
> What anyone does when a prowler comes around. (*Off look.*) Call the police.

The First Thug looks at Crane. Points at the large hole.

> FIRST THUG
> You want the cops here?

> CRANE
> At this point, they can't stop us. But the Batman has a talent for
> disruption. Force him outside, the police will take him down.
> (*indicates inmates*)
> Get them out of here.

> FIRST THUG
> (*indicates Rachel*)
> What about her?

> CRANE
> She's gone. I gave her a concentrated dose. The mind can only
> take so much . . .

> SECOND THUG
> The things they say about him . . . Can he really fly?

EXT. ARKHAM ASYLUM – CONTINUOUS   166

*Batman's cape flutters as he swings down two storeys, landing at the
high windows of the derelict corridor.*

INT. ABANDONED HYDROTHERAPY ROOM – CONTINUOUS   167.

> THIRD THUG
> I heard he can disappear –

*Crane backs into the shadows, smiling at the Third Thug. Rachel lies
in the corner, hyperventilating.*

> CRANE
> We'll find out, won't we?

*The Thugs move either side of the door . . . glass smashes, across the
room – a shadow drops from a high window. Rachel screams. The
two Thugs advance through the darkness.*

*Second Thug is grabbed from above – pulled up, screaming, into the
blackness of the rafters.*

The First Thug peers up into the darkness, gun aimed.

A shadow descends, shouting – First Thug fires – the shadow crumples onto him. It is the Second Thug – First Thug rolls the body off, scrambles to his feet – Batman strikes him from behind, knocking him unconscious.

Sirens outside, close.

Batman looks at Rachel –

Crane bursts from the shadows, arm high, aimed at Batman's face – Batman grabs his arm, ducking away from the puff of gas from Crane's sleeve . . . Batman spins Crane, ripping off his mask, wrenches his arm around to his own face, rips Crane's jacket open and pulls out the bladder full of toxin.

BATMAN

Taste of your own medicine, doctor?

Crane's eyes go wide as Batman squeezes the bladder and a choking cloud of dust sprays into Crane's face . . .

Crane falls to the ground, choking.

Batman turns him over, pulls his face up to meet his.

What have you been doing here?! Who are you working for?!

Crane's eyes are wide with terror –

Batman is a death's head – black eyes, fangs.

CRANE

Rā's . . . Rā's . . . al Ghūl . . .

Batman reacts, pulls Crane tighter.

BATMAN

Rā's al Ghūl is dead, Crane! Who are you working for?!
CRANE!!

But Crane just stares at him, eyes glazing – mind flying images cascading through his fevered brain . . . Crane smiles.

CRANE

Dr. Crane isn't here right now, but if you'd like to make an appointment–

98

Sirens outside. Batman turns to Rachel. Through her eyes:

Batman is a towering horned, winged demon . . .

Rachel lashes out at the demon with all her might . . . Batman applies a grip to her neck that renders her unconscious.

> COP
> (*over bullhorn*)
> BATMAN. PUT DOWN YOUR WEAPONS AND
> SURRENDER. YOU ARE SURROUNDED.

Batman rises, carrying Rachel.

EXT. ARKHAM ASYLUM – CONTINUOUS   168

Police cars surround the building. Cops have guns drawn, waiting. Staff emerge, blinking, from the darkened asylum. Flass and Gordon arrive. Flass shouts at the Uniforms:

> FLASS
> What're you waiting for?!.

> UNIFORMED COP
> Backup.

> FLASS
> Backup?

Flass gestures at the dozen police cars outside the building.

> UNIFORMED COP
> The Batman's in there. SWAT's on the way, but if you want to go now . . . (*Smiles.*) I'm right behind you, sir.

Flass turns to Gordon. Shrugs.

> FLASS
> SWAT's on the way.

Gordon shakes his head. Approaches the front doors.

INT. DERELICT CORRIDOR, DISUSED WING – CONTINUOUS   169

Batman carries Rachel, cloak billowing in his wake.

INT. LOBBY, ARKHAM ASYLUM – CONTINUOUS   170

Gordon moves through the dark, gun drawn, eyes flicking to terrified Nurses who make their way to the front door.

EXT. ARKHAM ASYLUM – CONTINUOUS   171

SWAT Officers pour out of vans, race up the front steps.

INT. CORRIDOR, ARKHAM ASYLUM – CONTINUOUS   172

Gordon tries the elevator – it is dead. He enters the stairs.

INT. LOBBY, ARKHAM ASYLUM – CONTINUOUS   173

The SWAT team bursts in – flashlights on rifles scan the darkness . . .

INT. STAIRWELL, ARKHAM ASYLUM – CONTINUOUS   174

Gordon looks down the stairwell – the way down to the disused wing is fenced off. He heads up – and is grabbed and swung out into the stairwell. Batman holds him as they rocket upwards.

GORDON
What –!

Batman covers Gordon's mouth. Down below: the door smashes open – SWAT team lights cross the darkened stairwell. Batman pulls Gordon into the rafters. Gordon turns, furious – sees –

Rachel. Lying in a storage space/open attic. Twitching.

(*Whispering.*) What's happened to her?

BATMAN
Crane poisoned her with a psychotropic hallucinogen. (*Off look.*) A panic-inducing toxin.

GORDON
Let me take her down to the medics –

BATMAN
They can't help her. But I can.

The lights come on – bleaching the stairwell – Batman, Rachel and Gordon are in the shadow of the attic.

Batman reaches down to his boot. Presses a switch in the heel, producing a barely audible high-frequency whine.

(*Indicates Rachel.*) I need to get her the antidote before the damage becomes permanent.

GORDON
How long does she have?

BATMAN
Not long.

EXT. ARKHAM ASYLUM — CONTINUOUS   175

A strange squealing sound rises. Flass looks around, curious. A dark cloud crosses the moon . . . not a regular cloud . . .

INT. STAIRWELL, ARKHAM ASYLUM — CONTINUOUS   176

Batman hands Rachel to Gordon. Gordon looks back at Batman.

BATMAN
Get her downstairs, meet me in the alley on the Narrows side.

GORDON
How will you get out?

BATMAN
I called for backup. (*Indicates boot.*) Crane was the third man at the docks. He's been smuggling his toxin hidden in Falcone's drugs. Refining and testing it here in the asylum . . . then dumping it into the water supply.

GORDON
What was he planning?

BATMAN
I don't know.

GORDON
Was he working for Falcone?

BATMAN
Someone else. Someone worse.

Gordon frowns at the loud squealing noise.

GORDON

What *is* that?

BATMAN

Backup.

EXT. ARKHAM ASYLUM – CONTINUOUS   177

*Flass screams – Cops dive for cover as bats – thousands upon
thousands – descend on the asylum, heading for the windows.*

INT. CORRIDOR, ARKHAM ASYLUM – CONTINUOUS   178

Windows shatter inwards as bats pour into the building

EXT. ARKHAM ASYLUM – CONTINUOUS   179

Gordon covers Rachel as he carries her down the steps.

INT. ARKHAM ASYLUM – CONTINUOUS   180

*Bats flood into the bright stairwell, soaring up past the cowering
SWATs, a black mass rising, darkening the stairwell.*

*Batman amidst the bats. Calm. Pulls the sounder out of his heel,
leans over the stairwell and drops it . . .*

*Bats cyclone down the stairwell, following the signal. Batman jumps
into the center of the black cyclone – hidden, falling . . .*

*Batman opens his cloak with a jolt – lands hard. He moves calmly
through the bats, slipping past cowering SWATS. Batman turns to
a cell door, pulls a packet from his utility belt . . .*

INT. CELL – CONTINUOUS   181

*Two Inmates flinch as the door lock blasts open and the door is
kicked in – Batman strides across the cell between them . . .*

BATMAN

Excuse me –

*And blasts the window of their cell. He slides out . . . one Inmate
turns to the other.*

LUNATIC
What'd I tell ya?

EXT. SIDE STREET – CONTINUOUS   182

Gordon lowers Rachel to the asphalt. She stirs.

BATMAN
(*out of shot*)
How is she?

Gordon looks up to see Batman standing there.

A searchlight from a chopper blasts them. Batman grabs Rachel. Gordon points back to the street.

GORDON
Take my car.

BATMAN
I brought mine.

Batman has disappeared into the dark end of the alley.

GORDON
Yours?

Blinding headlights flare. A massive engine roars.

Gordon dives out of the way as –

The Batmobile comes flying out of the darkness . . . the matt-black muscularity of the stealth-finished 'car' blows by. Gordon's jaw drops.

I *gotta* get me one of those.

INT. BATMOBILE – CONTINUOUS   183

Batman drives. Rachel, coming to, hangs on, terrified. A cop car pulls across the alley – Batman hits the accelerator.

EXT. ALLEY – CONTINUOUS   184

The Batmobile speeds towards the cop car –

INT. COP CAR – CONTINUOUS   185

The Cops gawp at the Batmobile, bracing –

EXT. ALLEY – CONTINUOUS   186

*The Batmobile smashes into the cop car, huge front tires crushing the
bonnet, bouncing the Batmobile right over the cop car in a messy
display of brute force.*

EXT. BRIDGE TO ARKHAM/NARROWS – CONTINUOUS   187

The Batmobile races across the bridge to Gotham proper.

INT. CRUSHED COP CAR – CONTINUOUS   188

The Cops are scrunched down. One of them grabs the radio.

> COP I
>
> He's in a vehicle!

> DISPATCHER
> (*over radio*)
>
> Make and color?

> COP I
>
> It's a black . . . (*Turns to partner, who shrugs.*) . . . tank.

> DISPATCHER
> (*over radio*)
>
> Tank?

EXT. SURFACE STREETS, GOTHAM – CONTINUOUS   189

The Batmobile weaves around traffic, dodging freeway supports.

INT. BATMOBILE – CONTINUOUS   190

*Rachel braces against the dash, breathing fast, staring at the road
ahead . . . through her eyes:*

*Speed: pure, visceral sensation – lights streaking, columns flashing
past at unthinkable velocity.*

BATMAN
You've been poisoned. Stay calm.

He looks at an intricate GPS display, then at the road ahead.

EXT. SUBTERRANEAN STREETS, GOTHAM – CONTINUOUS   191

The Batmobile races along – two cop cars join the pursuit from the cross streets, lights blazing, sirens blaring.

INT. BATMOBILE – CONTINUOUS   192

Batman spots the Cops on a rear-view monitor, flips a switch.

EXT. SURFACE STREETS, GOTHAM – CONTINUOUS   193

The Batmobile drops spike strips onto the road . . . the cop cars hit them – tires explode – rims light sparks as they grind, skidding sideways, one laying into the other.

Up ahead: the Batmobile slaloms outside of the pillars.

INT. CRUISER – CONTINUOUS   194

An impatient Cop is on the radio.

COP 3
At least tell me what it looks like . . .

His eyes widen: the Batmobile roars past. A shadowy monster.

Never mind.

EXT. SURFACE STREETS, GOTHAM   195

The Batmobile comes up onto the surface street and is hit by a spotlight from a chopper.

INT. BATMOBILE – CONTINUOUS   196

Batman glances at a row of buttons – each one a tiny screen showing different views. Batman pushes one – that view flicks onto the main display. Rachel is hyperventilating.

Breathe slowly. Close your eyes.

She does so. For an instant.

That's worse!

EXT. STREETS, GOTHAM – CONTINUOUS   197

Three cop cars pull across the intersection in a road block.

INT. BATMOBILE – CONTINUOUS   198

Batman spots the road block in front. Touches the GPS screen – the map becomes three-dimensional (heights of buildings, levels of streets). Batman skids into a turn –

EXT. SURFACE STREETS – CONTINUOUS   199

The Batmobile skids through the entrance to a multi-level parking garage – taking out the ticket machine and barrier.

INT. BATMOBILE – CONTINUOUS   200

Rachel flinches.

What're you doing?!

Short cut.

EXT. ROOF, PARKING GARAGE – CONTINUOUS   201

The Batmobile roars out onto the top level, and is lit up by the chopper.

The Batmobile reverses into a spot marked 'Compact', crushing the cars either side, then races forward . . . cop cars emerge onto the roof, blocking the only way down . . . The Batmobile screeches to a halt.

Batman glances at his three-dimensional GPS. Then looks at Rachel.

COP 3
(*over loudspeaker*)

TURN OFF YOUR ENGINE!

She recoils, terrified by his mask, clawing at her harness. Batman puts his gloved hand on her frantic arms.

BATMAN

Trust me.

Batman slides into the front driving position, body prone as if riding a motorcycle, head in a glass pod between the front wheels. He hits a button.

EXT. ROOF, PARKING GARAGE – CONTINUOUS   203

Cannons on the nose of the Batmobile blast the far wall . . . the massive jet at the back ignites, mouth adjusting . . . Flaps flare out like a python spreading its neck . . .

The Cops stare. The Batmobile rockets forward . . . heading for the gap in the far wall . . . accelerating . . .

INT. BATMOBILE – CONTINUOUS   204

Rachel screams. Batman hits another button –

EXT. ROOF, PARKING GARAGE – CONTINUOUS   205

An inverted spoiler jams into the airstream at the front of the car, bumping it just off the ground, a rampless jump.

EXT. ROOFTOPS – CONTINUOUS   206

The Batmobile jumps off the parking garage, soaring over a thirty-foot gap to land heavily on a neighboring flat roof.

The Cops stare at one another, open-mouthed.

EXT. ROOFTOPS – CONTINUOUS 207

The Batmobile turns – rockets for the edge of the roof – shoots over the gap to the next roof, chopper in pursuit.

INT. BATMOBILE – CONTINUOUS 208

Batman checks his 3D GPS, rockets forward, aiming at the next roof, a pitched chateau-style tile roof.

EXT. STREETS BELOW – CONTINUOUS 209

Cop cars shoot along, paralleling the rooftop chase . . .

From below: the chopper swoops low over the buildings – a glimpse of the Batmobile as it leaps across to the next building . . .

> COP 4
> (*over radio*)
> We're on him, we're on him . . .

EXT. ROOFTOPS – CONTINUOUS 210

The Batmobile lands on the pitched roof, racing along at a precarious angle, tiles sliding off the roof in its wake.

INT. BATMOBILE – CONTINUOUS 211

Batman's forward-slung position is gyroscopically balanced – he is the only vertical element in the angled car.

EXT. ROOFTOPS – CONTINUOUS 212

Chased by the low-flying chopper, the Batmobile swerves up over the gables, roof crumbling in its wake, racing for the end of the roof, which parallels an elevated freeway.

The Batmobile rockets forward – jumps the last gable . . . Drops onto the elevated freeway, traffic swerving to avoid it.

EXT. SURFACE STREETS – CONTINUOUS 213

Cop cars see the Batmobile disappear onto the freeway above.

COP 4
                 (*over radio*)
      Dammit!

INT. BATMOBILE – CONTINUOUS   214

*Batman's display shows a radar sweep. and plots a course through
the differing speeds of the lanes. He pilots, leaning left and right like
a motorcyclist . . .*

EXT. FREEWAY – CONTINUOUS   215

*The Batmobile swerves – the Chopper's light stays trained. Traffic
gets heavier. Cop cars are closing in from behind . . .*

INT. BATMOBILE – CONTINUOUS   216

*Batman lifts himself back into the rear driving position – throttles
back – kills all the lights, and the engine.*

EXT. FREEWAY – CONTINUOUS   217

*The Batmobile drops back, dark . . . the chopper loses it. The
Batmobile cruises across the lanes, a wraith.*

INT. BATMOBILE – CONTINUOUS   218

*Silence, but for the steady whine of the electric motor. Rachel
breathes in the sudden quiet. Eyes flickering.*

EXT. FREEWAY HEADING OUT OF GOTHAM – CONTINUOUS   219

*The Batmobile slices across lanes, a shadow only visible breaking the
glare of other cars' headlights. The cop cars pull forward, driving
parallel, an empty lane between them.*

INT. BATMOBILE – CONTINUOUS   220

*Rachel stares at Batman in the intimate quiet. Her eyes are glazing.
Her breathing is shallow.*

                              BATMAN
                              (*quiet*)
        Stay with me.

INT. COP CAR – CONTINUOUS   221

The Cop turns left to look at the other cop car.

                              COP 3
        Where'd he –?

He sees, between his car and the next, a black shape.

        THERE HE IS!

INT. BATMOBILE – CONTINUOUS   222

*The spotlight hits the car – Batman hits a button – the main engine
roars to life – Batman slips into the prone position – hits the boost.*

EXT. FREEWAY – CONTINUOUS   223

The Batmobile shoots forward from between the two cop cars.

INT. COP CAR – CONTINUOUS   224

*The Batmobile's jet wash blasts the windscreen, shattering it. The
Cop throws his hands in front of his face.*

EXT. FREEWAY – CONTINUOUS   225

*The cop car spins out of its lane, slamming into the guard rail as the
Batmobile races ahead, weaving through traffic.*

*The Batmobile smashes through barriers . . . Flies off the rising
freeway, down onto the disused frontage road below.*

INT. BATMOBILE – CONTINUOUS   226

*Batman kills the lights, running on night vision. Rachel's eyes flicker
at the eerie green view of ghostly trees, her breathing faster and still
more shallow.*

BATMAN

Hold on. Just hold on.

Batman yanks the wheel –

EXT. SMALL TURNOFF – CONTINUOUS   227

*Whipping the Batmobile right in a hard turn, down a small turnoff . . .
the Chopper loses the Batmobile, pursuing cop cars blaze past the
turnoff.*

INT. BATMOBILE – CONTINUOUS   228

*Rachel, crying, looks at the monstrous shapes of the trees: flickering,
jagged tree shapes spin past dizzyingly.*

BATMAN

Rachel? Rachel?!

*No reply. Up ahead: a lookout over a river gorge. Batman pushes
the Batmobile, speeding towards the lookout. Rachel's glazed eyes
register the danger – she twists, panicked . . .*

EXT. WOODED PATH – CONTINUOUS   229

*The Batmobile rockets off the edge of the lookout, over the gorge,
flying straight at the face of a waterfall.*

INT. BATMOBILE – CONTINUOUS   230

Rachel screams as they splash into the face of the waterfall –

INT. CAVERNS – CONTINUOUS   231

– and emerge through the curtain of water into the Batcave.

*The Batmobile's ground-anchors hook a steel cable, spinning an
inertia reel bolted to the cave wall, yanking the car to a halt like a jet
landing on an aircraft carrier.*

INT. BATMOBILE – CONTINUOUS   232

Rachel bounces in her seat. Passed out.

The canopy of the Batmobile hisses open in three complex sections, like insect wings unfolding. Batman lifts Rachel from the cockpit, steps down onto wet shale . . . carries her into the damp blackness of the caverns.

Cloak billowing in his wake, he heads for the glow of his work table. Gently lays Rachel on the table. Races up the scaffold to his computer station. A container sits there with paperwork from Fox. Batman opens it, removes a vial. He plugs it into a pneumatic syringe, puts the syringe between his teeth – glides off the scaffold, landing beside Rachel. He injects her in the biceps.

Batman steps back, watching Rachel's breathing slow.

INT. ABANDONED HYDROTHERAPY ROOM — CONTINUOUS   234

Cops photograph evidence, question Inmates. Gordon passes through the room, heading for the large hole, which is surrounded by Hazmat Techs examining it.

> GORDON
> Did they get any into the mains?

> HAZMAT TECH
> Oh, yeah.

> GORDON
> Notify the water board – there's gotta be a way of isolating the area's –

> HAZMAT TECH
> You don't understand – they put it *all* in the water supply . . .

The Hazmat Tech bangs one of the barrels – it echoes. Empty.

> . . . they've been doing this for weeks – Gotham's entire water supply is laced with it.

> GORDON
> Why haven't we felt any effects?.

> HAZMAT TECH
> It must be a compound that has to be absorbed through the lungs.

Rachel's eyes flicker open to the cavernous damp darkness. She sees bats hanging high above. Closes her eyes again.

> RACHEL
> (*under her breath*)

Oh. My. God.

> BATMAN
> (*out of shot*)

How do you feel?

His voice echoes as if spoken from all shadows at once.

> RACHEL
> (*hoarse*)

Where are we?

Nothing.

Why did you bring me here?

> BATMAN

If I hadn't . . . your mind would now be lost. You were poisoned.

Rachel thinks . . . concentrating . . . remembering.

> RACHEL

I remember . . . nightmares. This . . . face, this . . . *mask*.

> (*realizes*)

Crane. It was Crane

Rachel struggles off the table, trying to stand.

I have to tell the police – we've got –

She slips – Batman is there, catching her.

> BATMAN

Rest. Gordon has Crane.

In his arms, she looks up at him – he lays her gently back onto the table. Retreats into shadow.

> RACHEL

Is Sergeant Gordon your friend?

BATMAN

I don't have the luxury of friends.

Rachel watches this dark shadow hover just outside the light. Fascinated. Pitying. Batman steps into the light. Holding a pneumatic syringe and two vials. Rachel stares at him.

I'm going to give you a sedative. You'll wake up back at home . . .

Batman holds up the two vials.

And when you do, get these to Gordon, and Gordon alone. Trust no one.

RACHEL

What are they?

BATMAN

The antidote. One for Gordon to inoculate himself, the other to start mass production.

Batman hands Rachel the vials. She looks at him, curious.

RACHEL

Mass production?

BATMAN

Crane was just a pawn. We need to be ready.

Batman approaches with the syringe. Rachel offers her arm. Batman injects her. Her eyes close. Batman removes his cowl. Wayne stands above the sleeping Rachel. Stares at her for an inexpressibly lonely moment.

INT. STUDY, WAYNE MANOR – EVENING   236

Wayne emerges from the mirror. The noise of a party outside the door. Alfred is there, dinner jacket over his arm. Wayne grabs the shirt – dressing hastily.

ALFRED

When you told me your grand plan to save Gotham, one thing stopped me calling the men in white coats . . . (*Off look.*) You said it wasn't about thrill-seeking.

WAYNE

It's not.

Alfred points at the television.

ALFRED
(*stern*)

Well, what do you call that?

Alfred indicates the television: footage of the chase.

WAYNE

Damn good television.

ALFRED

It's a miracle no one was injured.

WAYNE

I didn't have time to observe the highway code, Alfred.

ALFRED

You're getting lost in this creature of yours.

WAYNE

I'm using this creature to help people like my father did –

ALFRED

For Thomas Wayne, helping others was never about proving anything to anyone. Including himself.

WAYNE

It's Rachel, Alfred. She was dying.

Alfred reacts.

She's downstairs, sedated. I need you to take her home.

Alfred nods. Moves towards the bookcase. He stops. Turns.

ALFRED

We both care about Rachel, sir. But what you're doing has to be beyond that. It can't be personal. Or you're just a vigilante.

Wayne looks from Alfred to the door.

WAYNE

Is Fox still here?

Alfred nods.

We need to send these people away.

ALFRED

Those are Bruce Wayne's guests out there. You have a name to maintain –

WAYNE

I don't care about my name.

ALFRED

It's not just your name, it's your father's. And it's all that's left of him. Don't destroy it.

Alfred exits through the bookcase. Wayne watches him go.

INT. MAIN HALL, WAYNE MANOR – CONTINUOUS   237

Hundreds of Guests. Music. Tables groaning with food.

FEMALE GUEST
(*out of shot*)

There he is!

Guests look up – Wayne wades into the throng, grinning and glad-handing. The band strikes up with 'Happy Birthday'.

EARLE
(*out of shot*)

Happy birthday, Bruce.

Wayne turns to Earle.

WAYNE

Mr. Earle, how did the stock offering go?

EARLE

Very well – the price soared.

WAYNE

Who was buying?

EARLE

A variety of funds and brokerages . . . it's all a bit technical – the key thing is, our company's future is secure.

Alfred gently arranges the unconscious Rachel on the rear seat of the car, frowning as her legs get stuck. He looks up to see a Caterer, cigarette in hand, staring, curious.

> ALFRED
> (*smiles*)
> Little the worse for wear, I'm afraid.

Alfred yanks Wayne's golf clubs to one side, Rachel settles.

INT. CELL, ARKHAM ASYLUM – CONTINUOUS   239

Gordon sits opposite Crane, who is handcuffed to a chair.

> GORDON
> What was the plan, Crane? How were you going to put your toxin into the air?

Crane stares, eyes abstracted. Gordon picks up Crane's mask.

> CRANE
> Scarecrow . . . scarecrow, scarecrow . . .

> GORDON
> Who are you working for, Crane?

No response. Gordon sighs. Hands the mask to an Officer.

> CRANE
> It's too late . . . you can't stop it.

Gordon turns to Crane. Who smiles.

INT. MAIN HALL, WAYNE MANOR – CONTINUOUS   240

Wayne circulates, charming, but distracted . . . finds Fox.

> WAYNE
> Thank you for that . . . *item.*

> FOX
> I'm sure you'll find a use for it.

> WAYNE
> I already have. How long would it take to manufacture on a large scale?

FOX
Weeks. Why?

Wayne looks at Fox, grave.

WAYNE

Someone's been planning to disperse it using the water supply.

FOX

The water supply isn't going to help you disperse an inhalant . . .
unless . . .

WAYNE

What?

FOX

Unless you have access to a microwave emitter powerful enough
to vaporize the water in the mains. The kind of microwave
emitter that Wayne Enterprises has recently misplaced.

WAYNE

Misplaced?

FOX

Earle just fired me for asking too many questions about it.

WAYNE

I need you to go back to Wayne Enterprises and start making
more of the antidote. I think the police are going to need as
much as they can get their hands on.

FOX

My security access has been revoked.

WAYNE

That wouldn't stop a man like you, would it?

FOX
(*smiles*)

No, it probably wouldn't.

Fox heads for the door. Wayne turns, striding across the room.
An elderly Society Dame grabs Wayne's elbow.

SOCIETY DAME

Bruce, there's somebody here you simply *must* meet . . .

Not just now, Mrs. Delane –

She turns Wayne to face an Asian Man in his fifties.

SOCIETY DAME
Now, am I pronouncing it right . . . ?

In the Asian Man's buttonhole is a double-bloomed blue poppy.

. . . Mr. *al Ghūl?*

The Asian Man nods. Wayne stares at him.

WAYNE
You're not Rā's al Ghūl. I watched him die.

The Society Dame laughs nervously, confused.

VOICE
(*out of shot*)
But is Rā's al Ghūl *immortal* . . . ?

Wayne turns. Standing there. Smiling. Ducard.

DUCARD
Are his methods supernatural?

WAYNE
(*understanding*)
Or cheap parlor tricks to conceal your true identity . . . Rā's?

Ducard – the real Rā's al Ghūl – smiles acknowledgment.

DUCARD/RĀ'S AL GHŪL
Surely a man who spends his nights scrambling over the
rooftops of Gotham wouldn't begrudge me dual identities?

WAYNE
(*disgusted*)
I saved you from the fire.

RĀ'S AL GHŪL
(*smiles*)
I warned you about compassion, Bruce.

*Wayne notices certain Guests staring at him: members of the League
of Shadows. Wayne looks at the Guests.*

WAYNE

Your quarrel is with me. Let these people go.

RĀ'S AL GHŪL
(amused)
You're welcome to explain the situation to them.

Wayne looks at Rā's. Grabs a glass from a tray.

WAYNE

Everyone! Everyone!

People turn to Wayne. He raises his glass. Unsteady.

I just want to thank you all for . . . drinking my booze.

People laugh.

No, really, the thing about being a Wayne is you're never short of a few freeloaders to fill up your mansion . . . So here's to you people . . .

Wayne downs his drink. People look away, embarrassed. Fredericks takes Wayne by the elbow.

FREDERICKS

That's enough, Bruce.

Wayne pulls his arm away. People are heading for the doors.

WAYNE

I'm not finished. (*Raises glass.*) To you false friends . . . and pathetic suck-ups who smile through your teeth at me . . . You had your fill, now leave me in peace! Get out. Everybody. Out!

Rā's watches Wayne, amused. Wayne turns to Fredericks. Who stares at him, disappointed.

FREDERICKS

The apple has fallen very far from the tree, Mr. Wayne.

Wayne watches Fredericks go. Rā's is at Wayne's shoulder.

RĀ'S AL GHŪL

Amusing. But pointless. None of these people have long to live—your antics at the Asylum have forced my hand . . .

                    WAYNE

Crane was working for you.

                  RĀ'S AL GHŪL

His toxin is derived from the organic compound in our blue
poppies. He was able to weaponize it.

                    WAYNE

He's not a member of the League of Shadows.

*As Guests filter out, a dozen of Rā's men remain, scattered around
the room.*

                  RĀ'S AL GHŪL

Of course not. He thought our plan was to hold the city to
ransom.

                    WAYNE

But really you're going to unleash Crane's poison on the entire
city . . .

                  RĀ'S AL GHŪL

Then watch Gotham tear itself apart through fear . . .

                    WAYNE

You're going to destroy millions of lives.

                  RĀ'S AL GHŪL

Only a cynical man would call what these people have 'lives',
Wayne.

Rā's steps out of the main hall and into a corridor.

INT. CORRIDOR, WAYNE MANOR – CONTINUOUS   240A

*The corridor is long and dark, lined with books and windows.
Outside, across the darkened hills: the glow of Gotham.*

                  RĀ'S AL GHŪL

People stacked like boxes. Families sleeping in garbage. Crime.
Despair. This is not how man was supposed to live.

Rā's al Ghūl gestures at the distant glow of Gotham.

The League of Shadows has been a check against human
corruption for thousands of years. We sacked Rome. Loaded

trade ships with plague rats. Burned London to the ground.
Every time a civilization reaches the pinnacle of its decadence,
we return to restore the balance.

WAYNE

Gotham isn't beyond saving. There are good people here, people
who –

RĀ'S AL GHŪL

You're defending a city so corrupt we infiltrated every level of
its infrastructure.

INT. CELL, ARKHAM ASYLUM – CONTINUOUS   241

Something drops into Crane's lap: his burlap mask. He looks up.
Two SWATS stand in the doorway.

SWAT 1

Time to play . . .

INT. SECURITY CONTROL ROOM, ARKHAM ASYLUM – MOMENTS
LATER   242

The SWATs enter the control room, grab the Guard, move to the
control room, unlock the cells . . .

INT. CORRIDOR, ARKHAM ASYLUM – CONTINUOUS   243

The electronic locks clang open.

INT. VARIOUS CELLS – CONTINUOUS   244

A rogue's gallery of criminal lunatics, including Zsaz, react to the
doors unlocking. Zsaz, curious, moves to the door . . .

INT. BEDROOM, RACHEL'S APARTMENT – CONTINUOUS   245

Rachel stirs. On her bed, fully clothed. Trying to remember a strange
dream. She sees the two vials of antidote sitting on her bedside table.
Hurries to her feet.

Rā's al Ghūl turns to Wayne.

RĀ'S AL GHŪL

You have no illusions about the world, Bruce. When I found
you in that jail you were lost. But I believed in you. I took
away your fear, and showed you a path. You were my greatest
student . . . it should be you standing at my side, saving the
world.

WAYNE

I'll be standing right where I am now – between you and the
people of Gotham.

Rā's al Ghūl looks at Wayne, hard. A door closing.

RĀ'S AL GHŪL

No one can save Gotham. When a forest grows too wild,
a purging fire is inevitable, and natural.

*Rā's looks at his Men. Nods. The Men start setting fire to the drapes.
Flames rise, smoke gathering at the ceiling . . .*

Tomorrow the world will watch in horror as its greatest city
destroys itself. The movement back to harmony will be
unstoppable this time.

WAYNE

You've tried to attack Gotham before?

RĀ'S AL GHŪL

Of course. Over the ages our weapons have grown more
sophisticated . . . with Gotham we tried a new one . . .
Economics.

Wayne stares at Rā's al Ghūl, realizing.

WAYNE

You created the depression twenty years ago.

RĀ'S AL GHŪL
(nods)

Create enough hunger, and everyone becomes a criminal. But
we underestimated certain of Gotham's citizens . . . such as your
parents.

Wayne stares at Rā's al Ghūl, enraged. Rā's smiles.

Unfortunate casualties of the fight for justice. Gunned down
by one of the very people they were trying to help. Their deaths
galvanized the city into saving itself, and Gotham has limped on
ever since. We're back to finish the job.

EXT. EXERCISE YARD, ARKHAM ASYLUM – CONTINUOUS   247

Inmates emerge. The two SWATs set charges on the back wall.

INT. ABANDONED HYDROTHERAPY ROOM – CONTINUOUS   248

Gordon searches the room.

Boom! An explosion echoes . . .

EXT. EXERCISE YARD, ARKHAM ASYLUM – CONTINUOUS   249

*Gordon and another Detective race out the back door – Flass and
several Uniforms are examining the hole in the wall.*

GORDON
They're all gone?

*Gordon looks through the hole . . . into the Narrows. The other
Cops suit up and check weapons.*

How many were in maximum security?

FLASS
Dozens . . . serial killers, rapists, assorted sociopaths.

GORDON
Get 'em to raise the bridges, we don't want any getting off the
island.

FLASS
(*sarcastic*)
Sure, I'll raise the bridges . . . as soon as we get every available
unit over here to help us find the *homicidal maniacs* running
loose out there.

They pass through the wall, heading into the Narrows.

Rā's squares up to Wayne.

> RĀ'S AL GHŪL
>
> And this time, no misguided idealists will be allowed to stand in
> the way. Like your father, you lack the courage to do all that is
> necessary. If someone stands in the way of true justice, you
> simply walk up behind him and stab him in the heart . . .

*Wayne and Rā's stare at each other . . . A shadow drops behind
Wayne as he spins, grabbing the Ninja's throat –*

Rā's draws a sword from his cane –

*Wayne, holding the Ninja, spins to block the killing stroke – the
sword slicing into his arm and side as he wraps his arm around the
sword, grasping it painfully.*

> WAYNE
>
> Perhaps you taught me too well.

> RĀ'S AL GHŪL
>
> Or perhaps you'll never learn . . .

*Rā's al Ghūl smashes the cane/scabbard against a column – Wayne
looks up –*

> To mind your surroundings as well as your opponent.

*A burning ceiling beam comes crashing down onto Wayne, pinning
him.*

*Rā's looks down at Wayne, unconscious, pinned under burning
timbers. Rā's bends, pulls his sword from Wayne's grasp.*

> Justice is balance. You burned down my house and left me for
> dead. Consider us even.

Rā's walks out of the burning building. Motions to a Ninja.

> RĀ'S AL GHŪL
>
> No one comes out. Make sure.

He walks towards the open doors of a waiting truck. Climbs in the back. Inside two SWATs flank a large industrial machine – the microwave emitter.

INT. STUDY, WAYNE MANOR – CONTINUOUS   252

Wayne, unconscious, pinned by burning timbers, flames rising.

EXT. SIDE DOOR, WAYNE MANOR – CONTINUOUS   253

A Ninja guards the side door, staring into the flames . . .

Whack! He goes down . . . Alfred is standing there, nine iron in hand. He looks down at the Ninja.

                          ALFRED
    I sincerely hope you're not from the Fire Department.

Alfred rushes in to the burning house.

INT. STUDY, WAYNE MANOR – CONTINUOUS   254

Alfred moves to Wayne, tries to shift the burning wood from Wayne's chest. He moves to Wayne's face. Slaps it, hard.

                          ALFRED
    Master Wayne! Master Wayne!!

Wayne's eyes flicker open. He pushes, but can't move.

    (*Exasperated.*) Sir, whatever is the point of all those push-ups if
    you can't even –

Wayne glares at Alfred, forces the weight from his chest. Wayne and Alfred push through the burning room. Wayne jabs at the flaming piano keys . . .

INT. WROUGHT-IRON SPIRAL STAIRCASE – CONTINUOUS   255

Alfred and Wayne crawl onto the lift.

EXT. WAYNE MANOR – CONTINUOUS   256

The burning house collapses . . .

Smoke and flames explode through the passage – Alfred yanks the lever, dropping them out of the heat – they speed down . . .

. . . landing hard. Smoldering. Wayne stares up the spiral: high above, sparks and firelight. The crash of collapsing timbers echoes down as Wayne Manor dies. Tears form in Wayne's eyes.

> WAYNE
> (*whispers*)
> What have I done, Alfred? Everything my family . . . my father built . . .

Alfred struggles to Wayne, removes his jacket. Wayne's shirt is thick with blood.

> ALFRED
> (*hoarse*)
> The Wayne legacy is more than bricks and mortar, sir.

Wayne stares up at the glowing shaft. Lost in his despair. Alfred rips Wayne's shirt open . . . a large gash in his arm.

> WAYNE
> I thought I could . . . help Gotham . . . but I've failed . . .

Alfred rips the shirt. Binds the wound.

> ALFRED
> And why do we fall, sir?

Wayne looks at Alfred's bruised, smudged, yet dignified face.

> So that we might better learn to pick ourselves up.

Wayne looks up at his old friend.

> WAYNE
> Still haven't given up on me?

Alfred offers him a trembling hand.

> ALFRED
> (*conviction*)
> Never.

An army of police vehicles and Mounted Police pour across. Rachel argues with a Police Officer.

POLICE OFFICER
Look, lady, we're about to raise the bridges – you won't have time to get back over –

RACHEL
Officer, I'm a Gotham City District Attorney with information relevant to this situation – so let me pass.

Flass and two Cops tackle a Lunatic. Residents watch from doorways. A Resident shouts.

RESIDENT
Harassment! I see harassment!

Flass points his gun at the Resident.

FLASS
Wanna see excessive force?

GORDON
Flass, cool it!

COP
(out of shot)
Gordon, there's someone to see you.

Gordon turns. Rachel is there.

GORDON
What're you doing here?

RACHEL
Our mutual friend sent me with this . . . it counteracts Crane's toxin.

She pulls out the syringe. Gordon takes it, curious.

Hopefully you won't need it.

Gordon frowns, looking around at the volatile slum.

GORDON

Not unless he's got some way of getting that crap into the air.
Thanks. Now, please, get off the island before they raise the
bridges.

Gordon motions to the Cop, who leads Rachel away.

EXT. BRIDGE TO ARKHAM/NARROWS – CONTINUOUS   261

*The Police Officer moves towards the bridge control booth. Signals.
A SWAT truck squeals up. The Police Officer turns. Looks at them.
Rā's al Ghūl is in the passenger seat. The Police Officer waves them
on.*

POLICE OFFICER

All right, last one across!

Rā's al Ghūl checks his watch. Nods at the driver.

INT. MONORAIL STATION – CONTINUOUS   262

The Train Driver checks his watch. Hits the intercom.

TRAIN DRIVER
(*over loudspeaker*)

This train is no longer in service.

Passengers groan, get to their feet.

EXT. BRIDGE TO ARKHAM/NARROWS – CONTINUOUS   263

All five bridges steadily rise up. Cutting off the island.

INT. THE BATCAVE – CONTINUOUS   264

*Close on: black, scalloped gauntlets thrust onto purposeful hands.
A dark cloak whipped around strong shoulders. A graphite cowl
placed over an implacable face.*

Bats flutter as an engine roars to life . . .

EXT. WATERFALL – CONTINUOUS   265

Moving in on water tumbling hypnotically . . .

The Batmobile explodes through the water, rocketing onto the opposite bank.

INT. MONORAIL TRAIN ABOVE FOGBOUND NARROWS –
CONTINUOUS   266

The Driver looks down, stopping the train above the Narrows.

EXT. NARROWS – CONTINUOUS   267

Rachel follows the Cop down an alley which opens up into a square at the base of a monorail tower. A SWAT van is parked there, surrounded by SWATs in a defensive ring. Rachel spots a Little Boy tugging at the arm of a Large SWAT. It is the same Little Boy the Batman encountered earlier.

> LITTLE BOY
>
> I can't find my mom.

The Large SWAT shoves the kid to one side as the van doors open – the Little Kid stumbles back – Rachel rushes over.

> RACHEL
>
> Hey! What the hell are you doing?!

Rachel picks up the kid, looks up at the Large SWAT.

> Hey, you!

The Large SWAT turns, pulls his sidearm, pointing it at Rachel . . .

> RĀ'S AL GHŪL
> (out of shot)
>
> Gentlemen . . .

Large SWAT turns, as do the others, spreading . . . beyond them Rachel can see Rā's al Ghūl step down from the truck, standing next to the microwave emitter . . .

> Time to spread the word . . . and the word is . . .

Rā's al Ghūl rests his hand on the machine's switch . . .

> Panic.

Rā's hits the button – a wave of energy pulses from the machine

Manhole covers burst into the air – fire hydrants explode – pipes rip – SWATs crouch – Rachel huddles over the Little Boy.

Gordon and Flass hit the deck as pipes and sewers explode.

INT. WATER BOARD CONTROL ROOM, WAYNE TOWER —
CONTINUOUS 269

An Older Technician and a Younger Technician monitor the system,
Young Tech's feet up on the desk. Lights flash — the Younger Tech
jerks upright.

> YOUNGER TECHNICIAN
> Jesus! The pressure . . . it's spiking . . .

The Older Tech looks over. The Young Tech points.

> Right there.

Older Tech comes over.

> OLDER TECHNICIAN
> That's the water main under the Narrows . . . something's
> vaporizing the water.

> YOUNGER TECHNICIAN
> How?

> OLDER TECHNICIAN
> The temperature's going through the roof!

EXT. THE NARROWS — CONTINUOUS 270

Rachel crawls through the steam with the Little Boy . . .

Rā's al Ghūl calmly watches steam pour from every orifice of the
Narrows . . . Steam filling the streets as fog . . . He puts on his gas
mask. The Ninjas follow suit.

EXT. ALLEY, THE NARROWS — CONTINUOUS 271

Gordon reaches into his pocket, coughing on the fog. Flass turns
around in the fog, blind, panicking — he points his gun at shapes
emerging . . . Residents, piling outside.

> FLASS
> Hold it! Stay back!

Gordon pulls out the pneumatic syringe – injects himself . . . The Residents stare at Flass, wide-eyed, terrified.

Flass makes eye contact with a Teenager who blinks – to Flass: his eyes become pools of black . . .

Down on the ground! Now!

> GORDON

Flass, he's unarmed!

Flass cocks his weapon, aiming at the Teenager, trembling . . .

Wham – Gordon takes Flass to the ground – they tear at each other – Flass gets his hands around Gordon's throat – Gordon elbows his face, knocks him cold. Gordon drags him to a drainpipe. Handcuffs him to it.

EXT. NARROWS – CONTINUOUS   272

Rachel crouches in a doorway, holding the Little Boy, who is clutching something, crying, looking around, terrified.

> RACHEL

It's OK, it's OK . . . no one's going to hurt you.

> VOICE
> (out of shot)

Of course they are . . .

Rachel turns – a massive shape emerges from the mist . . . a horse – dragging from the stirrup . . . a dead Cop. The rider –

Crane, in burlap mask, Crown Prince of the Insane. Other shapes emerge from the fog behind him, Arkham Inmates.

> RACHEL

Crane!

> CRANE
> (shakes head)

Scarecrow . . .

Rachel grabs the Little Boy, who drops what he was clutching: Batman's optic. Rachel dives into the fog carrying him – Crane gallops after . . .

Rachel runs blindly down the alley clutching the Little Boy – They hit a dead end. Rachel pushes the shivering child down. Turns to face Crane, who towers over them on horseback

Let me help you . . .

The horse rears up, hooves high.

>   RACHEL
> Try shock therapy.

She fires her tazer at Crane – the barbs catch in the sacking of his mask, arcing between his eyes . . . Crane lolls back in the saddle. The horse turns, dragging the limp Crane into the fog. The Inmates scatter.

INT. MONORAIL TRAIN ABOVE FOGBOUND NARROWS –
CONTINUOUS   273

The Driver looks down, stopping the train above the Narrows.

EXT. BRIDGE TO ARKHAM/NARROWS – CONTINUOUS   274

Loeb and a Lieutenant get out of a car at the blockade. Staring across: fog hangs over the island.

>   LOEB
>   (into radio)
> What the hell's going on in there?

EXT. NARROWS – CONTINUOUS   275

Gordon, on the other end, looks over to the Gotham side.

>   GORDON
> We need reinforcements – Tac teams, SWATS, riot cops – get
> 'em in masks and –!

>   LOEB
>   (over radio)
> Gordon, all the city's riot police are on the island with you!

>   GORDON
> Well, they're completely incapacitated –

Loeb looks at the raised bridge.

> LOEB
>
> There's nobody left to send in . . .

Behind Loeb, unnoticed, the Batmobile arcs across the river . . .

EXT. NARROWS – CONTINUOUS 277

Gordon does not see the headlights in mid-air behind him . . .

> GORDON
>
> So I'm on my own –?

The Batmobile smashes through the balustrade, sending Gordon sprawling . . . The car opens – Batman emerges.

> Nice landing.

Batman approaches.

> Rachel's in there . . . the Narrows is tearing itself to pieces.

> BATMAN
>
> This is just the beginning. They intend to destroy the entire city.

> GORDON
>
> They've incapacitated all of the riot police here on the island.

> BATMAN
>
> If they hit the whole city with the toxin, there's no one to stop Gotham tearing itself apart in mass panic.

EXT. NARROWS – CONTINUOUS 278

Rā's al Ghūl's Ninjas climb the monorail support, the microwave emitter sitting on the ground beneath, guarded by two more Ninjas . . .

EXT. NARROWS – CONTINUOUS 279

Gordon looks at the raised bridge.

> GORDON
>
> How could they do that? There's no way to get the machine off the island. Except –

                              BATMAN
They'll be using the train.

                              GORDON
How do you know?

                              BATMAN
The monorail follows the water mains right into the central hub
beneath Wayne Tower. If they drive their machine into Wayne
Station it'll cause a chain reaction that'll vaporize the entire
city's water supply . . .

                              GORDON
Covering Gotham with a fog of fear toxin.

Batman looks up to the monorail tracks overhead.

                              BATMAN
I'm going to stop them loading that train . . .

                              GORDON
And if you can't?

Batman considers.

                              BATMAN
Can you drive stick?

EXT. NARROWS – CONTINUOUS   280

*Rachel and the Little Boy hug the side of a building, picking their
way through the fog. Suddenly, Crane's Inmates emerge in front
of them.*

*Rachel darts back, grabs the Little Boy and tries to lift him up to
a fire escape, but he can't quite reach . . .*

Rachel drops to the ground, covers the Little Boy protectively.

                           LITTLE BOY
                      (*whispered, crying*)
The Batman will rescue us. I know him, he's my friend – he'll
come . . .

*The Lunatics draw closer, smiling . . . Rachel sees a Cop's body lying
in front of her – darts forward – grabs the gun from his holster –
fumbles the safety, takes a deep breath –*

RACHEL

Don't peek, OK?

Victor Zsaz steps forward, smiling . . . Rachel closes her eyes . . .
starts squeezing the trigger – a voice from above.

VOICE
(*out of shot*)

Grab the boy.

Rachel opens her eyes – Zsaz looks up: a winged wraith drops out of
the fog, kicking Zsaz to the ground – Rachel grabs the Little Boy –
Batman grabs her and shoots up . . .

EXT. SHANTY ROOF – CONTINUOUS   281

They climb onto the roof. Rachel wraps her coat around the Little
Boy. Batman turns to the Narrows: the maze of streets filled with
fog, glowing from street lights and flickering fires down below.

As Rachel rubs the Little Boy's arms he looks past her at Batman and
manages a small smile.

LITTLE BOY

Told you he'd come . . .

Rachel glances at Batman, then smiles at the Little Boy.

Batman turns to the city, stares at the wide sweep of the monorail
tracks. The 'spokes' that lead in to Wayne Tower . . .

He steps up to the ledge . . .

RACHEL

Wait!

Batman turns.

You could die. At least tell me your name.

Wayne's eyes stare out from the black cowl.

BATMAN

It's not who I am underneath . . . (*Touches his chest.*) But what
I do that defines me.

Rachel steps forward, recognizing her own words, realizing.

RACHEL

Bruce –

But he is already falling . . .

*Batman falls, sliding his gloves into the activating pockets . . . the
cloak goes rigid – smashing the wind like a parachute . . . Batman's
arms control his cloak, gliding . . .*

*He noses down, accelerating into one of the fogbound channels of
the maze . . . Buildings whip by, fire escapes and lampposts burst out
of the fog – Batman steers, but he's dropping so fast he can't help but
take a few knocks . . . he whips around a turn, dropping and
dropping into an alley . . .*

*Inhabitants of the Narrows stare up, cowering or screaming as they
see a black dragon streaking overhead . . .*

EXT. ROOFTOP BY MONORAIL SUPPORT – CONTINUOUS   283

*Ninjas are hoisting the emitter up to the train. Rā's al Ghūl looks up
at the sound of the screams. Curious.*

BATMAN
(*out of shot*)

It ends here.

Batman emerges from the fog. Rā's marvels.

RĀ'S AL GHŪL

You took my advice about theatricality a bit literally, don't you
think?

Two Ninjas step forward in front of Rā's.

Sorry, friend, but I've done you the honor of killing you once
today already, and I can't save the world by killing one man at a
time.

BATMAN

I can't beat *two* of your pawns?

Four more Ninjas rappel out of the fog on ropes.

RĀ'S AL GHŪL

As you wish.

Rā's smiles, loops a hand around a rope and swings up . . .

Batman tackles the Ninja nearest him – both fly over the edge, drop into the fog – the other Ninjas dive after . . .

Batman and the Ninja drop through the fog, obstacles jump up through the white . . . Batman uses the Ninja as a human shield to bounce off a fire escape, rolling him to cushion his landing on the next roof down.

The other Ninjas land on the roof. Crouched around him . . .

EXT. STREET, NARROWS – CONTINUOUS   284

Gordon runs out of an alley to the parked Batmobile. He looks at the car, then at the key. He pushes a button – nothing. He moves closer, leaning in, hitting the button.

GORDON

How the hell –

Gordon recoils as the canopy flips open with a hiss. He smiles, keys his radio.

This is Gordon – prepare to lower the bridge.

EXT. ROOFTOP, NARROWS – CONTINUOUS   285

Batman draws a Batarang, flies it from the hip, kicks right, sending a Ninja off the roof – Batman aims his grappling gun, fires – but a cord wraps his wrist and jerks the gun out of his hand, over into the fog . . . A Ninja flings something at Batman's feet – a small explosion sends him tumbling towards the edge – he grabs a Ninja's arm as he goes over . . .

EXT. STREET, NARROWS – CONTINUOUS   286

Batman and the Ninja smash through corrugated iron and drop to the street, painfully. Batman struggles to his feet . . .

Across the street, a Baffled Resident picks up Batman's grappling gun and looks it over. The length of monofilament wire stretches off into the fog . . .

INT. MONORAIL TRAIN – CONTINUOUS   287

Rā's moves past the microwave emitter which fills the front compartment, humming. Rā's starts the train moving.

EXT. STREET, NARROWS – CONTINUOUS   288

The Ninjas land beside Batman . . . an enormous Mob appears through the mist behind them. Batman rises – in their eyes: Batman is a towering demon with eyes of black fire . . .

The mob swarms Batman, pulling at his arms and legs . . . The train overhead is gathering speed . . .

The Baffled Resident holding the grappling gun pulls its trigger – the wire retracts at frightening speed . . . the grapple hook pops into view, hurtling towards him – snaps back into the gun with such velocity that it pushes him off his feet, and slides across the street – through the forest of legs . . .

Batman dives at it – rolls onto his back – shoots for the sky –

The grappling hook catches the moving train, ripping Batman out of the arms of his attackers, dragging him into the air . . . the Ninjas watch him go. Look at one another.

EXT. STREET, NARROWS – CONTINUOUS   289

The Batmobile's enormous rear wheels begin spinning – the front wheels are locked up – the spinning wheels belch smoke as the car begins to rotate . . .

INT. BATMOBILE – CONTINUOUS   290

Gordon frowns. His eyes dart as he looks for the front brakes. He hits a switch – the car bolts . . .

EXT. STREET, NARROWS – CONTINUOUS   291

The Batmobile rockets forward, taking out a police cruiser . . .

EXT. BRIDGE TO ARKHAM/NARROWS – CONTINUOUS   292

Loeb and the Lieutenant watch in astonishment as the train emerges from the fog, trailing Batman, who skims overhead . . .

Loeb and the other Cops dive for cover as manhole covers and fire hydrants explode in the train/emitter's furious wake.

INT. CONTROL ROOM, WATER BOARD – CONTINUOUS   293

Alarms sound – the Technicians look at the map – lights flash.

> YOUNGER TECHNICIAN
> What's that?

> OLDER TECHNICIAN
> The pressure's moving along the mains . . . blowing all the pipes . . . some kind of chain reaction . . .

> YOUNGER TECHNICIAN
> Where is it moving?

> OLDER TECHNICIAN
> Towards us.

INT. MONORAIL TRAIN – CONTINUOUS   294

Rā's pulls off his mask, watching the city speed around him.

EXT. SURFACE STREETS BELOW THE MONORAIL – CONTINUOUS
295

A small Crowd outside a store watch news on stacked TVs. The train streaks overhead. People look up, shocked to see –

Batman hanging from the train by his grappling cable, flying along, fifteen feet in the air, dodging stoplights and awnings . . .

The train crosses over a busy intersection – Batman flies over cars, between tall trucks . . . behind him, in the train's wake, manhole covers explode, fire hydrants burst . . .

Batman struggles to fasten his grappling gun into his utility belt, but he's being tossed too violently. The train is heading for a tunnel . . .

Batman latches the grappling gun into his belt – shoots up, skirting the lip of the tunnel.

INT. MONORAIL TRAIN – CONTINUOUS   296

Batman smashes through a side window . . .

RĀ'S AL GHŪL
You!

The Technicians stare at the map: blinking lights reach closer and closer to Wayne Tower . . .

OLDER TECHNICIAN
Pressure's building underneath us . . . we'd better evacuate the building . . .

YOUNGER TECHNICIAN
Why?

OLDER TECHNICIAN
Because Wayne Tower sits right on the central hub, if that pressure reaches us, the water supply across the whole city will blow.

The Technician, worried, looks at a pressure gauge: the needle is moving steadily higher, towards the red zone.

EXT. STREETS, GOTHAM – CONTINUOUS   298

The Batmobile, racing, sideswipes a row of parked cars . . .

INT. BATMOBILE – CONTINUOUS   299

Gordon winces. Mouths 'Sorry.'

INT. MONORAIL TRAIN – CONTINUOUS   300

Rā's al Ghūl moves back past the emitter, draws his sword from his cane. Batman advances, cloak flapping. The train streaking through the canyons of Gotham . . .

Rā's lunges, swinging his sword – Batman parries with his gauntlet, sparks striking off the metal scallops.

INT. CONTROL ROOM, WATER BOARD – CONTINUOUS   301

Alarms: the Technicians watch the blinking lights move close to the hub . . . the pressure gauge needle tips into the red.

OLDER TECHNICIAN

Everybody out! We're *sitting* on the hub – and she's gonna blow big!!

The Younger Technician looks at the Older Technician. Then grabs his coat.

INT. MONORAIL TRAIN – CONTINUOUS   302

Rā's swings his cane – Batman traps it in his scallop – twists his arm – sends the cane spinning away.

RĀ'S AL GHŪL

Familiar . . .

Rā's thrusts his sword at Batman's chest, Batman dodges left, ducks at Rā's, who knees him sideways

Batman regains footing – Rā's strikes down at his head . . . Batman crosses his arms, catching the sword in the scallops of both gauntlets, holding fast . . .

Don't you have anything new?

BATMAN

How about *this*?

Batman yanks his arms in opposite directions, breaking Rā's al Ghūl's sword in two. Rā's stumbles back – Batman jumps over him to the train control panel – looks ahead to Wayne Tower . . .

INT. CONTROL ROOM, WATER BOARD, WAYNE TOWER –
CONTINUOUS   303

The Older Technician watches the pressure gauge needle slide up through the red. He closes his eyes.

INT. TRAIN – CONTINUOUS   304

Batman reaches for the controls – Rā's jams his broken sword into the brake. Sparks explode as the train's brakes die – Rā's smashes Batman to the ground – Rā's is choking Batman, thumbs pushed deep into the flesh above Batman's neckpiece . . . Batman looks up at Rā's . . .

RĀ'S AL GHŪL

Don't be afraid, Bruce . . . you hate this city as much as I do,
but you're just an ordinary man in a cape. That's why you
couldn't fight injustice in this city . . . and that's why you can't
stop this train . . .

BATMAN

Who said anything about stopping it?

EXT. GOTHAM STREET, BELOW MONORAIL SUPPORT – CONTINUOUS

305

*A Pedestrian ducks back as the Batmobile smashes into a monorail
support. The canopy flies open, ejects Gordon.*

PEDESTRIAN

Nice ride, man.

Gordon pulls him away, glances up at the approaching train . . .

INT. MONORAIL TRAIN – CONTINUOUS   306

Rā's looks up at the track ahead, confused . . .

BATMAN

You'll never learn to mind your surroundings . . .

EXT. GOTHAM STREET, BELOW MONORAIL SUPPORT – CONTINUOUS

307

*Gordon twists the electronic key in two halves. The Batmobile
explodes, tearing apart the monorail support . . .*

INT. MONORAIL TRAIN – CONTINUOUS   308

*Rā's sees the track ahead obliterated – looks at his own sword sticking
out of the destroyed brake panel . . .*

BATMAN

. . . as much as your opponent . . .

*Batman smashes his gauntlet across Rā's al Ghūl's face – knocking
him aside – forcing him to the floor – Batman grabs Rā's' hair in one
hand, Batarangs clasped in his fist, steel points protruding like claws,
poised to strike a killing blow . . .*

Rā's looks up at him with scorn . . .

> RĀ'S AL GHŪL
> Have you finally learned to do what's necessary?

Batman flings the Batarangs at the front windscreen, shattering it . . .

> BATMAN
> I won't kill you . . .

Batman pulls a mini-mine from his belt and flings it at the back door, blowing it apart, uncoupling the rear cars. Wind howls, funneled through the train . . .

> But I don't have to save you . . .

Batman's cloak goes rigid – catches the wind – like pulling a ripcord. Batman, yanked from Rā's al Ghūl's hands, flies back through the car . . . And out . . .

Rā's looks up to see the exploding monorail tower ahead . . .

EXT. MONORAIL STATION – CONTINUOUS   309

The train derails . . . crashing down into Wayne Plaza – digging through the concrete – metal shredding, marble shattering, dust clouds flying, parked cars exploding . . .

The train has disintegrated into burning rubble just short of the entrance to Wayne Station . . .

INT. CONTROLS ROOM, WATER BOARD, WAYNE TOWER –
CONTINUOUS   310

The Older Technician opens one eye. Then the other. And starts breathing again.

EXT. GOTHAM STREETS NEAR WAYNE PLAZA – CONTINUOUS 311

Gordon lifts his head up to see the massive fiery destruction. And, further up, above it all . . .

Batman soars in a high bank, riding the thermals, staring down at Rā's al Ghūl's funeral pyre . . .

And we dissolve to –

INT. CORRIDOR, WAYNE ENTERPRISES – DAY 312

Earle strides towards the boardroom, tossing his coat at his Assistant, who catches it, awkward.

ASSISTANT
Ah, Mr. Earle, the meeting's started –

EARLE
What?

INT. BOARDROOM, WAYNE ENTERPRISES – CONTINUOUS 313

Earle throws open the doors. Fox is standing at the head of the table, holding some paperwork.

EARLE
Fox, what are you doing here? I seem to remember firing you.

FOX
You did, but I found a new job. Yours. (*Relish.*) Didn't you get the memo?

Fredericks watches Earle, smiling. Earle's lips are thin with rage.

EARLE
Whose authority?

Fox leans forward to the intercom.

FOX
Jessica, put Mr. Wayne on the line, please.

Intercut with:

INT. ROLLS ROYCE (PARKED) 314

Alfred leafs through a newspaper. Holds it up to show Wayne.

ALFRED
Batman may have made the front page, but Bruce Wayne got pushed to eight . . .

Wayne looks at the paper: DRUNKEN BILLIONAIRE BURNS DOWN HOME. *Wayne smiles. Shakes his head. The phone rings.*

EARLE
(*over phone*)
What on earth makes you think you have authority to decide

who runs this company, Bruce?

WAYNE

The fact that I'm the owner?

EARLE

What are talking about? Wayne Enterprises went public a week
ago –

WAYNE

And I bought most of the shares. Through various charitable
foundations, trusts and so forth . . .

Alfred is smiling in the front seat.

Look, it's all a bit technical, but the important thing is . . . my
company's future is secure. Right, Mr. Fox?

In the boardroom, Fox smiles.

FOX

Right you are, Mr. Wayne.

Earle is speechless.

INT. ORANGERY – CONTINUOUS   315

*Soot-stained glass crunches underfoot as Rachel picks her way
through the smoking remnants of the greenhouse.*

EXT. DISUSED KITCHEN GARDEN – CONTINUOUS   316

*Rachel finds Wayne hammering a board across the disused well.
He looks up at her. She approaches. He turns to the well.*

WAYNE

Do you remember the day I fell?

RACHEL

Of course. I was so scared for you. (*Looks at him.*) I've spent
a lot of time being scared for you.

WAYNE

Rachel . . . I'm –

RACHEL

No, Bruce. I'm sorry. The day Chill died – I said terrible things . . .

WAYNE

True things. Justice is about more than revenge.

RACHEL

I never stopped thinking about you . . . about us . . . when
I heard you were back . . . I started to hope . . .

Rachel kisses him. Pulls back, looks into his eyes. Troubled.

Then I found out about your mask.

WAYNE

Batman's just a symbol, Rachel.

Wayne looks confused. Rachel gently brushes his face with her fingers.

RACHEL

This is your mask. Your real face is the one criminals now fear.
The man I loved . . . the man who vanished . . . never came
back at all.

Wayne stares at her, heartbroken.

But maybe he's still out there somewhere. Maybe one day, when
Gotham no longer needs Batman. I'll see him again.

Wayne looks down at the black gap yet to be covered.

WAYNE

As I lay there, I *knew* . . . I could sense it . . .

RACHEL

What?

WAYNE

That things would never be the same.

Wayne picks up another board. Places it over the gap. Closing the well.

EXT. SMOKING RUINS OF WAYNE MANOR – MOMENTS LATER 317

Wayne walks Rachel past the ruins.

RACHEL

Well, you proved me wrong.

WAYNE

About what?

147

RACHEL

Your father would be proud of you. Just like I am.

She walks away. Wayne looks down. Sees something in the rubble.
He crouches, digging out: his father's stethoscope. Rachel stops.
Turns. Points at the ruins.

What will you do?

Wayne, crouched, holding the stethoscope, looks up. Glorious
purpose in his eyes.

WAYNE

I'm going to rebuild it just the way it was. Brick for brick.

Rachel nods. Walks off. Wayne stares after her. Alone. But Alfred is
at Wayne's shoulder. Watching his gaze.

ALFRED

Just the way it was, sir?

Wayne turns to Alfred.

WAYNE

Yes, why?

They stroll, side by side, towards the smoking ruins.

ALFRED

I thought we might take the opportunity of making some
improvements to the foundation.

WAYNE

In the south-east corner?

ALFRED

Precisely, sir.

Dissolve to:

The irregular shadow of a bat symbol cast up onto turbulent clouds.
And we are –

EXT. ROOF, POLICE STATION – NIGHT   318

Gordon sips coffee from a Styrofoam cup. Beside him – an upturned
spotlight with a metal stencil bolted to it.

A dark fluttering, and Batman is standing the other side of the spotlight. He reaches out, taps the stencil.

BATMAN

Nice.

GORDON

Couldn't find any mob bosses to strap to the light.

Gordon kills the searchlight. The two men stand opposite each other in the dark.

BATMAN

Well, Sergeant?

GORDON

It's *Lieutenant*, now. Commissioner Loeb had to promote me. And he had to disband the task force hunting you. Amazing what saving a city can do for your image. (*Crushes his cup.*) You've started something – bent cops running scared, hope on the streets . . .

Gordon leaves his sentence hanging between them.

BATMAN

But?

GORDON

But there's a lot of weirdness out there right now . . . the Narrows is *lost* . . . we still haven't picked up Crane or half the inmates of Arkham that he freed . . .

BATMAN

We will. Gotham will return to normal.

GORDON

Will it? What about escalation?

BATMAN

Escalation?

GORDON

We start carrying semiautomatics, they buy automatics . . . we start wearing kevlar, they buy armor-piercing rounds . . .

BATMAN

And?

149

Gordon leans closer to Batman. Points at him.

GORDON

And . . . you're wearing a *mask* and jumping off rooftops . . .

Gordon fishes in his pocket.

Take this guy . . .

He pulls out a clear plastic evidence bag.

. . . armed robbery, double homicide . . .

Inside the clear plastic bag is a playing card.

Got a taste for theatrics, like you . . .

Gordon hands Batman the bag.

Leaves a calling card.

Batman turns the card over. It is a Joker.

BATMAN

I'll look into it.

He steps up onto the balustrade. Gordon looks at him.

GORDON

I never said thank you.

Batman looks out at the lights of Gotham. Cloak billowing around him.

BATMAN

And you'll never have to.

Batman drops from the rooftop, gliding on the night wind.

Gordon smiles. He can't help it.

Fade out.

Credits.

End.

Batman Begins

THE STORYBOARDS

HOW IT BEGINS

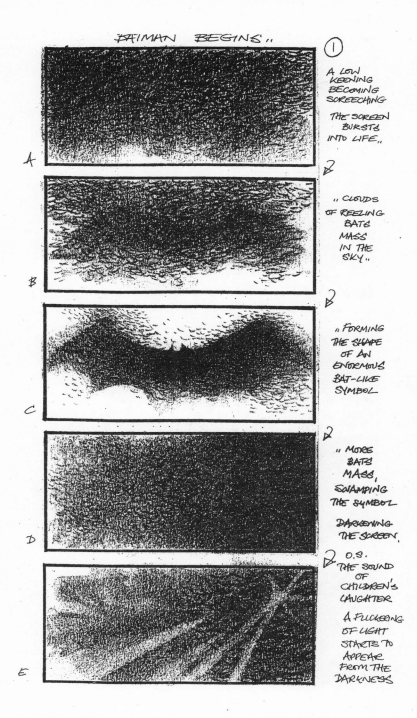

BATMAN BEGINS...

① A LOW
KEENING
BECOMING
SCREECHING

THE SCREEN
BURSTS
INTO LIFE...

A

②
" CLOUDS
OF REELING
BATS
MASS
IN THE
SKY "

B

③
" FORMING
THE SHAPE
OF AN
ENORMOUS
BAT-LIKE
SYMBOL

C

④
" MORE
BATS
MASS,
SWAMPING
THE SYMBOL

DARKENING
THE SCREEN.

D

⑤ O.S.
THE SOUND
OF
CHILDREN'S
LAUGHTER

A FLICKERING
OF LIGHT
STARTS TO
APPEAR
FROM THE
DARKNESS

E

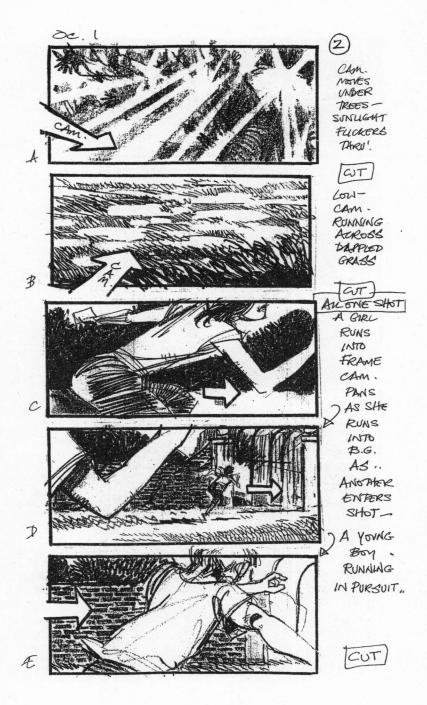

SC. 1

(2)

A

CAM.
MOVES
UNDER
TREES —
SUNLIGHT
FLICKERS
THRU'.

CUT

B

LOW-
CAM.
RUNNING
ACROSS
DAPPLED
GRASS

CUT
ALL ONE SHOT

C

A GIRL
RUNS
INTO
FRAME
CAM.
PANS
AS SHE
RUNS
INTO
B.G.
AS..
ANOTHER
ENTERS
SHOT—

D

A YOUNG
BOY
RUNNING
IN PURSUIT..

E

CUT

156

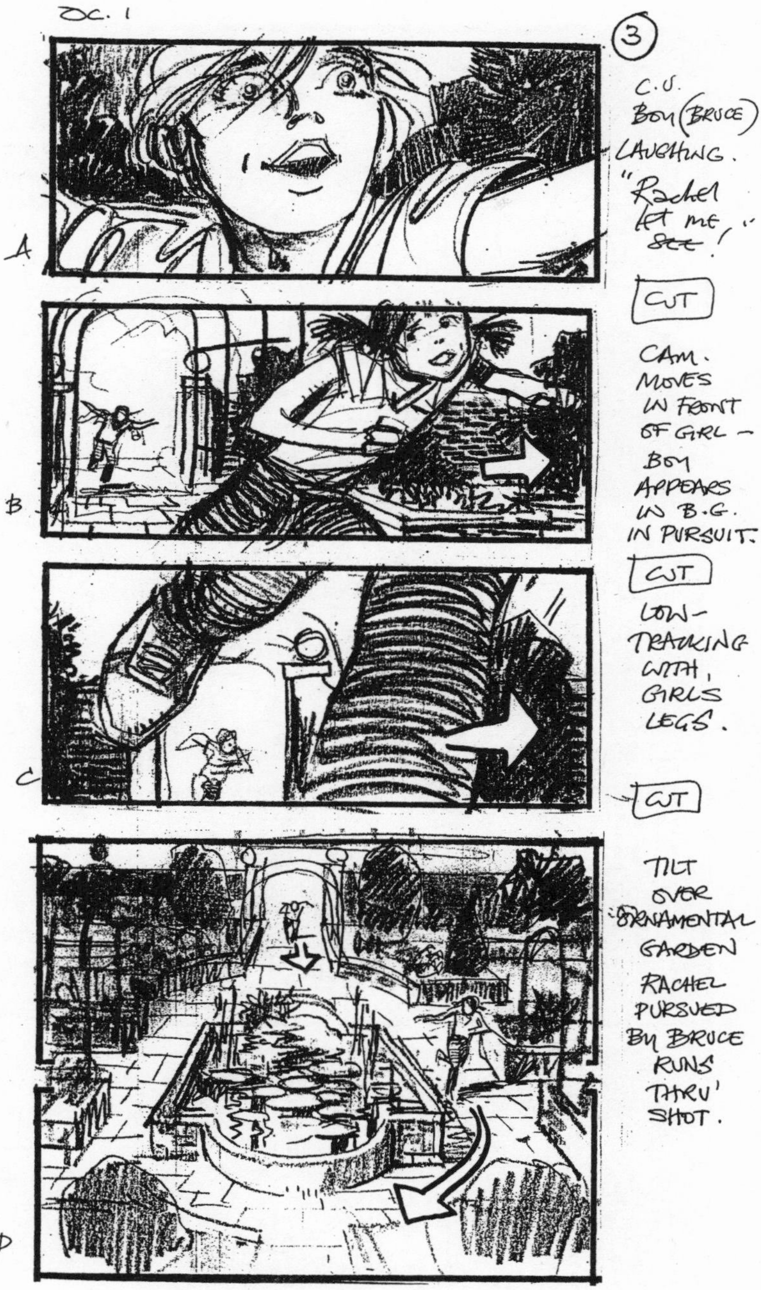

OC. 1

③

A — C.U. BOY (BRUCE) LAUGHING. "Rachel let me see!"

CUT

B — CAM. MOVES IN FRONT OF GIRL — BOY APPEARS IN B.G. IN PURSUIT.

CUT

C — LOW-TRACKING WITH, GIRLS LEGS.

CUT

D — TILT OVER ORNAMENTAL GARDEN RACHEL PURSUED BY BRUCE RUNS THRU' SHOT.

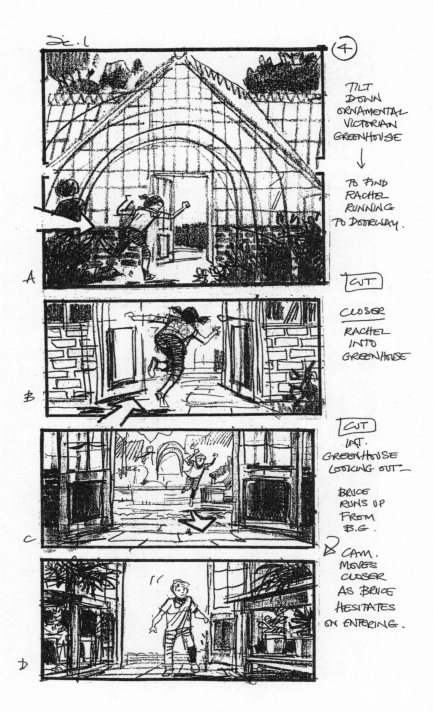

Sc. 1

(4)

TILT
DOWN
ORNAMENTAL
VICTORIAN
GREENHOUSE

↓

TO FIND
RACHEL
RUNNING
TO DOORWAY.

A

CUT

CLOSER

RACHEL
INTO
GREENHOUSE

B

CUT
INT.
GREENHOUSE
LOOKING OUT.

BRUCE
RUNS UP
FROM
B.G.

C

→ CAM.
MOVES
CLOSER
AS BRUCE
HESITATES
ON ENTERING.

D

158

SC. 2

(5)

CAM.
MOVES
BEHIND
HIM AS
HE WALKS
DOWN ROWS
OF PLANTS
ON TABLES.

A

CUT

ANGLE —
WE
SEE
RACHEL
HIDING
UNDER
TABLE
AS HE
PASSES —
SHE REACHES
OUT.

B

CUT

INSERT

HER HAND
GRABBING
HIS ANKLE

C

CUT

LOW ANGLE
HE DROPS
DOWN
TO FIND
HER.
"Rachel
can I see?"

D

"Finders
keepers etc

CUT

OVER
RACHEL
TO BRUCE.

"In my
garden."

E

159

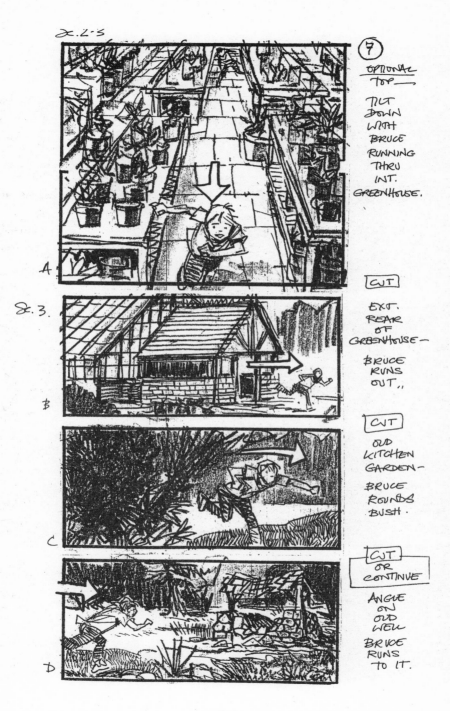

X.L.S

⑦

A

OPTIONAL
TOP —

TILT
DOWN
WITH
BRUCE
RUNNING
THRU
INT.
GREENHOUSE.

Sc.3.

B

CUT

EXT.
REAR
OF
GREENHOUSE —

BRUCE
RUNS
OUT.,

C

CUT

OLD
KITCHEN
GARDEN —

BRUCE
ROUNDS
BUSH.

D

CUT
OR
CONTINUE

ANGLE
ON
OLD
WELL

BRUCE
RUNS
TO IT.

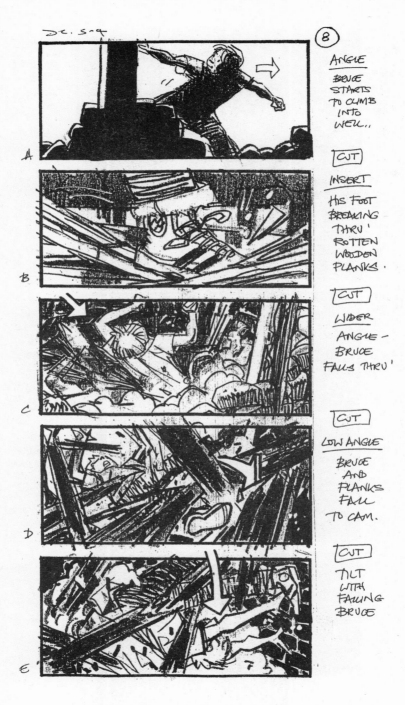

JC. 5-9

⑧

A ANGLE

BRUCE STARTS TO CLIMB INTO WELL..

CUT

B INSERT

HIS FOOT BREAKING THRU' ROTTEN WOODEN PLANKS.

CUT

C WIDER ANGLE - BRUCE FALLS THRU'

CUT

D LOW ANGLE

BRUCE AND PLANKS FALL TO CAM.

CUT

E TILT WITH FALLING BRUCE

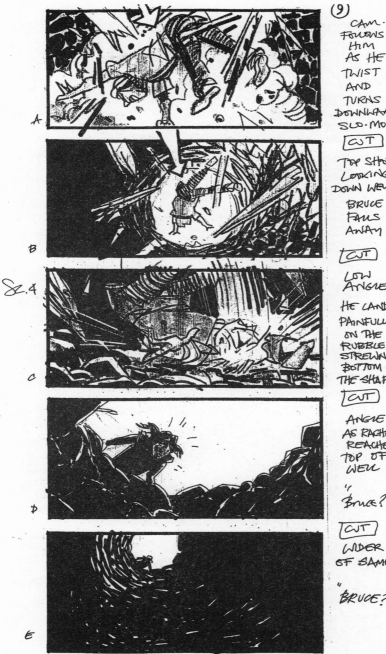

CAM. FOLLOWS HIM AS HE TWIST AND TURNS DOWNWARD SLO·MO?

A

CUT

TOP SHOT LOOKING DOWN WELL — BRUCE FALLS AWAY..

B

CUT

Sc. 4

LOW ANGLE —

HE LANDS PAINFULLY ON THE RUBBLE STREWN BOTTOM OF THE SHAFT.

C

CUT

ANGLE AS RACHEL REACHES TOP OF WELL

"BRUCE?"

D

CUT

WIDER OF SAME—

"BRUCE??"

E

163

10

CLOSE
ON
BRUCE
LIFTS
HIS HEAD..
""
GROANING.

CUT

ANGLE
M.C.U.
RACHEL
REACTION
TO..

CUT

HER P.O.V.
BRUCE
FAR BELOW.

CUT

C.U.
RACHEL
SHE
TWISTS
OUT OF
SHOT.

CUT

Sc. 7

CAM. PANS WITH HER
AS SHE
RUNS
OUT OF
GARDEN.

SHOT
CONTINUES

164

PREVIOUS SHOT CONTINUES PANNING> AS SHE RUSHES UP HOUSE STEPS (11)

MOM!
MISTER ALFRED!

Sc. 7

A

Sc. 8

B

CUT
BACK
TO..

TOP SHOT
OF BRUCE
AT BOTTOM
OF WELL.
IN SHOCK.—
HE GROANS

CUT

C

M.C.U.
HE LOOKS
OFF..
FREEZES

D

CUT
P.O.V.
OUT OF
TUNNEL

BATS
EXPLODE
FROM THE
DARKNESS

E

CUT
CLOSER
OF THE
SAME.

165

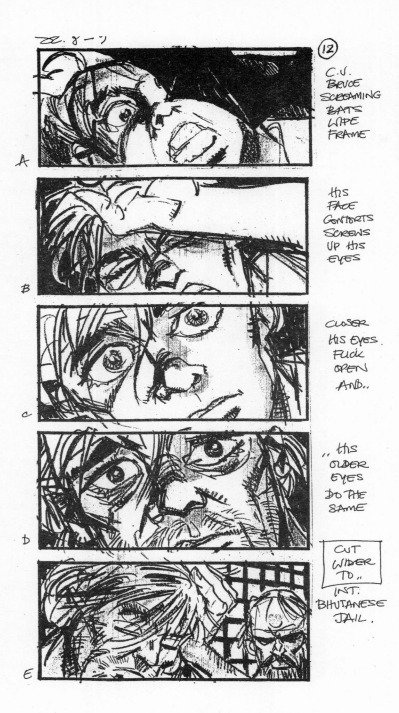

12

A
C.V.
BRUCE
SCREAMING
BATS
WIPE
FRAME

B
HIS
FACE
CONTORTS
SCREWS
UP HIS
EYES

C
CLOSER
HIS EYES.
FLICK
OPEN
AND..

D
.. HIS
OLDER
EYES
DO THE
SAME

CUT
WIDER
TO..
INT.
BHUTANESE
JAIL.

E

THE MONASTERY

INT. THRONE ROOM - MONASTERY "

① WIDE INT. THRONE ROOM + ALTAR

A

CUT

C.U. DUCARD

B

CUT

C.U. HIS HAND REACHES DOWN CRUSHES POPPY.

C

② "DROPS CRUSHED BLOOM INTO MORTAR & PESTLE

D

CUT

WAYNE APPROACHES IN B.G..

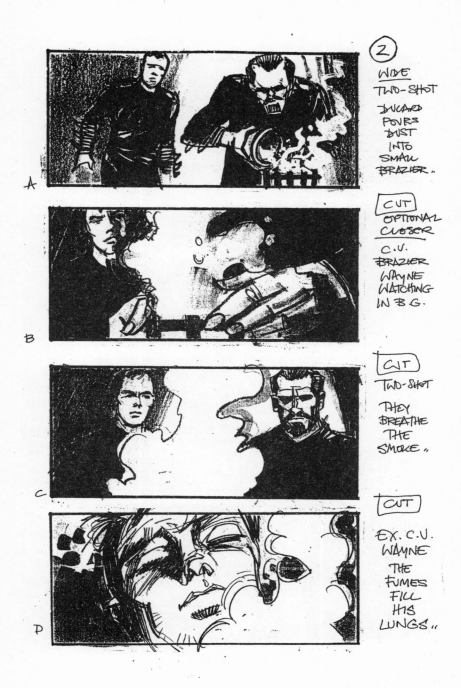

② WIDE
TWO-SHOT

DUCARD
POURS
DUST
INTO
SMALL
BRAZIER."

A

CUT
OPTIONAL
CLOSER

C.U.
BRAZIER
WAYNE
WATCHING
IN B.G.

B

CUT
TWO-SHOT

THEY
BREATHE
THE
SMOKE."

C

CUT
EX. C.U.
WAYNE
THE
FUMES
FILL
HIS
LUNGS."

D

171

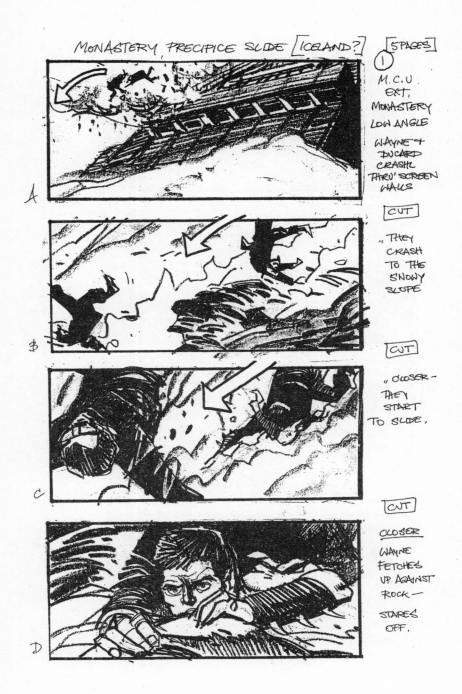

MONASTERY, PRECIPICE SLIDE [ICELAND?] [5 PAGES]

① M.C.U
EXT.
MONASTERY
LOW ANGLE

WAYNE +
DUCARD
CRASH
THRU' SCREEN
WALLS

A

[CUT]

"THEY
CRASH
TO THE
SNOWY
SLOPE

$

[CUT]

"CLOSER—
THEY
START
TO SLIDE.

C

[CUT]

CLOSER
WAYNE
FETCHES
UP AGAINST
ROCK—

STARES
OFF.

D

②

A — OVER F.G. WAYNE SEEING DUCARD SPINNING DOWN TOWARD EDGE OF PRECIPICE

CUT

B — ANGLE - WAYNE LAUNCHES HIMSELF AFTER DUCARD,

CUT

C — EX. WIDE SEE THE TWO SLIDING TOWARD THE EDGE,

CUT

D — CLOSER DUCARD FALLS OFF SLOPE - WAYNE SLIDES INTO FRAME

173

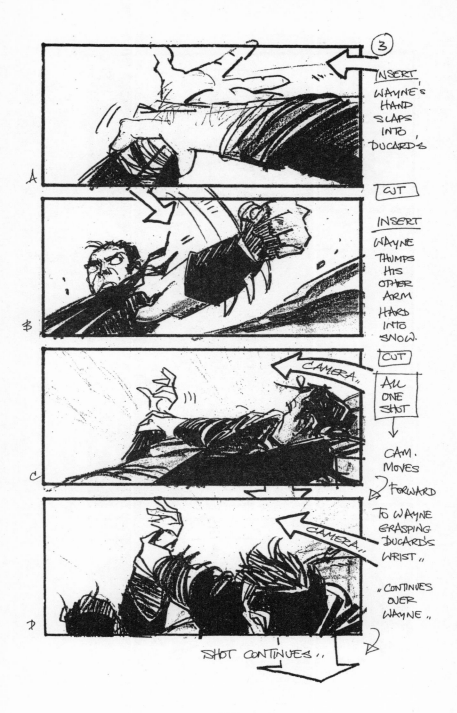

③

INSERT
WAYNE'S
HAND
SLAPS
INTO
DUCARD'S

A

[CUT]

INSERT
WAYNE
THUMPS
HIS
OTHER
ARM
HARD
INTO
SNOW.

B

[CUT]

CAMERA..

ALL
ONE
SHOT

CAM.
MOVES
FORWARD

C

TO WAYNE
GRASPING
DUCARD'S
WRIST..

CAMERA..

"CONTINUES
OVER
WAYNE"

D

SHOT CONTINUES..

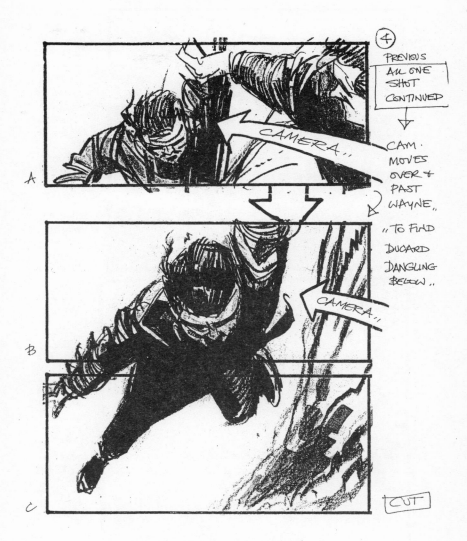

4

PREVIOUS
ALL ONE
SHOT
CONTINUED

CAM.
MOVES
OVER &
PAST
WAYNE...

"TO FIND
DUCARD
DANGLING
BELOW...

CAMERA...

CAMERA...

A

B

C

CUT

175

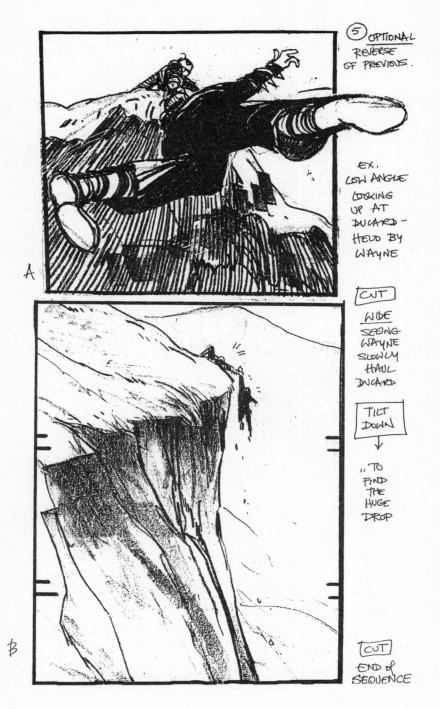

⑤ OPTIONAL
REVERSE
OF PREVIOUS.

EX.
LOW ANGLE
LOOKING
UP AT
DUCARD -
HELD BY
WAYNE

A

CUT

WIDE
SEEING
WAYNE
SLOWLY
HAUL
DUCARD

TILT
DOWN
↓

" TO
FIND
THE
HUGE
DROP

B

CUT
END of
SEQUENCE

176

WAYNE AND DUCARD ON THE PRECIPICE

Scs. 78-79   [5 PAGES] ①

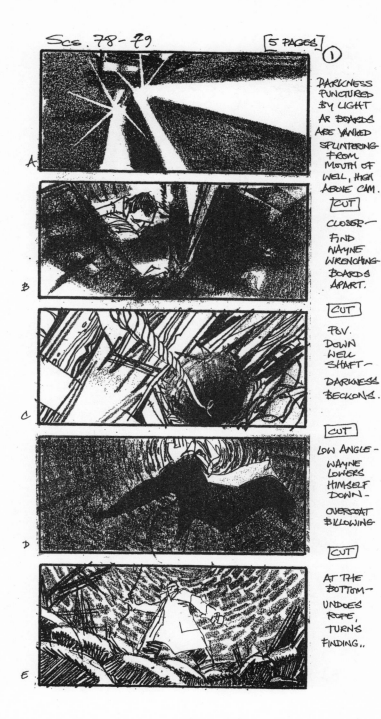

A

DARKNESS
PUNCTURED
BY LIGHT
AS BOARDS
ARE YANKED
SPLINTERING
FROM
MOUTH OF
WELL, HIGH
ABOVE CAM.

CUT

B

CLOSER—
FIND
WAYNE
WRENCHING
BOARDS
APART.

CUT

C

P.O.V.
DOWN
WELL
SHAFT—
DARKNESS
BECKONS.

CUT

D

LOW ANGLE—
WAYNE
LOWERS
HIMSELF
DOWN—
OVERCOAT
BILLOWING

CUT

E

AT THE
BOTTOM—
UNDOES
ROPE,
TURNS
FINDING..

Scs. 78-79   ⑫

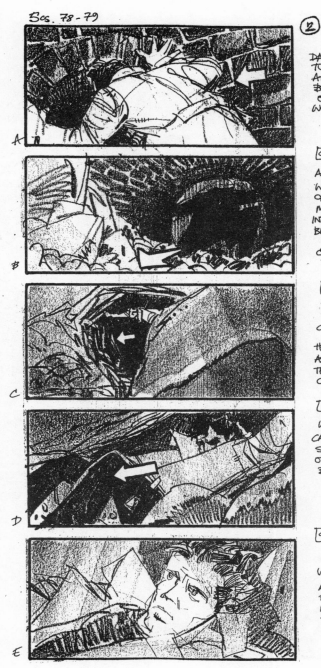

DARK
TUNNEL
AT THE
BOTTOM
OF
WELL-SHAFT

CUT

ANGLE
WAYNE
CROUCHES
MOVING
INTO THE
BLACKNESS

CRAWLING
THRU'
INTO.,

CUT

JAGGED
ROCK
CREVICE —

HE CROUCHES,
ADVANCES
THRU' LOW
CHAMBER.

CUT

WAYNE
CAREFULLY
SLIDES
ON HIS
BACK.,

CUT

C.U.
WAYNE
AIR
BLOWS
IN HIS
FACE.

③

HE STANDS..

O.S. SOUND
OF
ROARING
WATER

CUT

INSERT

HIS HANDS
AS HE
CRACKS
OPEN A
CHEMICAL
TORCH.

TOP SHOT — PAN ← FROM WAYNE TO DISCOVER CAVERN + UNDERGROUND RIVER ..

CUT

LOW ANGLE
BEHIND
WAYNE —
A VAST
CAVERN ..

TILT UP

A JAGGED
BLACK
CEILING
HIGH ABOVE ..

A

B

C

D

E

181

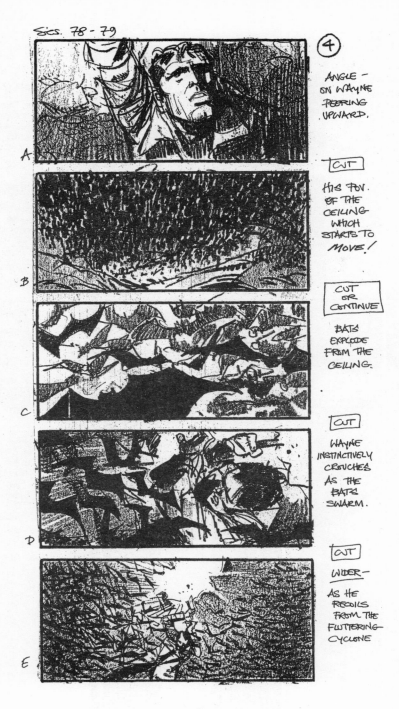

Scs. 78 - 79

④

A — ANGLE — ON WAYNE PEERING UPWARD.

CUT

B — HIS POV. OF THE CEILING WHICH STARTS TO MOVE!

CUT OR CONTINUE

C — BATS EXPLODE FROM THE CEILING.

CUT

D — WAYNE INSTINCTIVELY CROUCHES AS THE BATS SWARM.

CUT

E — WIDER — AS HE RECOILS FROM THE FLUTTERING CYCLONE

Scs. 78 - 79

⑤

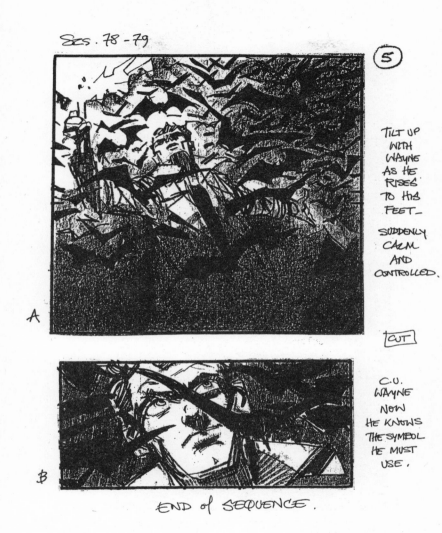

A

TILT UP
WITH
WAYNE
AS HE
RISES
TO HIS
FEET -

SUDDENLY
CALM
AND
CONTROLLED.

CUT

𝔹

C.U.
WAYNE
NOW
HE KNOWS
THE SYMBOL
HE MUST
USE.

END OF SEQUENCE.

BATMAN IN FLAMES

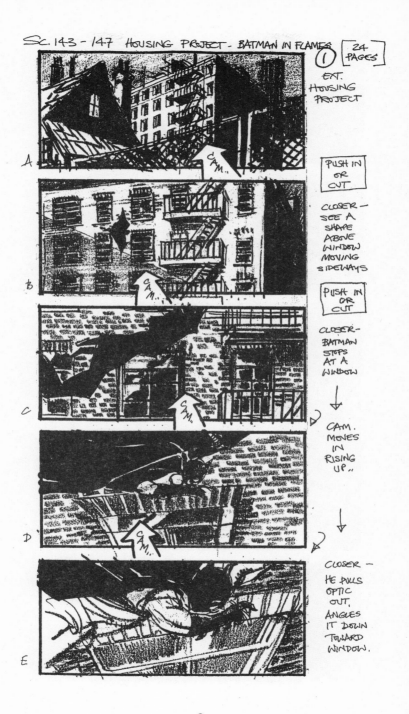

SC. 143 - 147 HOUSING PROJECT - BATMAN IN FLAMES   ① 24 PAGES

EXT. HOUSING PROJECT

A

PUSH IN OR CUT

CLOSER - SEE A SHAPE ABOVE WINDOW MOVING SIDEWAYS

B

PUSH IN OR CUT

CLOSER - BATMAN STOPS AT A WINDOW

↓

C

CAM. MOVES IN RISING UP..

↓

D

CLOSER - HE PULLS OPTIC OUT, ANGLES IT DOWN TOWARD WINDOW.

E

187

Sc. 143

②

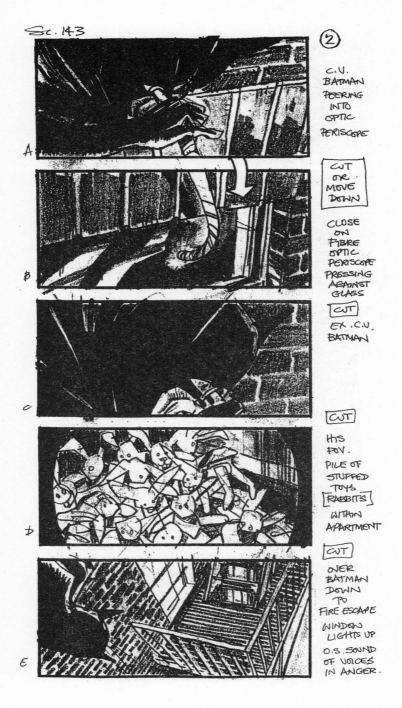

A
C.U.
BATMAN
PEERING
INTO
OPTIC
PERISCOPE

CUT
OR
MOVE
DOWN

B
CLOSE
ON
FIBRE
OPTIC
PERISCOPE
PRESSING
AGAINST
GLASS

CUT
EX. C.U.
BATMAN

C

CUT
HIS
POV.
PILE OF
STUFFED
TOYS
RABBITS
WITHIN
APARTMENT

D

CUT
OVER
BATMAN
DOWN
TO
FIRE ESCAPE
WINDOW
LIGHTS UP
O.S. SOUND
OF VOICES
IN ANGER.

E

188

Sc. 143

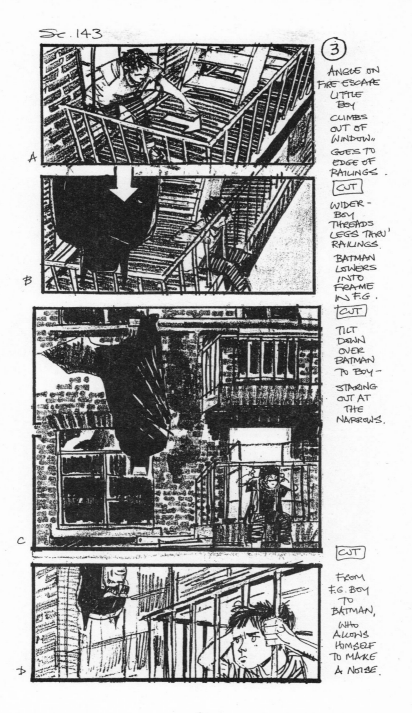

③

ANGLE ON
FIRE ESCAPE
LITTLE
BOY
CLIMBS
OUT OF
WINDOW..
GOES TO
EDGE OF
RAILINGS.

CUT

WIDER -
BOY
THREADS
LEGS THRU'
RAILINGS.
BATMAN
LOWERS
INTO
FRAME
IN F.G.

CUT

TILT
DOWN
OVER
BATMAN
TO BOY -

STARING
OUT AT
THE
NARROWS.

CUT

FROM
F.G. BOY
TO
BATMAN,
WHO
ALLOWS
HIMSELF
TO MAKE
A NOISE.

A

B

C

D

189

SC. 143

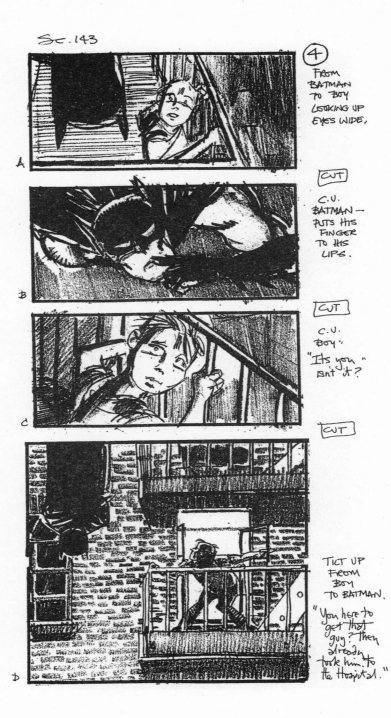

A

CUT

B

CUT

C

CUT

D

④
FROM
BATMAN
TO BOY
LOOKING UP
EYES WIDE.

C.U.
BATMAN —
PUTS HIS
FINGER
TO HIS
LIPS.

C.U.
BOY "
"Its you "
Isn't it ?

TILT UP
FROM
BOY
TO BATMAN.

" You here to
get that
guy? They
already
took him to
the Hospital. "

190

Sc. 143 - 144

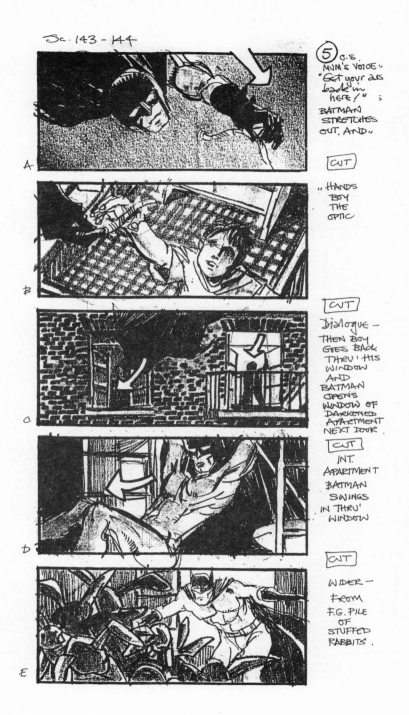

(5) O.S.
MUM'S VOICE:
"Get your ass
back in
here!"
BATMAN
STRETCHES
OUT, AND"

CUT

"HANDS
BOY
THE
OPTIC

CUT

Dialogue —
THEN BOY
GOES BACK
THRU' HIS
WINDOW
AND
BATMAN
OPENS
WINDOW OF
DARKENED
APARTMENT
NEXT DOOR.

CUT

INT.
APARTMENT
BATMAN
SWINGS
IN THRU'
WINDOW

CUT

WIDER —

FROM
F.G. PILE
OF
STUFFED
RABBITS.

Sc. 144

⑥

INSERT
C.U.
RABBIT
IT HAS
BEEN SPLIT
OPEN.

A

CUT

O.S.
SOUND

ANGLE C.U.
BATMAN
LOOKS OFF.

B

CUT

SILHOUETTE
OF
BATMAN
WIPES
FRAME IN
F.G. AS
DOOR
CRACKS
OPEN

C

CUT

CLOSER
ON DOORWAY
CRANE &
TWO THUGS
ENTER.
"Get rid of
all traces."

D

CUT

CRANE

PAN

◁ PAN WITH CRANE TO WINDOW - PASSING F.G. RABBITS AND
THUG #1 DOUSING THEM WITH GASOLINE.

JC · 144 - 145

⑦

A — CLOSER — CRANE NOTICES RAIN — CLOSES WINDOWS!

B — CUT — LOW CAM. FOLLOWS GASOLINE SLOSHING ONTO FLOOR

C — CUT OR TILT UP TO .. "THUG #1 BACKING WITH CAN TOWARD BATHROOM

D — CUT — WITHIN BATHROOM — THUG #1 BACKS IN ..

E — CUT — OPTIONAL HE SEES TOILET AND ..

193

Sc. 145·146

8

PUTS
GASOLINE
CAN.
ON FLOOR

A

RAISES
TOILET
SEAT ,,

B

CROSS
CUT

C.U.
THUG #2
IN MAIN
ROOM —
PREPARING
MOLOTOV
COCKTAIL ,,

CROSS
CUT

INT.
BATHROOM,

THUG #1
RAISES
HEAD TO
LOOK IN
CRACKED
MIRROR.
OPENS
MOUTH
TO SCREAM ,,

C

CUT

.. AND
IS SMASHED
INTO
MIRROR.

D

E

SC·146

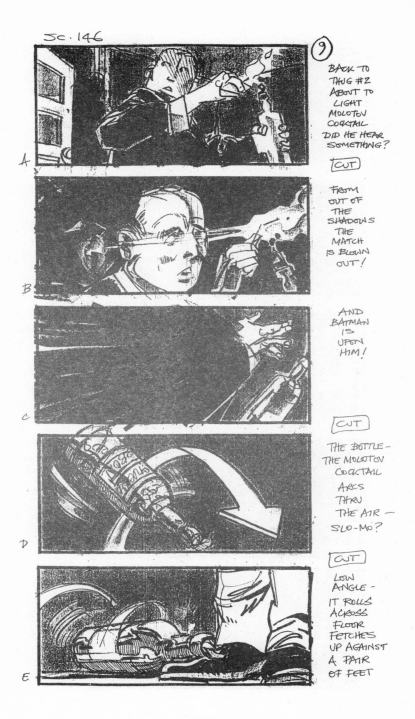

⑨

A — BACK TO THUG #2 ABOUT TO LIGHT MOLOTOV COCKTAIL DID HE HEAR SOMETHING?

CUT

B — FROM OUT OF THE SHADOWS THE MATCH IS BLOWN OUT!

C — AND BATMAN IS UPON HIM!

CUT

D — THE BOTTLE — THE MOLOTOV COCKTAIL ARCS THRU THE AIR — SLO-MO?

CUT

E — LOW ANGLE — IT ROLLS ACROSS FLOOR FETCHES UP AGAINST A PAIR OF FEET

Sc. 146

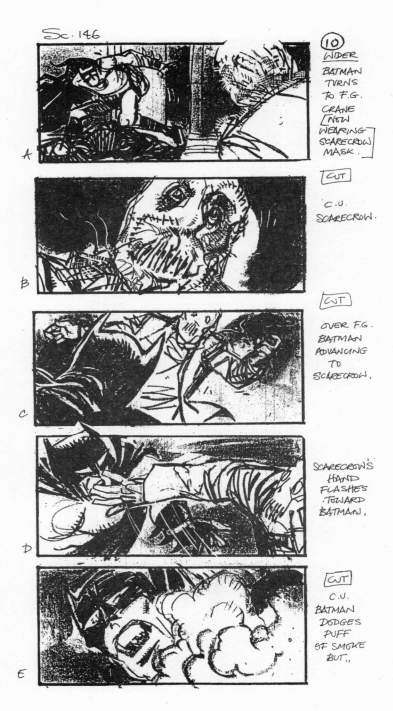

(10)
WIDER
BATMAN
TURNS
TO F.G.
CRANE
[NOW
WEARING
SCARECROW
MASK.]

CUT
C.U.
SCARECROW.

CUT
OVER F.G.
BATMAN
ADVANCING
TO
SCARECROW.

SCARECROW'S
HAND
FLASHES
TOWARD
BATMAN,

CUT
C.U.
BATMAN
DODGES
PUFF
OF SMOKE
BUT,,

A

B

C

D

E

SC 146

⑪
" HE
REACTS,
STAGGERS,
LOOKS
OFF —
SEES ,,

CUT

A

POV.

C.U.
DISTORTING
FACE OF
SCARECROW ..

B

CUT
POV.

CAM.
MOVES
OVER
ELONGATED
MONSTROUS
SCARECROW
CAPERING
AND
CAVORTING .
EYES
SMOKING
:

C

D

CUT

BATMAN
GASPING
REELS
BACK

E

197

Sc. 146

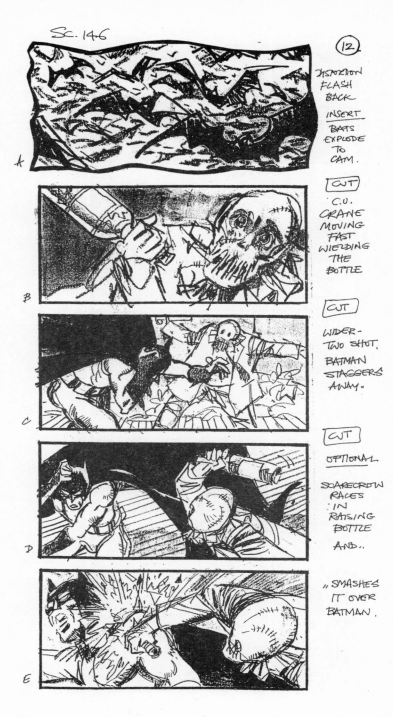

(12)

DISTORTION
FLASH
BACK

INSERT
BATS
EXPLODE
TO
CAM.

CUT
C.U.
CRANE
MOVING
FAST
WIELDING
THE
BOTTLE

CUT
WIDER —
TWO SHOT.
BATMAN
STAGGERS
AWAY."

CUT
OPTIONAL
SCARECROW
RACES
IN
RAISING
BOTTLE
AND..

"SMASHES
IT OVER
BATMAN.

Sc. 146

(13)

A

INSERT
CUT?

BATS
TEEMING
TO CAM.

CUT

B

ANGLE
BATMAN
MOVING
AWAY
GASOLINE
POURING
OFF HIM

CUT

C

C.U.
SCARECROW.

"Need
a light?"

CUT

D

WIDE
TWO-SHOT

SCARECROW
THREATENING
THEN,,

CUT

E

,,TOSSES
THE
LIGHTER
TO CAM.

199

Sc · 146 ~ 147

(14)

WIDER ANGLE —
EXPLOSION
AND ,,

A

CUT

BATMAN
BURSTS
INTO
FLAMES.

B

CUT

DISTORTION
FLASH
BACK —
INSERT

RA'S AL
GHUL
OPENS
BOX —
BATS
BURSTING
FORTH.

C

BATMAN
IN FLAMES
LEAPS
DESPERATELY
TO THE
WINDOWS!

D

CUT
EXT.
HE SMASHES
THRU!

E

Sc. 147

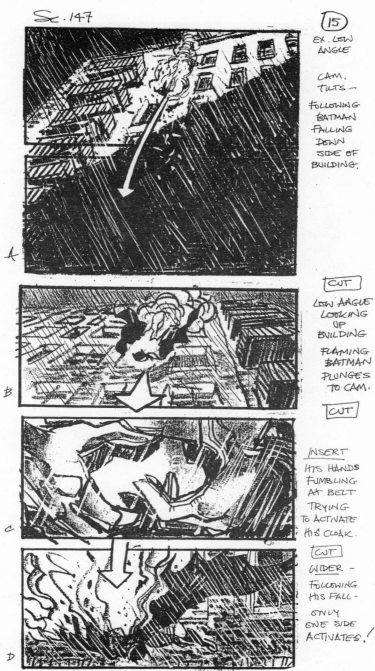

A

B

C

D

(15)
EX. LOW
ANGLE

CAM.
TILTS —

FOLLOWING
BATMAN
FALLING
DOWN
SIDE OF
BUILDING.

CUT

LOW ANGLE
LOOKING
UP
BUILDING

FLAMING
BATMAN
PLUNGES
TO CAM.

CUT

INSERT
HIS HANDS
FUMBLING
AT BELT
TRYING
TO ACTIVATE
HIS CLOAK.

CUT

WIDER —
FOLLOWING
HIS FALL —

ONLY
ONE SIDE
ACTIVATES!

SC.147

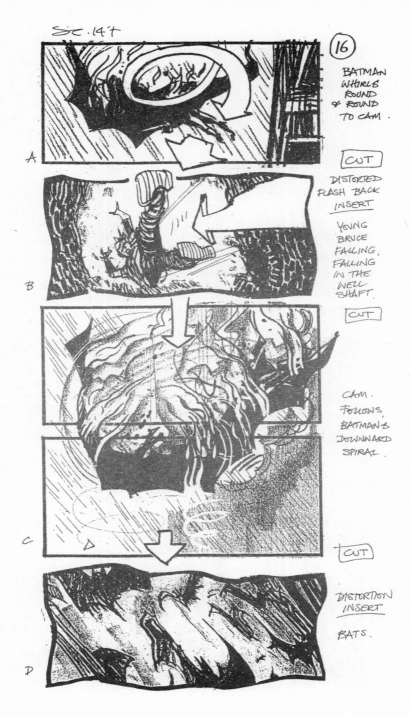

(16)

BATMAN
WHIRLS
ROUND
& ROUND
TO CAM.

A   CUT

DISTORTED
FLASH BACK
INSERT

YOUNG
BRUCE
FALLING,
FALLING
IN THE
WELL
SHAFT.

B   CUT

CAM.
FOLLOWS,
BATMAN'S
DOWNWARD
SPIRAL.

C   D   CUT

DISTORTION
INSERT

BATS.

D

202

Sc. 147

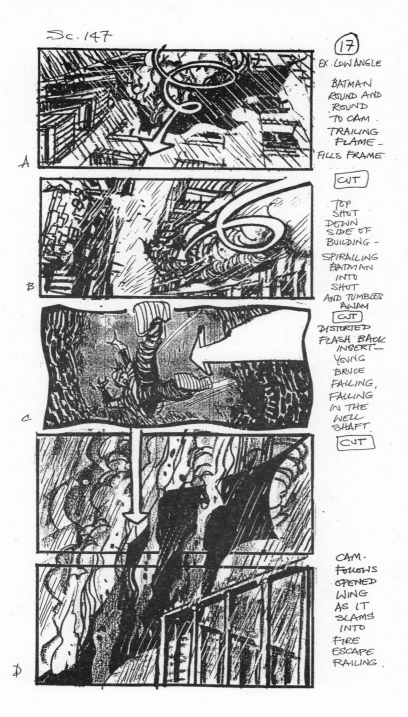

(17)
EX. LOW ANGLE
BATMAN
ROUND AND
ROUND
TO CAM.
TRAILING
FLAME -
FILLS FRAME

CUT

TOP
SHOT
DOWN
SIDE OF
BUILDING -

SPIRALLING
BATMAN
INTO
SHOT
AND TUMBLES
AWAM

CUT

DISTORTED
FLASH BACK
INSERT—
YOUNG
BRUCE
FALLING,
FALLING
IN THE
WELL
SHAFT.

CUT

CAM.
FOLLOWS
OPENED
WING
AS IT
SLAMS
INTO
FIRE
ESCAPE
RAILING.

A

B

C

D

203

Sc. 147

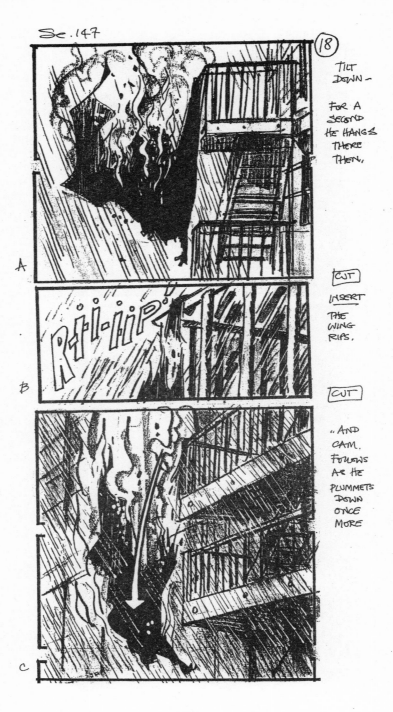

A

TILT
DOWN –

FOR A
SECOND
HE HANGS
THERE
THEN,

CUT

INSERT

THE
WING
RIPS,

B

CUT

".. AND
CAM.
FOLLOWS
AS HE
PLUMMETS
DOWN
ONCE
MORE

C

Sc. 147

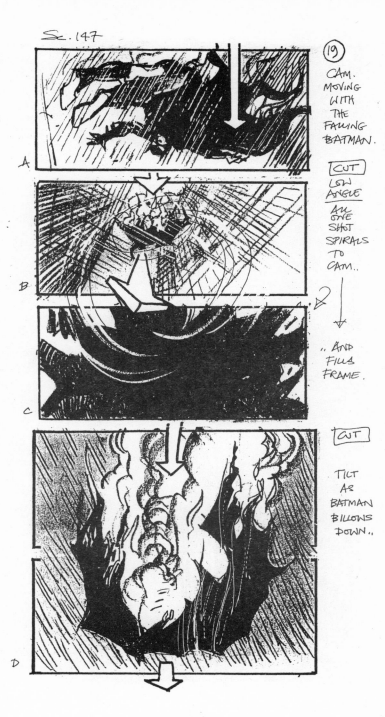

19
CAM.
MOVING
WITH
THE
FALLING
BATMAN.

A

CUT
LOW
ANGLE
ALL ONE
SHOT
SPIRALS
TO
CAM..

B

.. AND
FILLS
FRAME.

C

CUT

TILT
AS
BATMAN
BILLOWS
DOWN..

D

205

Sc. 147

20

IMPACT
ON
THE
WET
PAVEMENT!

A

CUT

OPTIONAL
TOP SHOT
LOOKING
DOWN
BUILDING
TO
STREET
BELOW —
BATMAN
NOT MOVING

B

CUT

M.C.U.
THE
FALLEN
BATMAN —
SLOWLY
HE RAISES
HIS HEAD

C

THEN..

HE ROLLS
TO CAM..

D

OVER
THE
SODDEN
COBLES..

" FETCHING
UP
BREATHING
HARD —
THE FLAMES
EXTINGUISHED.

E

206

Sc. 147

21

A
F.G.
SMOULDERING
BATMAN.

TWO MEN
IN B.G.
LOOK UP.

CUT

B
EX.
C.U.
BATMAN
LOOKS
OFF..

C
C.U.
POV.
THE
MEN
DISTORT
LOOM
MENACINGLY.

CUT

D
F.G.
BATMAN
STUMBLES
UPRIGHT

CUT
WIDER

E
..STAGGERS
INTO
ALLEY.

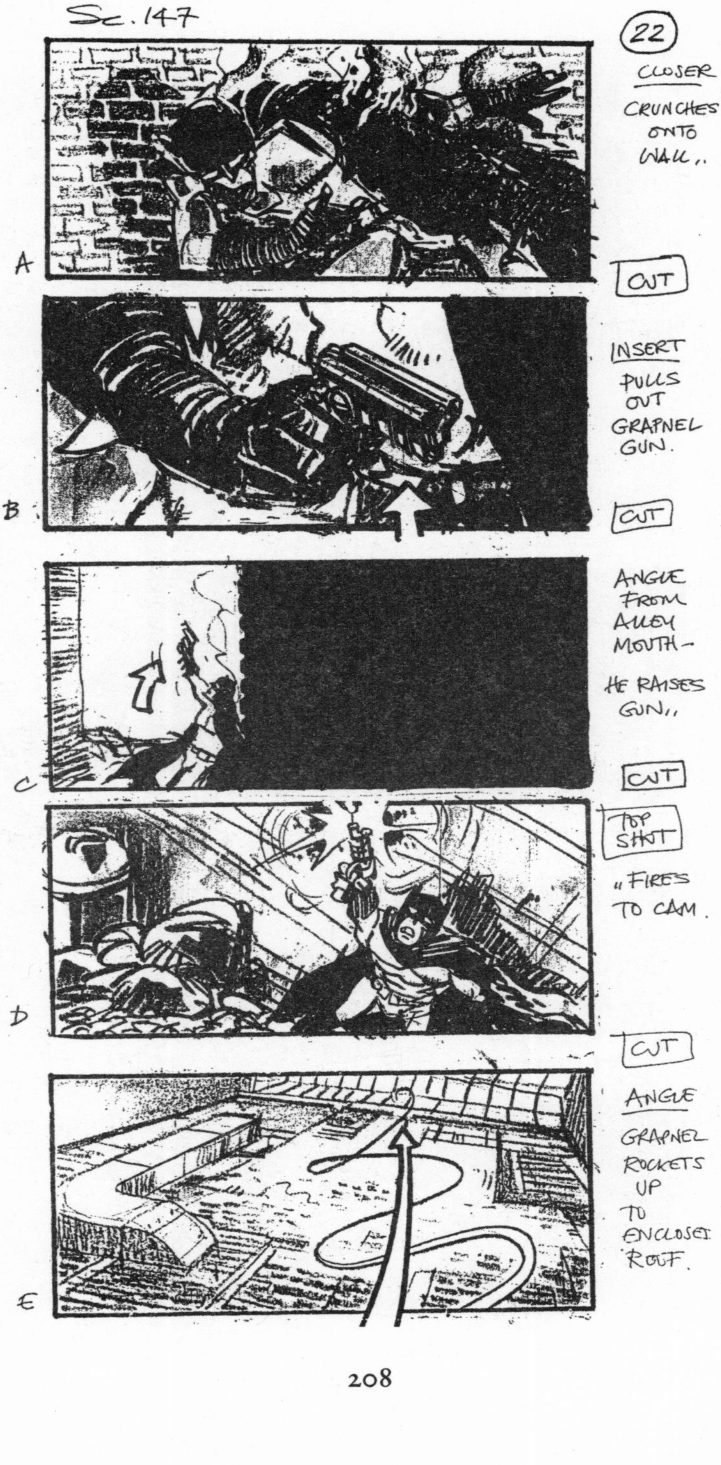

Sc. 147

(22)
CLOSER
CRUNCHES
ONTO
WALL,.

A

CUT

INSERT
PULLS
OUT
GRAPNEL
GUN.

B

CUT

ANGLE
FROM
ALLEY
MOUTH—

HE RAISES
GUN,,

C

CUT

TOP
SHOT

"FIRES
TO CAM.

D

CUT

ANGLE

GRAPNEL
ROCKETS
UP
TO
ENCLOSED
ROOF.

E

208

Sc. 147

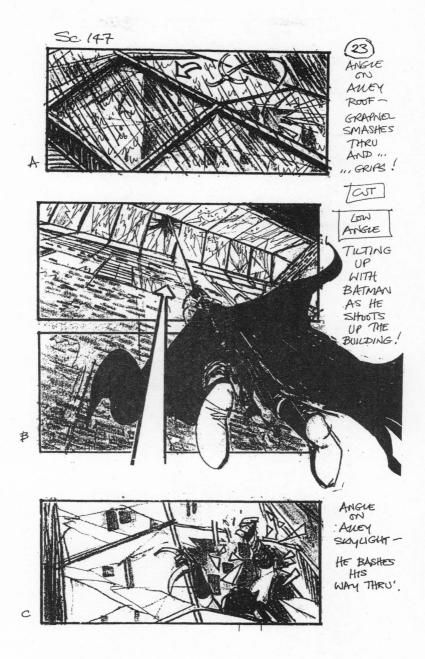

A

B

C

(23)
ANGLE
ON
ALLEY
ROOF —
GRAPNEL
SMASHES
THRU
AND ...
... GRIPS !

CUT

LOW
ANGLE

TILTING
UP
WITH
BATMAN
AS HE
SHOOTS
UP THE
BUILDING !

ANGLE
ON
ALLEY
SKYLIGHT —

HE BASHES
HIS
WAY THRU'.

SC. 147   (24)

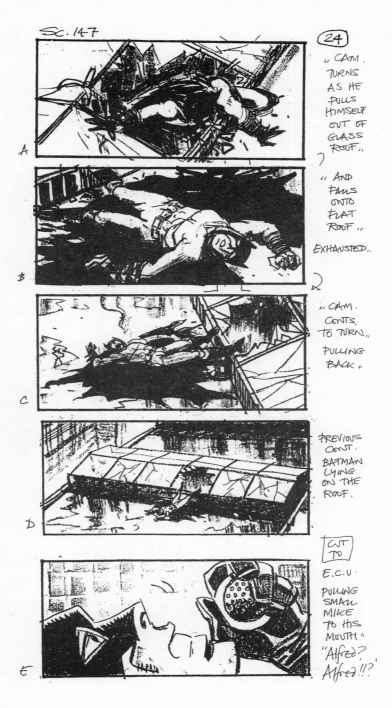

A   "CAM. TURNS AS HE PULLS HIMSELF OUT OF GLASS ROOF."

B   "AND FALLS ONTO FLAT ROOF." EXHAUSTED..

C   "CAM. CONTS. TO TURN." PULLING BACK "

D   PREVIOUS CONT. BATMAN LYING ON THE ROOF.

E   CUT TO
     E.C.U. PULLING SMALL MIKE TO HIS MOUTH "
     "Alfred? Alfred!!?"

210

BATS DESCEND ON THE ASYLUM

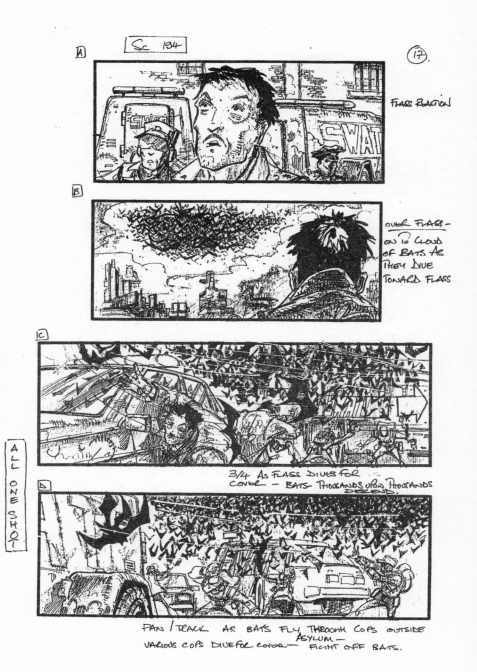

Sc 134

A

17.

FLASS REACTION

B

OVER FLASS —
ON TO CLOUD
OF BATS AS
THEY DIVE
TOWARD FLASS

A
L
L

O
N
E

S
H
O
T

C

3/4 AS FLASS DIVES FOR
COVER — BATS- THOUSANDS UPON THOUSANDS
DESCEND.

D

PAN / TRACK AS BATS FLY THROUGH COPS OUTSIDE
ASYLUM —
VARIOUS COPS DIVE FOR COVER — FIGHT OFF BATS.

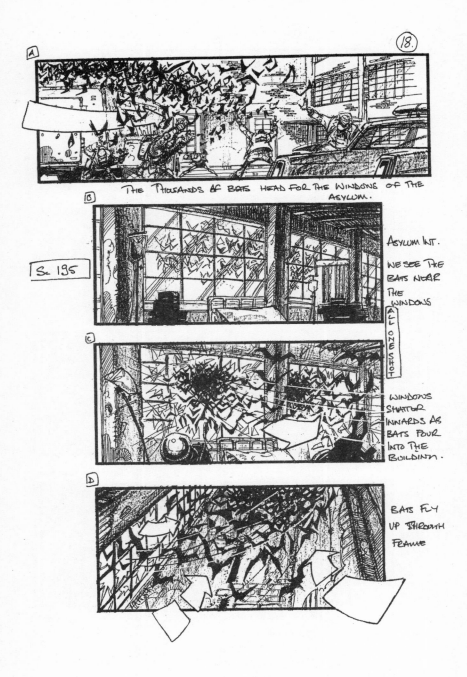

A

THE THOUSANDS OF BATS HEAD FOR THE WINDOWS OF THE ASYLUM.

B

Sc 195

ASYLUM INT.

WE SEE THE BATS NEAR THE WINDOWS

ALL ONE SHOT

C

WINDOWS SHATTER INWARDS AS BATS POUR INTO THE BUILDING.

D

BATS FLY UP THROUGH FRAME

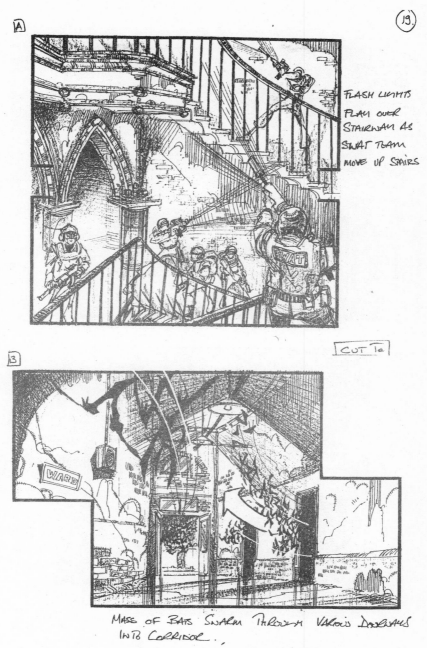

A

FLASH LIGHTS
PLAY OVER
STAIRWAY AS
SWAT TEAM
MOVE UP STAIRS

CUT To

B

MASS OF BATS SWARM THROUGH VARIOUS DOORWAYS
INTO CORRIDOR.
TRACK BACK AS BATS SWARM PAST CAMERA.
(THOUSANDS UPON THOUSANDS OF BATS).

215

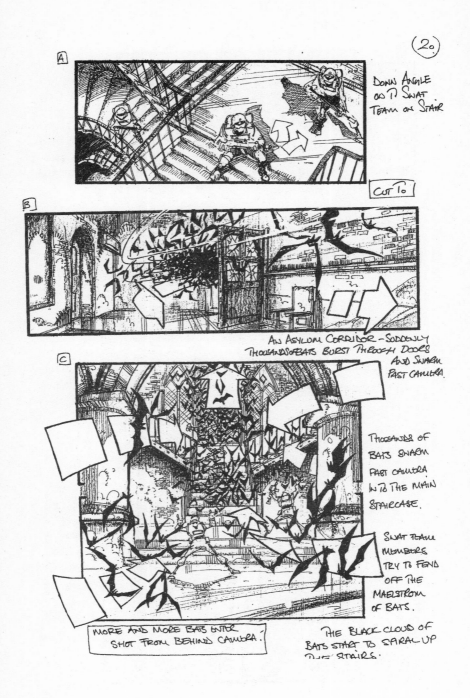

(20.)

A — DOWN ANGLE ON 7 SWAT TEAM ON STAIR

CUT TO

B — AN ASYLUM CORRIDOR — SUDDENLY THOUSANDS OF BATS BURST THROUGH DOORS AND SWARM PAST CAMERA.

C — THOUSANDS OF BATS SWARM PAST CAMERA INTO THE MAIN STAIRCASE.

SWAT TEAM MEMBERS TRY TO FEND OFF THE MAELSTROM OF BATS.

MORE AND MORE BATS ENTER SHOT FROM BEHIND CAMERA.

THE BLACK CLOUD OF BATS START TO SPIRAL UP THE STAIRS.

216

ALL ONE SHOT

TILT UP WITH BATS.
AS THE BLACK
LIVING MASS
SWIRLS UP
PAST THE
STARTLED SWAT
TEAM.

217

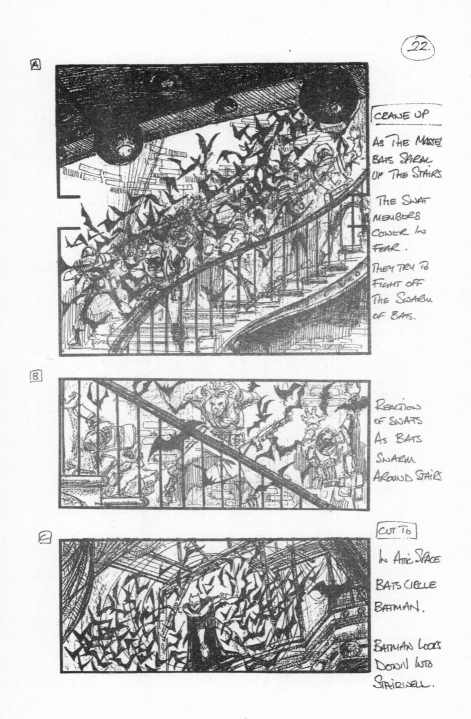

A

CRANE UP

AS THE MASSE
BATS SPIRAL
UP THE STAIRS

THE SWAT
MEMBERS
COWER IN
FEAR.

THEY TRY TO
FIGHT OFF
THE SWARM
OF BATS.

B

REACTION
OF SWATS
AS BATS
SWARM
AROUND STAIRS

C

CUT TO

IN ATTIC SPACE
BATS CIRCLE
BATMAN.

BATMAN LOOKS
DOWN INTO
STAIRWELL.

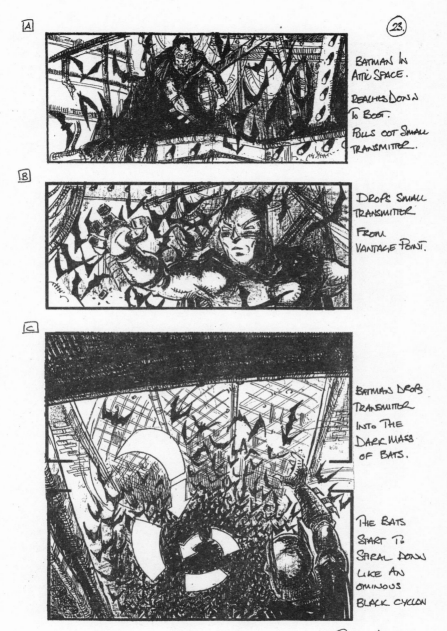

A

BATMAN IN
ATTIC SPACE.

REACHES DOWN
TO BOOT.

PULLS OOT SMALL
TRANSMITTER.

B

DROPS SMALL
TRANSMITTER
FROM
VANTAGE POINT.

C

BATMAN DROPS
TRANSMITTER
INTO THE
DARK MASS
OF BATS.

THE BATS
START TO
SPIRAL DOWN
LIKE AN
OMINOUS
BLACK CYCLON

THEY DIVE
DOWN AFTER THE
TRANSMITTER

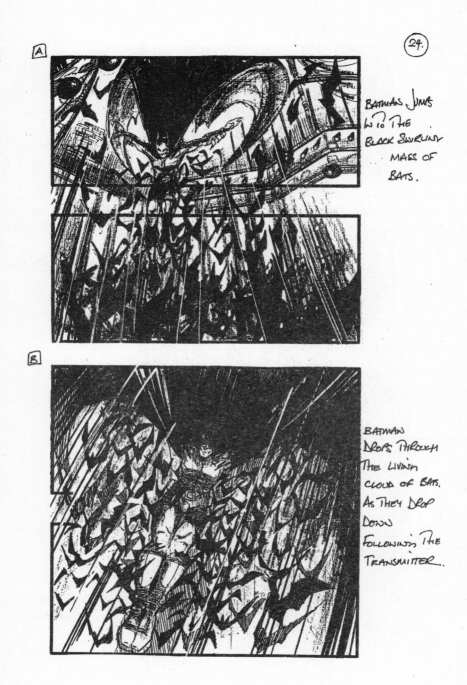

A

BATMANS JUMPS
W TO THE
BLACK SWIRLING
MASS OF
BATS.

B

BATMAN
DROPS THROUGH
THE LIVING
CLOUD OF BATS.
AS THEY DROP
DOWN
FOLLOWING THE
TRANSMITTER.

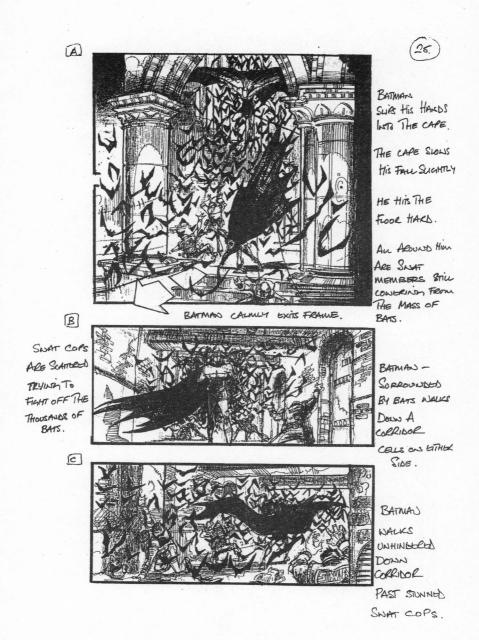

A.

BATMAN
SLIPS HIS HANDS
INTO THE CAPE.

THE CAPE SLOWS
HIS FALL SLIGHTLY

HE HITS THE
FLOOR HARD.

ALL AROUND HIM
ARE SWAT
MEMBERS STILL
COWERING FROM
THE MASS OF
BATS.

BATMAN CALMLY EXITS FRAME.

B.

SWAT COPS
ARE SCATTERED
TRYING TO
FIGHT OFF THE
THOUSANDS OF
BATS.

BATMAN —
SORROUNDED
BY BATS WALKS
DOWN A
CORRIDOR

CELLS ON EITHER
SIDE.

C.

BATMAN
WALKS
UNHINDERED
DOWN
CORRIDOR
PAST STUNNED
SWAT COPS.

221

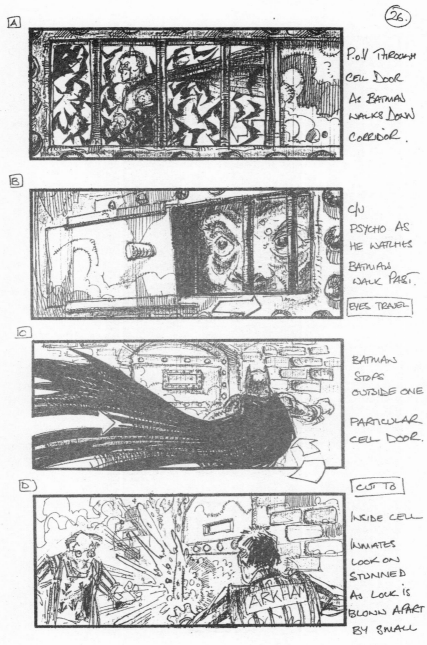

A P.O.V THROUGH CELL DOOR AS BATMAN WALKS DOWN CORRIDOR.

B C/U PSYCHO AS HE WATCHES BATMAN WALK PAST.

EYES TRAVEL

C BATMAN STOPS OUTSIDE ONE PARTICULAR CELL DOOR.

D CUT TO

INSIDE CELL INMATES LOOK ON STUNNED AS LOCK IS BLOWN APART BY SMALL EXPLOSIVE CHARGE.

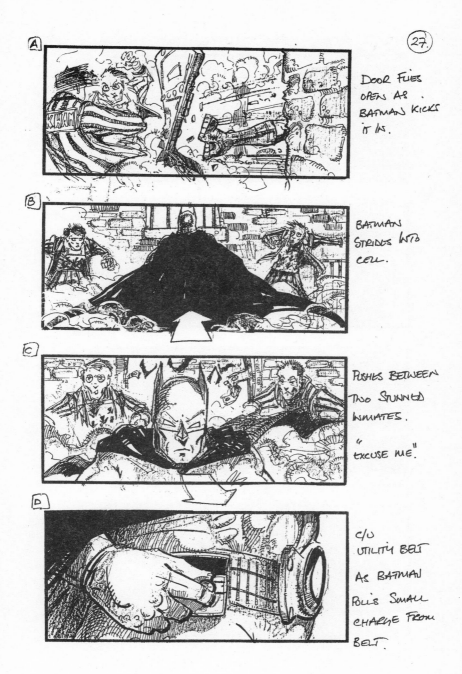

A — DOOR FLIES OPEN AS BATMAN KICKS IT IN.

B — BATMAN STRIDES INTO CELL.

C — PUSHES BETWEEN TWO STUNNED INMATES.

"EXCUSE ME"

D — C/U UTILITY BELT AS BATMAN PULLS SMALL CHARGE FROM BELT.

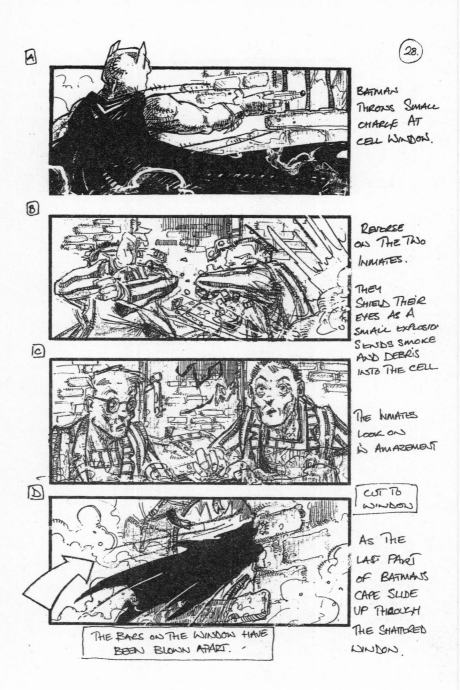

A.

BATMAN THROWS SMALL CHARGE AT CELL WINDOW.

B.

REVERSE ON THE TWO INMATES.

THEY SHIELD THEIR EYES AS A SMALL EXPLOSION SENDS SMOKE AND DEBRIS INTO THE CELL

C.

THE INMATES LOOK ON IN AMAZEMENT

D.

CUT TO WINDOW

AS THE LAST PART OF BATMANS CAPE SLIDE UP THROUGH THE SHATTERED WINDOW.

THE BARS ON THE WINDOW HAVE BEEN BLOWN APART.

224

WAYNE BECOMES BATMAN

Sc 291   INT BATCAVE -   .   ①.

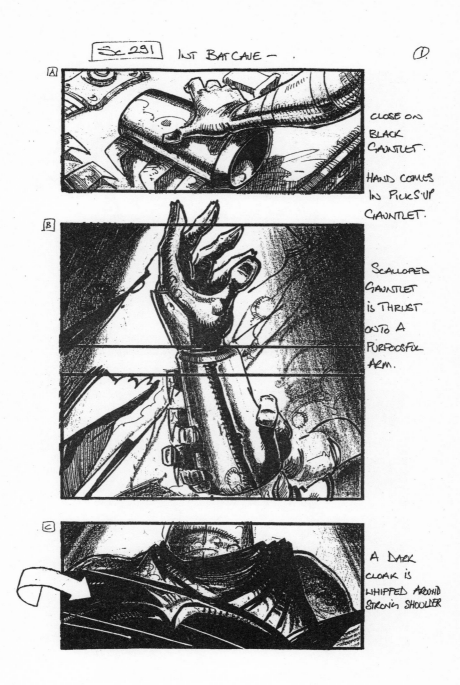

A   CLOSE ON
    BLACK
    GAUNTLET.

    HAND COMES
    IN PICKS·UP
    GAUNTLET.

B   SCALLOPED
    GAUNTLET
    IS THRUST
    ONTO A
    PURPOOSFUL
    ARM.

C   A DARK
    CLOAK IS
    WHIPPED AROUND
    STRONG SHOULLER

227

CRANE DOWN AS A GRAPHITE COAL IS PLACED OVER AN IMPLACABLE FACE.

CAMERA CRANES DOWN AS....

THE FIGURE OF BATMAN RUNS THROUGH CAVE-

228

Sc 291 – CONTINUED.   4-PAGES.

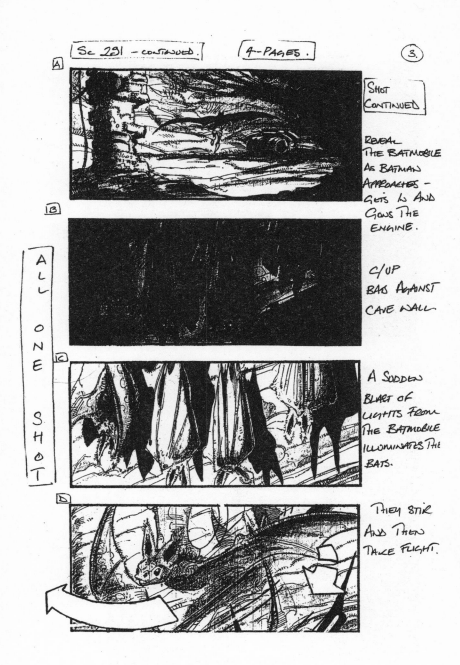

A SHOT CONTINUED.

REVEAL THE BATMOBILE AS BATMAN APPROACHES – GETS IN AND GUNS THE ENGINE.

B C/UP BATS AGAINST CAVE WALL

ALL ONE SHOT

C A SUDDEN BLAST OF LIGHTS FROM THE BATMOBILE ILLUMINATES THE BATS.

D THEY STIR AND THEN TAKE FLIGHT.

Sc 291 - CONTINUED.

(4)

A

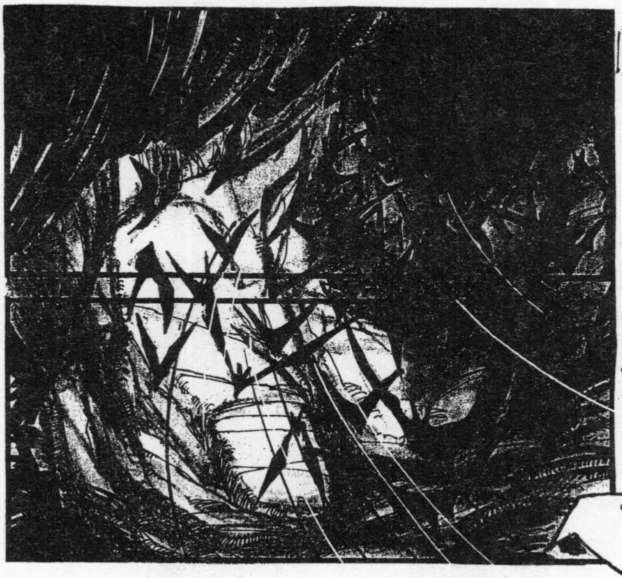

SHOT CONTINUED

PAN LEFT
AS WE SEE
MORE BATS –
ALOT MORE
ALL TAKE TO
THE AIR IN A
LIVING MASS OF
BLACK.

RACHEL ASKS BATMAN WHO HE IS

THE NARROWS. SC 281-311. END SEQUENCE.

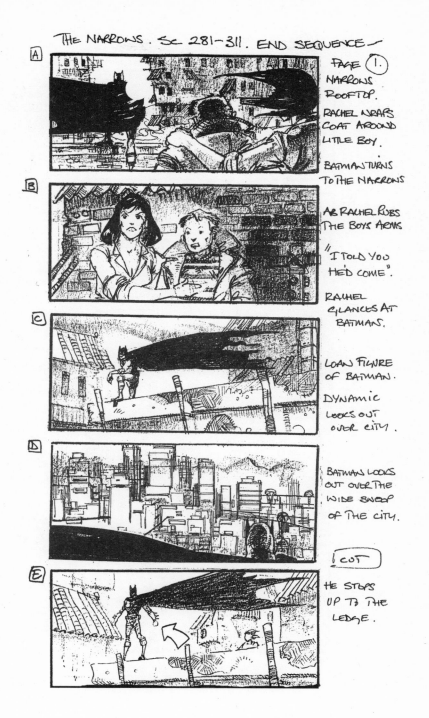

Ⓐ

PAGE ①

NARROWS ROOFTOP.

RACHEL WRAPS COAT AROUND LITTLE BOY.

BATMAN TURNS TO THE NARROWS

Ⓑ

AS RACHEL RUBS THE BOYS ARMS

"I TOLD YOU HE'D COME".

RACHEL GLANCES AT BATMAN.

Ⓒ

LOAN FIGURE OF BATMAN.

DYNAMIC LOOKS OUT OVER CITY.

Ⓓ

BATMAN LOOKS OUT OVER THE WIDE SWEEP OF THE CITY.

CUT

Ⓔ

HE STEPS UP TO THE LEDGE.

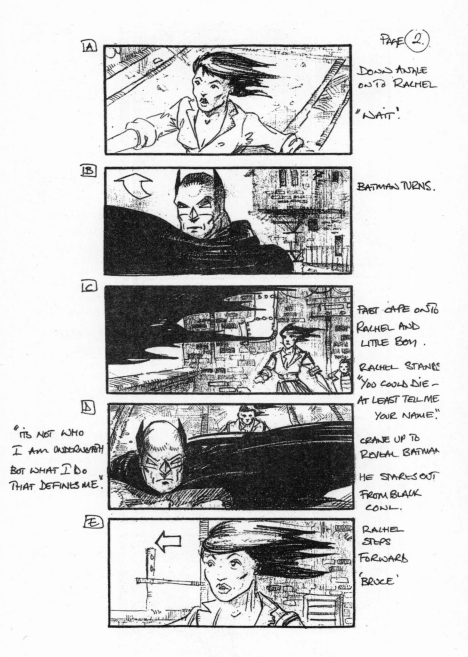

A — DOWN ANGLE ON TO RACHEL

"WAIT."

B — BATMAN TURNS.

C — FAST CAPE ON TO RACHEL AND LITTLE BOY.

RACHEL STANDS "YOU COULD DIE — AT LEAST TELL ME YOUR NAME."

"IT'S NOT WHO I AM UNDERNEATH BUT WHAT I DO THAT DEFINES ME."

D — CRANE UP TO REVEAL BATMAN

HE STARES OUT FROM BLACK COWL.

E — RACHEL STEPS FORWARD 'BRUCE'

234

A

BUT BATMAN
IS ALREADY
FALLING.

B

RACHEL RUNS UPTO
AND LEANS OVER
THE LEDGE.

C

RACHELS P.O.V
AS BATMAN
FALLS/DIVES
AWAY FROM
CAMERA - INTO
THE MISTS OF
THE NARROWS.

D

TRAVELS WITH
BATMAN AS
HE PLUNGES
INTO THE
MISTS.

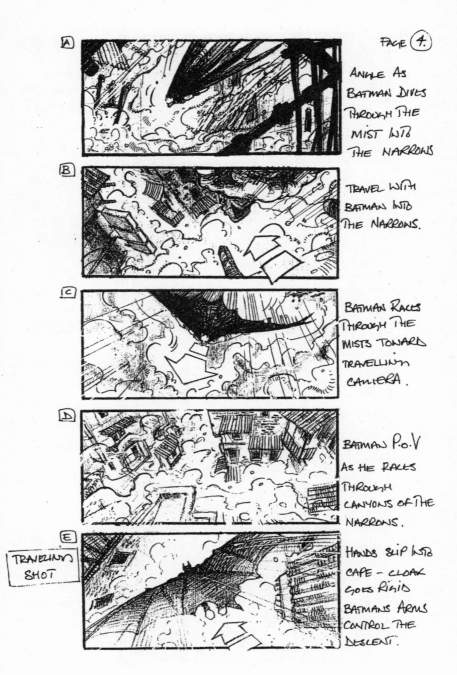

Ⓐ ANGLE AS
BATMAN DIVES
THROUGH THE
MIST INTO
THE NARROWS

Ⓑ TRAVEL WITH
BATMAN INTO
THE NARROWS.

Ⓒ BATMAN RACES
THROUGH THE
MISTS TOWARD
TRAVELLING
CAMERA.

Ⓓ BATMAN P.O.V
AS HE RACES
THROUGH
CANYONS OF THE
NARROWS.

TRAVELLING SHOT

Ⓔ HANDS SLIP INTO
CAPE - CLOAK
GOES RIGID
BATMANS ARMS
CONTROL THE
DESCENT.

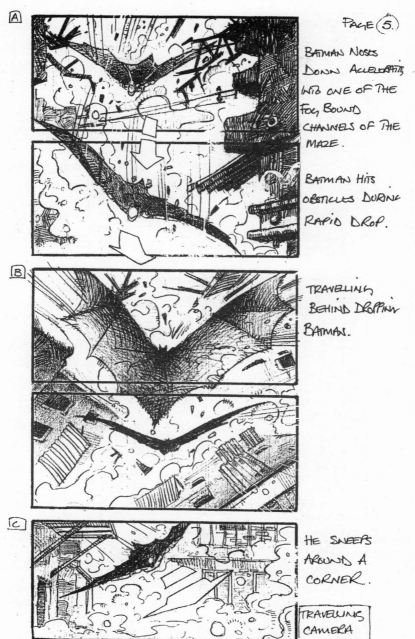

BATMAN NOSES
DOWN ACCELERATES
INTO ONE OF THE
FOG BOUND
CHANNELS OF THE
MAZE.

BATMAN HITS
OBSTICLES DURING
RAPID DROP.

TRAVELLING
BEHIND DROPPING
BATMAN.

HE SWEEPS
AROUND A
CORNER.

TRAVELLING
CAMERA

237

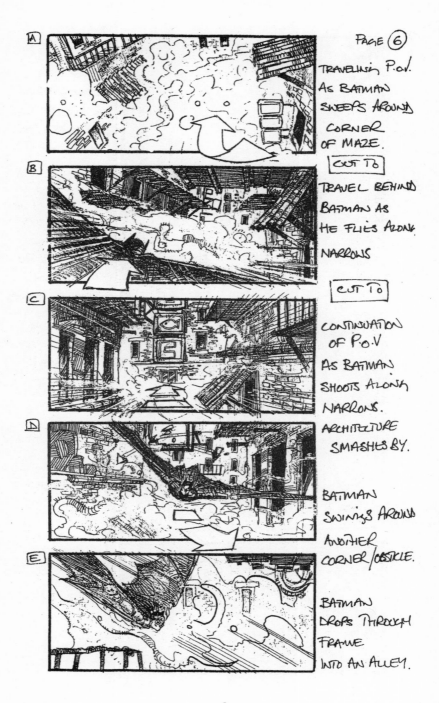

A — PAGE ⑥
TRAVELLING P.O.V.
AS BATMAN
SWEEPS AROUND
CORNER
OF MAZE.

B — CUT TO
TRAVEL BEHIND
BATMAN AS
HE FLIES ALONG
NARROWS

C — CUT TO
CONTINUATION
OF P.O.V
AS BATMAN
SHOOTS ALONG
NARROWS.
ARCHITECTURE
SMASHES BY.

D — BATMAN
SWINGS AROUND
ANOTHER
CORNER/OBSTICLE.

E — BATMAN
DROPS THROUGH
FRAME
INTO AN ALLEY.

238

A

TRAVEL WITH
BATMAN AS
HE DROPS
DOWN INTO THE
ALLEY.

B

INHABITANTS OF
NARROWS STARE UP

COWERING OR
SCREAMING AS
THEY SEE A BLACK
DRAGON/DEMON
STREAKING OVERHEA

UP ANGLE

C

DOWN ANGLE.

ANGLE ON
CRAZED INHABITANT

D

ANGLE ON

CRAZED MAN
ATTACKING —
LOOKS UP
SCREAMING.

CAR CHASE

CAR CHASE

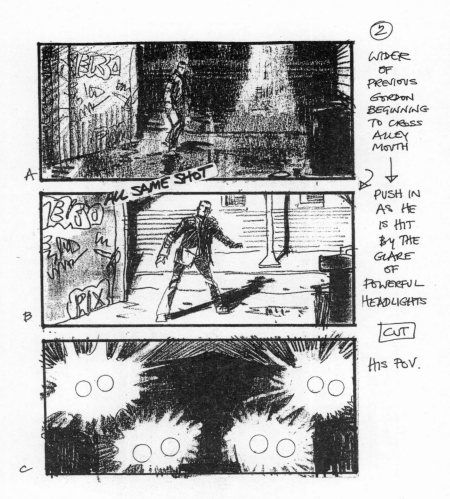

② WIDER
OF
PREVIOUS
GORDON
BEGINNING
TO CROSS
ALLEY
MOUTH

↓

PUSH IN
AS HE
IS HIT
BY THE
GLARE
OF
POWERFUL
HEADLIGHTS

CUT

HIS POV.

A

ALL SAME SHOT

B

C

244

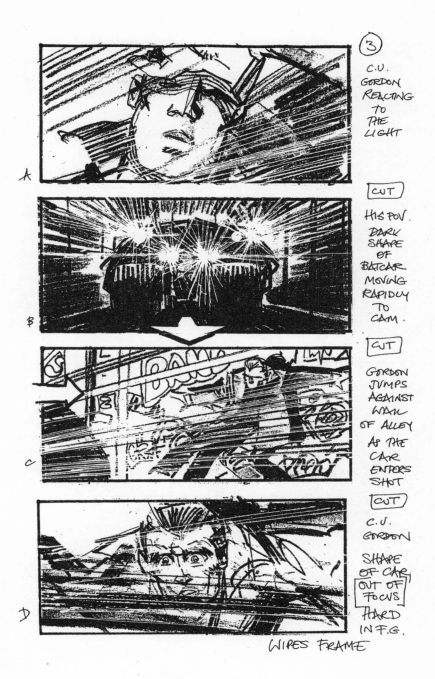

③

C.U.
GORDON
REACTING
TO
THE
LIGHT

A

CUT

HIS P.O.V.
DARK
SHAPE
OF
BATCAR
MOVING
RAPIDLY
TO
CAM.

B

CUT

GORDON
JUMPS
AGAINST
WALL
OF ALLEY
AS THE
CAR
ENTERS
SHOT

C

CUT

C.U.
GORDON

SHAPE
OF CAR
OUT OF
FOCUS
HARD
IN F.G.

D

WIPES FRAME

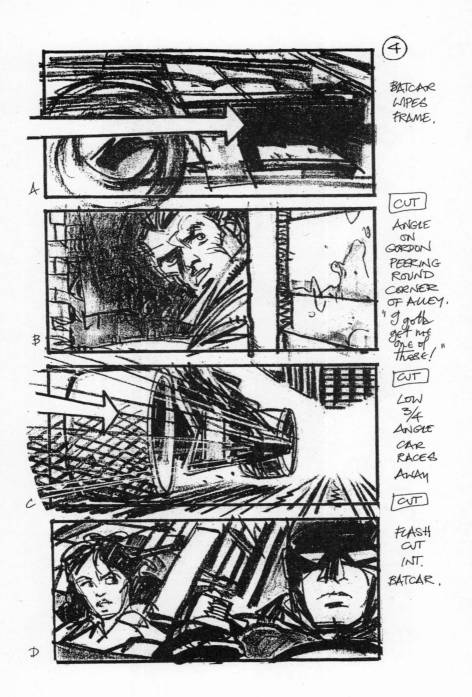

④

A   BATCAR WIPES FRAME.

CUT

B   ANGLE ON GORDON PEERING ROUND CORNER OF ALLEY. "I gotta get me one of those!"

CUT

C   LOW 3/4 ANGLE CAR RACES AWAY

CUT

D   FLASH CUT INT. BATCAR.

A.

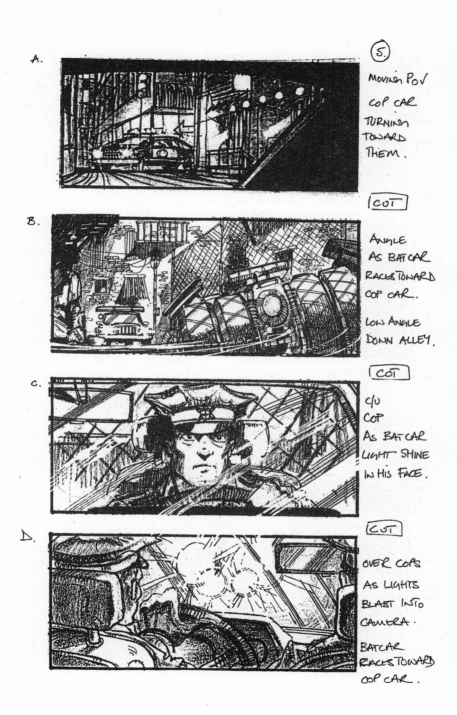

MOVING POV
COP CAR
TURNING
TOWARD
THEM.

COT

B.

ANGLE
AS BATCAR
RACES TOWARD
COP CAR.

LOW ANGLE
DOWN ALLEY.

COT

C.

C/U
COP
AS BATCAR
LIGHT SHINE
IN HIS FACE.

CUT

D.

OVER COPS
AS LIGHTS
BLAST INTO
CAMERA.

BATCAR
RACES TOWARD
COP CAR.

247

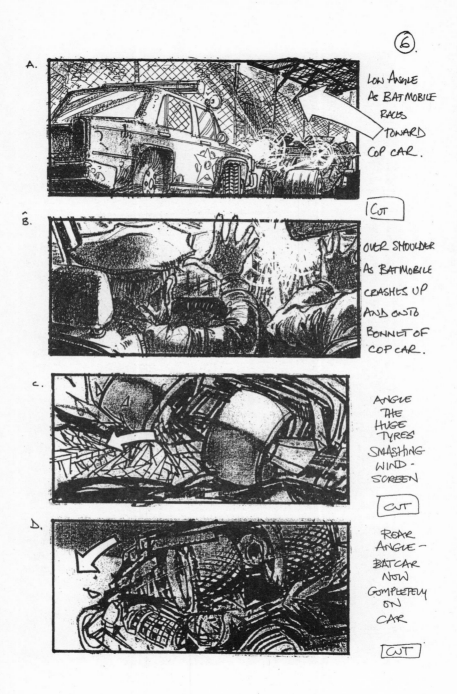

A.

⑥.

LOW ANGLE
AS BATMOBILE
RACES
TOWARD
COP CAR.

CUT

B̂.

OVER SHOULDER
AS BATMOBILE
CRASHES UP
AND ONTO
BONNET OF
COP CAR.

C.

ANGLE
THE
HUGE
TYRES
SMASHING
WIND-
SCREEN

CUT

D.

REAR
ANGLE -
BATCAR
NOW
COMPLETELY
ON
CAR

CUT

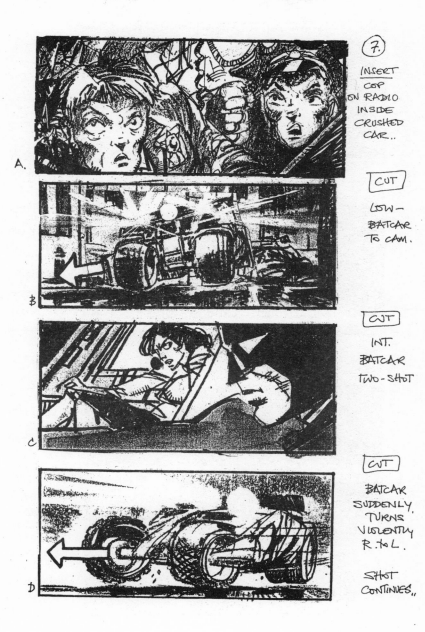

7.

INSERT
COP
ON RADIO
INSIDE
CRUSHED
CAR..

A.

CUT

LOW —
BATCAR
TO CAM.

B.

CUT

INT.
BATCAR
TWO-SHOT

C.

CUT

BATCAR
SUDDENLY
TURNS
VIOLENTLY
R. to L.

SHOT
CONTINUES,,

D.

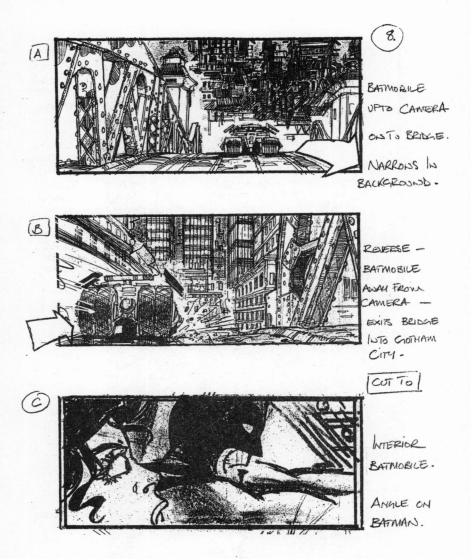

8.

A

BATMOBILE
UPTO CAMERA
ONTO BRIDGE.

NARROWS IN
BACKGROUND.

B

REVERSE —
BATMOBILE
AWAY FROM
CAMERA —
EXITS BRIDGE
INTO GOTHAM
CITY.

CUT TO

C

INTERIOR
BATMOBILE.

ANGLE ON
BATMAN.

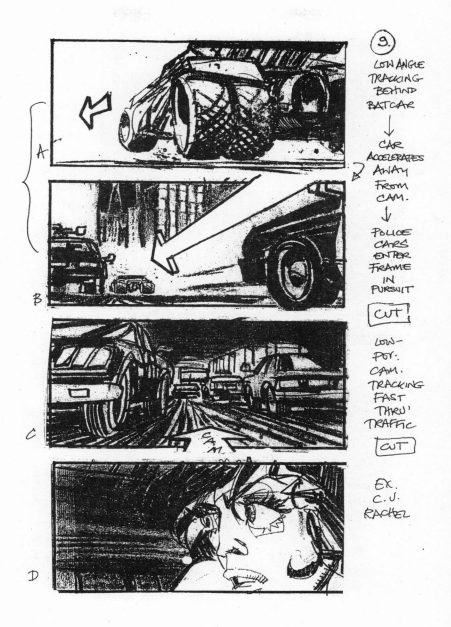

A

B

C

D

9.

LOW ANGLE
TRACKING
BEHIND
BATCAR

↓

CAR
ACCELERATES
AWAY
FROM
CAM.

↓

POLICE
CARS
ENTER
FRAME
IN
PURSUIT

CUT!

LOW-
POV.
CAM.
TRACKING
FAST
THRU'
TRAFFIC

CUT!

EX.
C.U.
RACHEL

10.

LOW
ANGLE
CAM
THRU'
TRAFFIC

CUT

DISTORTED
POV.

CUT

C.S.
RACHEL
REACTING.

CUT

MORE
MOVING
DISTORTED
IMAGES

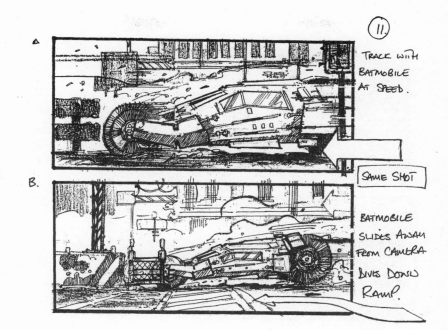

A.   TRACK WITH BATMOBILE AT SPEED.

SAME SHOT

B.   BATMOBILE SLIDES AWAY FROM CAMERA DIVES DOWN RAMP.

C.

"SAME ACTION FROM CHASE CAR."

LOW ANGLE.

AS BATMOBILE PULLS RIGHT AND HEAD DOWN RAMP.

TRAVEL BEHIND BATMOBILE BEFORE TURN/ MANOEUVRE

A.

THE
BATMOBILE
SPEEDS
DOWN
THE RAMP
INTO THE
UNDERPASS.

⑫

B.

PROFILE

TRAVEL +
CRANE DOWN
TO KEEP PACE
WITH SPEEDING
BATMOBILE.

C.

c/u
COP
AS HE TALKS
IN TO HAND SET.

o/s ENGINE
ROAR.
AS BATMOBILE
APPROACHES.

254

A.

⑬

LOW ANGLE
TRAVEL BEHIND
BATMOBILE.

B.

VIEW DOWN
INTO UNDERPASS

—

ON THE ROADS
BELOW WE
SEE A POLICE
ROAD BLOCK.

TRAVEL —

C.

255

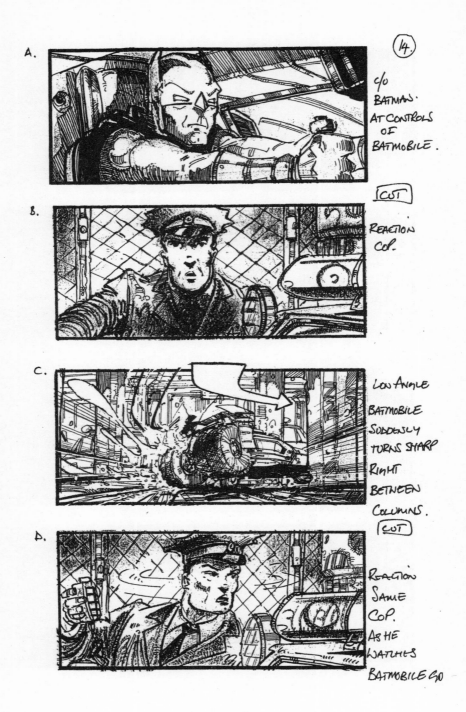

A.

⑭

c/o
BATMAN.
AT CONTROLS
OF
BATMOBILE.

CUT

B.

REACTION
COP.

C.

LOW ANGLE
BATMOBILE
SUDDENLY
TURNS SHARP
RIGHT
BETWEEN
COLUMNS.

CUT

D.

REACTION
SAME
COP.
AS HE
WATCHES
BATMOBILE GO

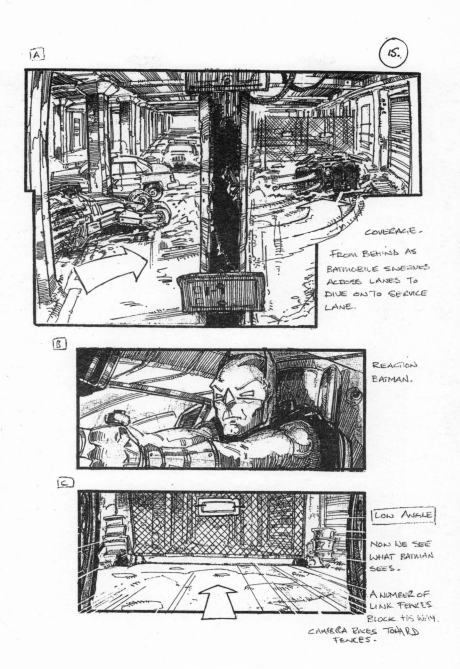

A

COVERAGE.

FROM BEHIND AS
BATMOBILE SWERVES
ACROSS LANES TO
DIVE ONTO SERVICE
LANE.

B

REACTION
BATMAN.

C

LOW ANGLE

NOW WE SEE
WHAT BATMAN
SEES.

A NUMBER OF
LINK FENCES
BLOCK HIS WAY.

CAMERA RACES TOWARD
FENCES.

257

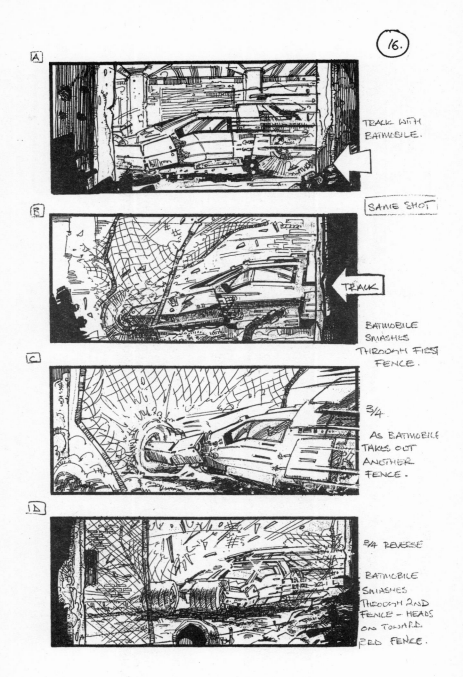

A TRACK WITH BATMOBILE.

SAME SHOT

B TRACK

BATMOBILE SMASHES THROUGH FIRST FENCE.

C 3/4

AS BATMOBILE TAKES OUT ANOTHER FENCE.

D 3/4 REVERSE

BATMOBILE SMASHES THROUGH 2ND FENCE - HEADS ON TOWARD RED FENCE.

258

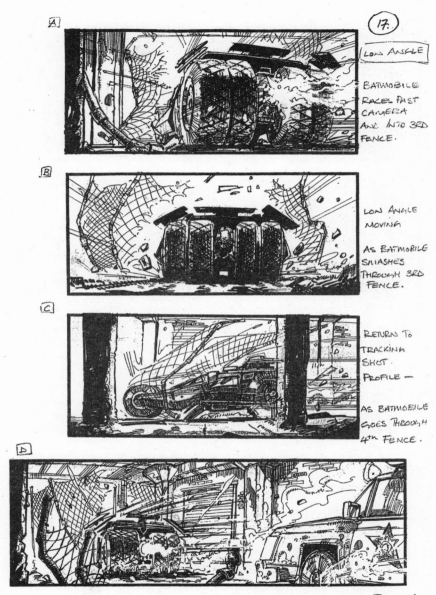

A

17.

LON ANGLE

BATMOBILE
RACES PAST
CAMERA
AND INTO 3RD
FENCE.

B

LON ANGLE
MOVING

AS BATMOBILE
SMASHES
THROUGH 3RD
FENCE.

C

RETURN TO
TRACKING
SHOT
PROFILE —

AS BATMOBILE
GOES THROUGH
4TH FENCE.

D

LON 3/4 AS BATMOBILE RACES THROUGH
4TH FENCE — POLICE CAR RACES ALONG
IN PURSUIT.

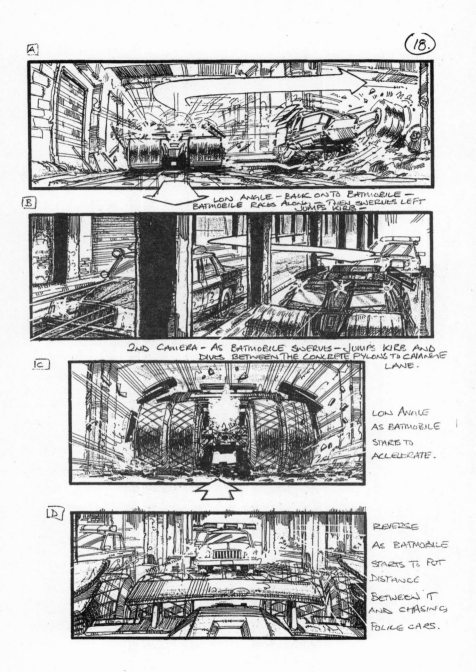

A

LON ANGLE - BACK ONTO BATMOBILE -
BATMOBILE RACES ALONG - THEN SWERVES LEFT
JUMPS KIRB -

B

2ND CAMERA - AS BATMOBILE SWERVES - JUMPS KIRB AND
DIVES BETWEEN THE CONCRETE PYLONS TO CAIANBLE
LANE.

C

LON ANGLE
AS BATMOBILE
STARTS TO
ACCELERATE.

D

REVERSE
AS BATMOBILE
STARTS TO PUT
DISTANCE
BETWEEN IT
AND CHASING
POLICE CARS.

(19)
ANGLE
AS BAT-
CAR
RACES
AWAY

[CUT]

SIDE TRACK — PACING WITH BATCAR — CONCRET PILLARS STROBE

TRACK"   TRACK"

[CUT]
EX. LOW —
CAM.
FORCES
BETWEEN
CARS

[CUT]
EX. C.U.
RACHEL
SCREAMING

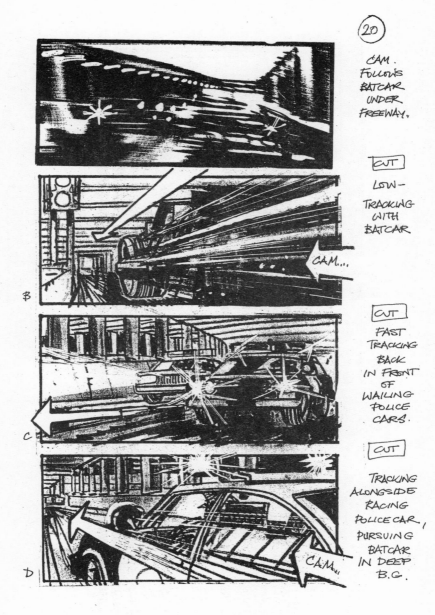

20

CAM.
FOLLOWS
BATCAR
UNDER
FREEWAY.

CUT

LOW-
TRACKING
WITH
BATCAR

CAM....

CUT

FAST
TRACKING
BACK
IN FRONT
OF
WAILING
POLICE
CARS.

CUT

TRACKING
ALONGSIDE
RACING
POLICE CAR,
PURSUING
BATCAR
IN DEEP
B.G.

CAM...

B

C

D

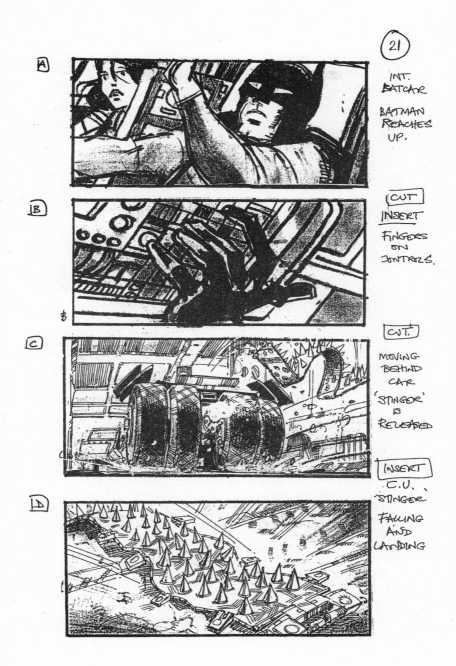

(21)

(A) INT.
BATCAR

BATMAN
REACHES
UP.

(B) CUT
INSERT

FINGERS
ON
CONTROLS.

(C) CUT.

MOVING
BEHIND
CAR
'STINGER'
IS
RELEASED

INSERT
C.U.
'STINGER'

(D) FALLING
AND
LANDING

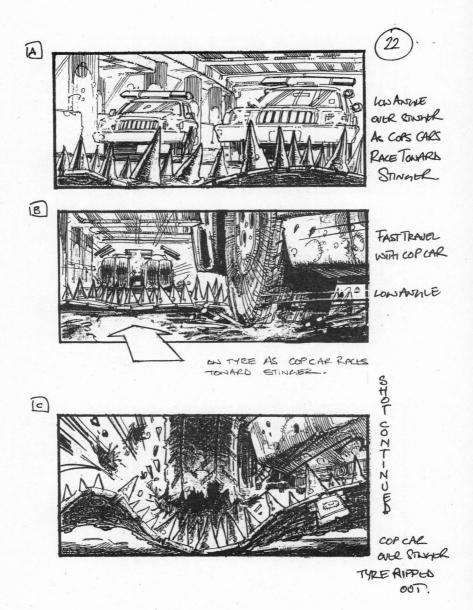

A

LOW ANGLE
OVER STINGER
AS COPS CARS
RACE TOWARD
STINGER

B

FAST TRAVEL
WITH COP CAR

LOW ANGLE

ON TYRE AS COP CAR RACES
TOWARD STINGER.

C

SHOT CONTINUED

COP CAR
OVER STINGER
TYRE RIPPED
OUT.

264

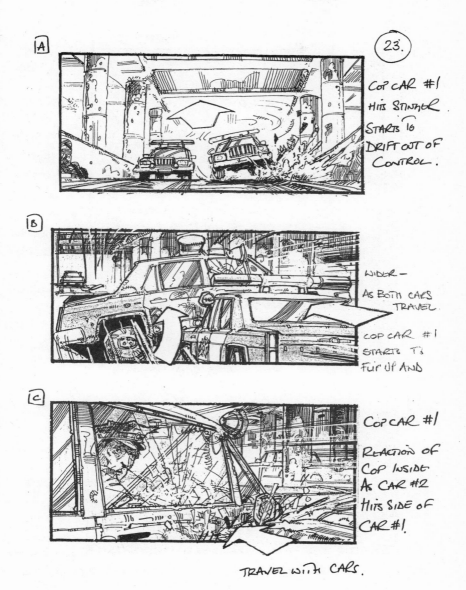

A

COP CAR #1
HITS STINGER.
STARTS TO
DRIFT OUT OF
CONTROL.

B

WIDER —

AS BOTH CARS
TRAVEL.

COP CAR #1
STARTS TO
FLIP UP AND

C

COP CAR #1

REACTION OF
COP INSIDE
AS CAR #2
HITS SIDE OF
CAR #1.

TRAVEL WITH CARS.

265

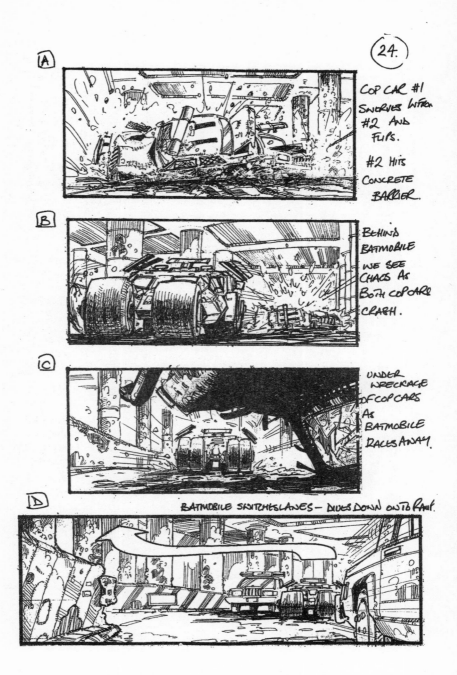

A

COP CAR #1
SWERVES INTO
#2 AND
FLIPS.

#2 HITS
CONCRETE
BARRIER.

B

BEHIND
BATMOBILE
WE SEE
CHAOS AS
BOTH COP CARS
CRASH.

C

UNDER
WRECKAGE
OF COP CARS
AS
BATMOBILE
RACES AWAY.

D

BATMOBILE SWITCHES LANES — DIVES DOWN ON TO RAMP.

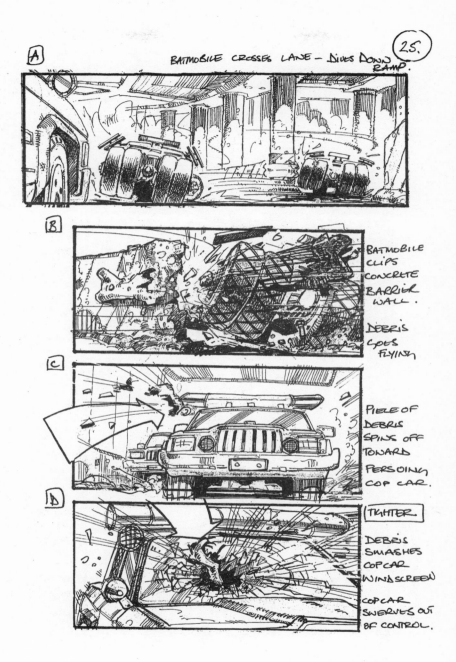

A

BATMOBILE CROSSES LANE – DIVES DOWN RAMP.

B

BATMOBILE CLIPS CONCRETE BARRIER WALL.

DEBRIS GOES FLYING

C

PIECE OF DEBRIS SPINS OFF TOWARD PERSOING COP CAR.

D

TIGHTER

DEBRIS SMASHES COP CAR WINDSCREEN

COP CAR SWERVES OUT OF CONTROL.

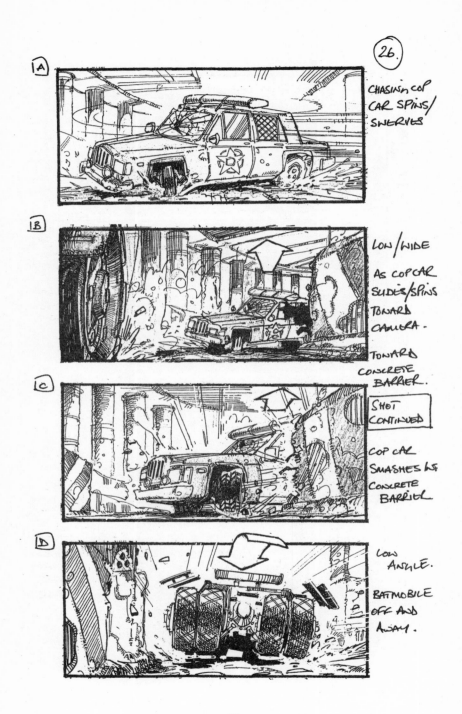

A

CHASIN'n COP
CAR SPINS/
SWERVES

B

LON/WIDE

AS COP CAR
SLIDES/SPINS
TOWARD
CAMERA.

TOWARD
CONCRETE
BARRIER.

C

SHOT
CONTINUED

COP CAR
SMASHES INTO
CONCRETE
BARRIER

D

LOW
ANGLE.

BATMOBILE
OFF AND
AWAY.

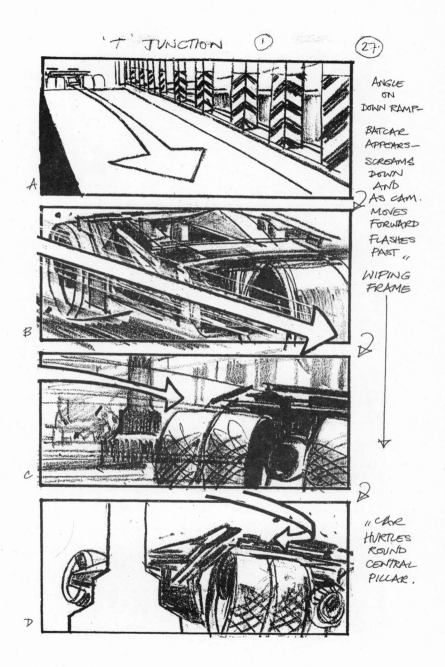

'T' JUNCTION   ①   ㉗

ANGLE
ON
DOWN RAMP

BATCAR
APPEARS—
SCREAMS
DOWN
AND
AS CAM.
MOVES
FORWARD
FLASHES
PAST "

WIPING
FRAME

" CAR
HURTLES
ROUND
CENTRAL
PILLAR.

A

B

C

D

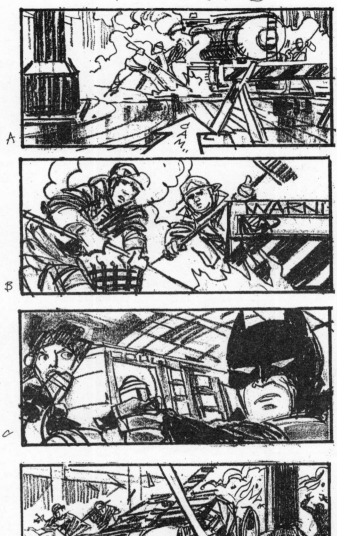

'T' JUNCTION ②   (28)

A   MOVING
                           POV.
                           RUSHING
                           TOWARD
                           ROAD
                           WORKS
                           GANG

                           CUT

B   FLASH
                           CUT
                           WORKERS
                           LOOKING
                           UP IN
                           HORROR

                           CUT

C   FLASH
                           CUT
                           C.U.
                           BATMAN
                           REACTING.

                           CUT

D   ANGLE
                           AS CAR
                           SWERVES
                           THRU'
                           FLAMING
                           TAR
                           AND
                           BARRIERS

270

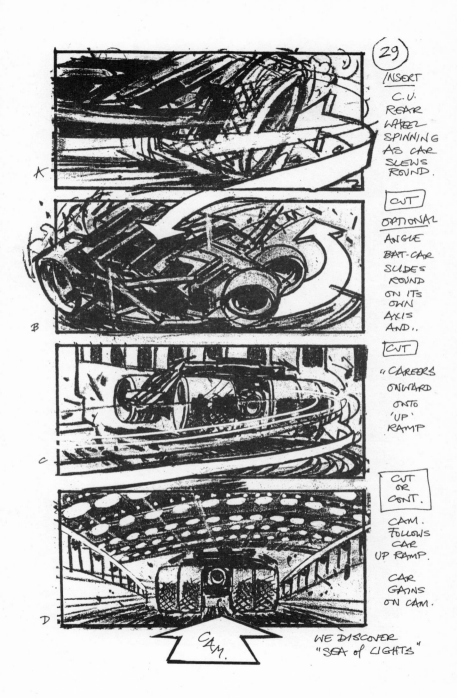

29

INSERT
C.U.
REAR
WHEEL
SPINNING
AS CAR
SLEWS
ROUND.

CUT

OPTIONAL
ANGLE
BAT-CAR
SLIDES
ROUND
ON ITS
OWN
AXIS
AND..

CUT

"CAREERS
ONWARD
ONTO
'UP'
RAMP

CUT
OR
CONT.

CAM.
FOLLOWS
CAR
UP RAMP.

CAR
GAINS
ON CAM.

WE DISCOVER
"SEA of LIGHTS"

CAM.

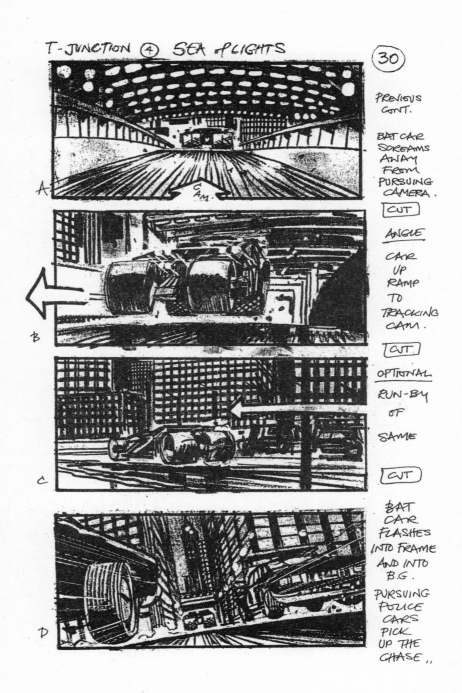

PREVIOUS
CONT.

BAT CAR
SCREAMS
AWAY
FROM
PURSUING
CAMERA.

CUT

ANGLE

CAR
UP
RAMP
TO
TRACKING
CAM.

CUT

OPTIONAL

RUN-BY

OF

SAME

CUT

BAT
CAR
FLASHES
INTO FRAME
AND INTO
B.G.

PURSUING
POLICE
CARS
PICK
UP THE
CHASE ,,

A.

31

UP ANGLE
ON 'WALK'
SIGN AS
LEGEND
CHANGES.

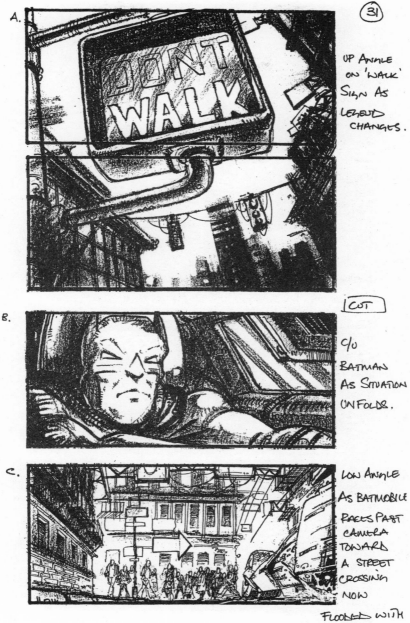

CUT

B.

C/U
BATMAN
AS SITUATION
UNFOLDS.

C.

LOW ANGLE
AS BATMOBILE
RACES PAST
CAMERA
TOWARD
A STREET
CROSSING
NOW
FLOODED WITH
PEDESTRIANS.

273

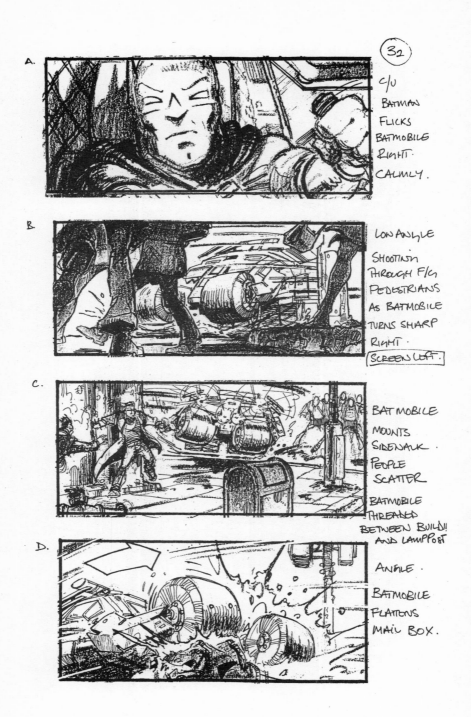

A.

C/U
BATMAN
FLICKS
BATMOBILE
RIGHT.
CALMLY.

B.

LOW ANGLE
SHOOTING
THROUGH F/G
PEDESTRIANS
AS BATMOBILE
TURNS SHARP
RIGHT.
SCREEN LEFT.

C.

BATMOBILE
MOUNTS
SIDEWALK.
PEOPLE
SCATTER

BATMOBILE
THREADED
BETWEEN BUILDI
AND LAMPPOST

D.

ANGLE.
BATMOBILE
FLATTENS
MAIL BOX.

274

A

REVERSE
AS BATMOBILE
SHOOTS OUT
ACROSS THE
ROAD.

CARS SLAM TO
A HALT.

B.

LOW ANGLE
AS BATMOBILE
CARVES ITS
WAY BETWEEN
THE SWERVING
TRAFFIC.

C.

BATMOBILE
SHOOTS TOWARD
OPPOSITE
SIDEWALK.

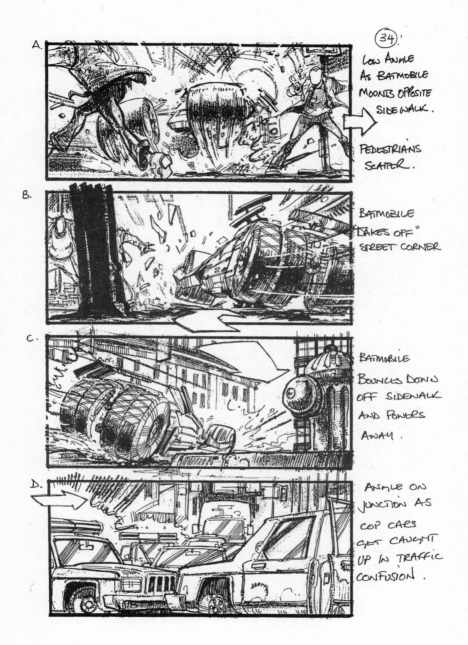

A.

(34)
Low Angle
As Batmobile
Mounts Opposite
Sidewalk.

Pedestrians
Scatter.

B.

Batmobile
"Takes Off"
Street Corner

C.

Batmobile
Bounces Down
Off Sidewalk
And Powers
Away.

D.

Angle On
Junction As
Cop Cars
Get Caught
Up In Traffic
Confusion.

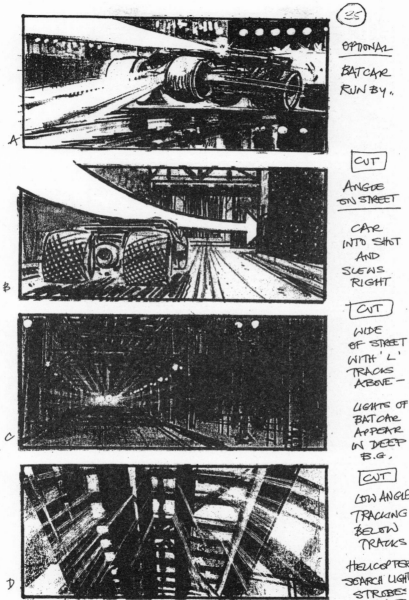

25

A

OPTIONAL
BATCAR
RUN BY.

CUT

ANGLE
ON STREET

CAR
INTO SHOT
AND
SLEWS
RIGHT

B

CUT

WIDE
OF STREET
WITH 'L'
TRACKS
ABOVE —

LIGHTS OF
BATCAR
APPEAR
IN DEEP
B.G.

C

CUT

LOW ANGLE
TRACKING
BELOW
TRACKS

HELICOPTER
SEARCH LIGHT
STROBES
DOWN TO
CAM.

D

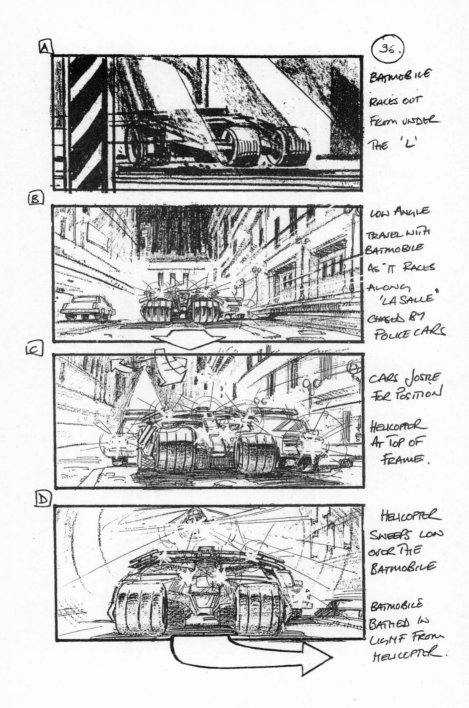

A   (36.)

BATMOBILE
RACES OUT
FROM UNDER
THE 'L'

B   LOW ANGLE
TRAVEL WITH
BATMOBILE
AS IT RACES
ALONG
'LA SALLE'
CHASED BY
POLICE CARS

C   CARS JOSTLE
FOR POSITION

HELICOPTER
AT TOP OF
FRAME.

D   HELICOPTER
SWEEPS LOW
OVER THE
BATMOBILE

BATMOBILE
BATHED IN
LIGHT FROM
HELICOPTER.

278

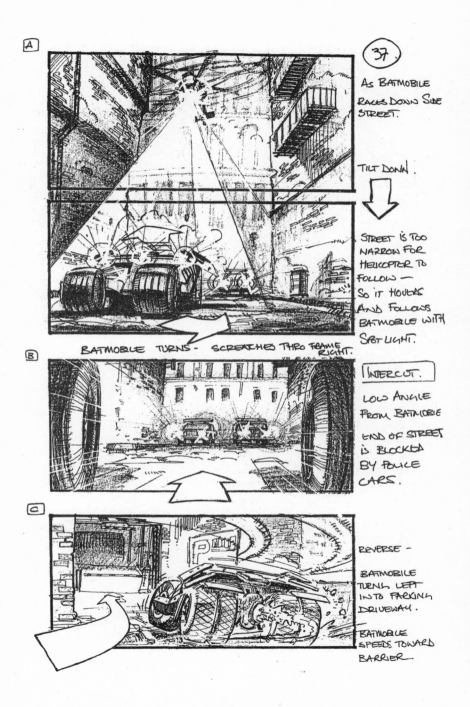

A

37

AS BATMOBILE
RACES DOWN SIDE
STREET.

TILT DOWN.

STREET IS TOO
NARROW FOR
HELICOPTER TO
FOLLOW —
SO IT HOVERS
AND FOLLOWS
BATMOBILE WITH
SPOT LIGHT.

BATMOBILE TURNS - SCREATCHES THRO FRAME RIGHT.

B

INTERCUT.

LOW ANGLE
FROM BATMOBILE

END OF STREET
IS BLOCKED
BY POLICE
CARS.

C

REVERSE -

BATMOBILE
TURNS LEFT
INTO PARKING
DRIVEWAY.

BATMOBILE
SPEEDS TOWARD
BARRIER.

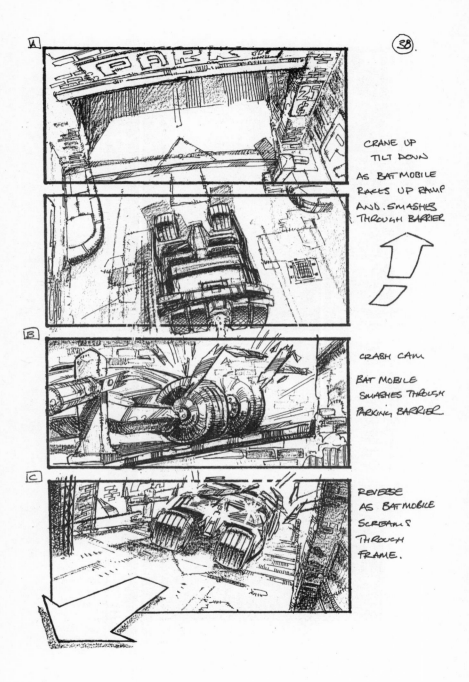

CRANE UP
TILT DOWN
AS BAT MOBILE
RACES UP RAMP
AND SMASHES
THROUGH BARRIER

CRASH CAM

BAT MOBILE
SMASHES THROUGH
PARKING BARRIER

REVERSE
AS BATMOBILE
SCREAMS
THROUGH
FRAME.

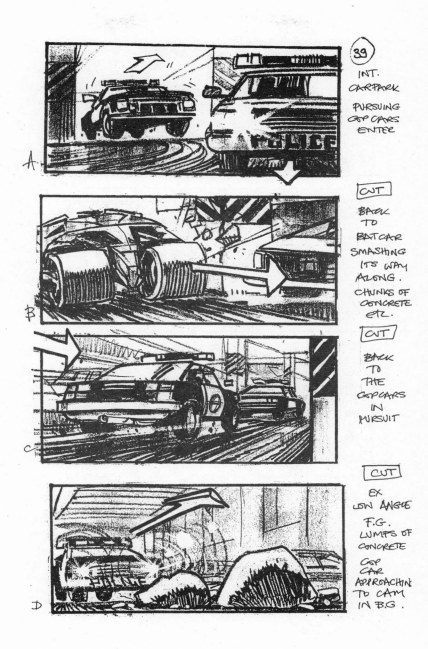

39

INT.
CARPARK

PURSUING
COP CARS
ENTER

CUT

BACK
TO
BATCAR
SMASHING
ITS WAY
ALONG.
CHUNKS OF
CONCRETE
ETC.

CUT

BACK
TO
THE
COPCARS
IN
PURSUIT

CUT

EX
LOW ANGLE
F.G.
LUMPS OF
CONCRETE
COP
CAR
APPROACHIN'
TO CAM
IN B.G.

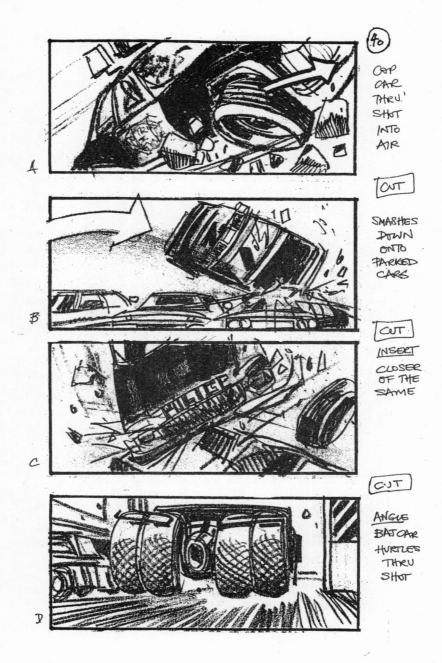

(40)

COP
CAR
THRU.'
SHOT
INTO
AIR

CUT

SMASHES
DOWN
ONTO
PARKED
CARS

CUT.

INSERT

CLOSER
OF THE
SAME

CUT

ANGLE
BATCAR
HURTLES
THRU
SHOT

A

B

C

D

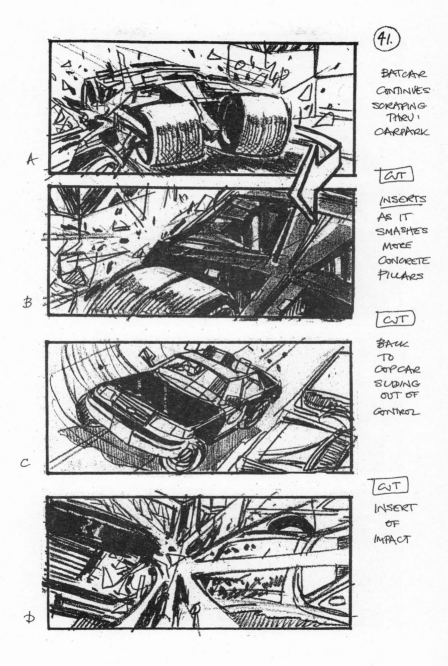

41.

BATCAR
CONTINUES
SCRAPING
THRU
CARPARK

CUT

INSERTS
AS IT
SMASHES
MORE
CONCRETE
PILLARS

CUT

BACK
TO
COPCAR
SLIDING
OUT OF
CONTROL

CUT

INSERT
OF
IMPACT

A

B

C

D

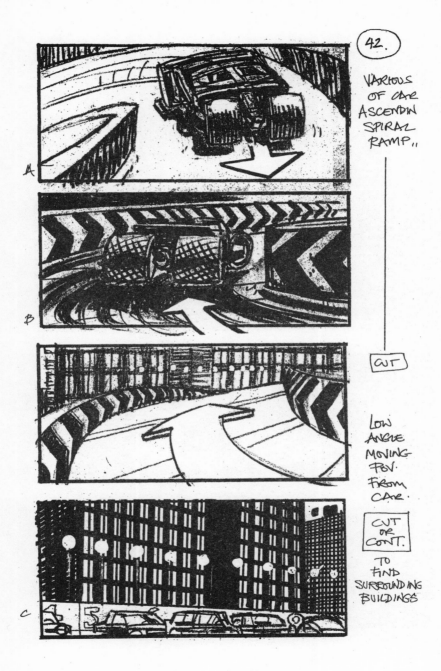

42.

VARIOUS
OF CAR
ASCENDIN
SPIRAL
RAMP,,

CUT

LOW
ANGLE
MOVING
P.O.V.
FROM
CAR.

CUT
OR
CONT.

TO
FIND
SURROUNDING
BUILDINGS

A

B

C

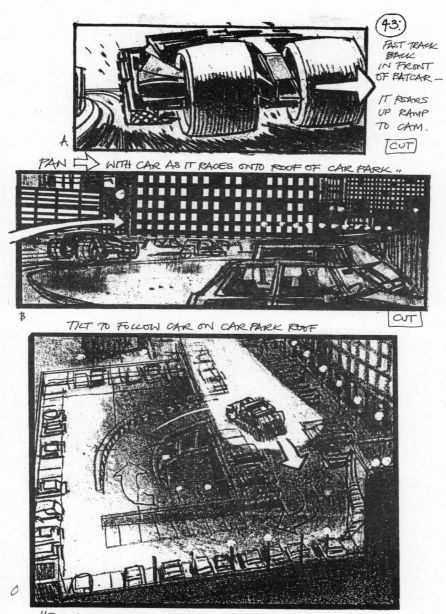

43.
FAST TRACK
BACK
IN FRONT
OF BATCAR —

IT ROARS
UP RAMP
TO CAM.

A

CUT

PAN ⟹ WITH CAR AS IT RACES ONTO ROOF OF CAR PARK ..

B

CUT

TILT TO FOLLOW CAR ON CAR PARK ROOF

C

HELICOPTER BEAM CATCHES CAR AND FOLLOWS ..

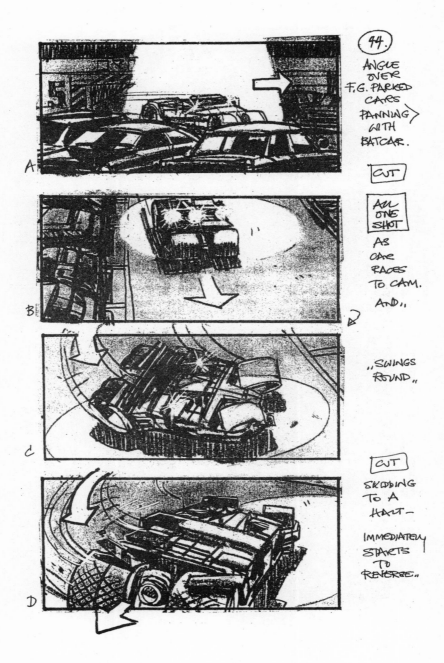

44.
ANGLE
OVER
F.G. PARKED
CARS
PANNING)
WITH
BATCAR.

CUT

ALL
ONE
SHOT
AS
CAR
RACES
TO CAM.
AND,,

,,SWINGS
ROUND,,

CUT

SKIDDING
TO A
HALT —

IMMEDIATELY
STARTS
TO
REVERSE,,

A

B

C

D

286

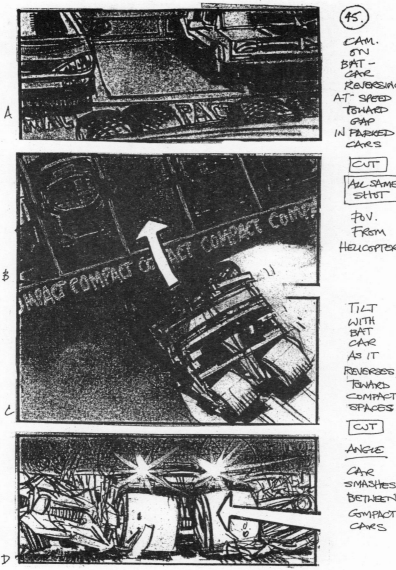

A

B

C

D

45.

CAM.
ON
BAT-
CAR
REVERSING
AT SPEED
TOWARD
GAP
IN PARKED
CARS

CUT

ALL SAME
SHOT

P.O.V.
FROM
HELICOPTER

TILT
WITH
BAT
CAR
AS IT
REVERSES,
TOWARD
COMPACT
SPACES..

CUT

ANGLE

CAR
SMASHES
BETWEEN
COMPACT
CARS

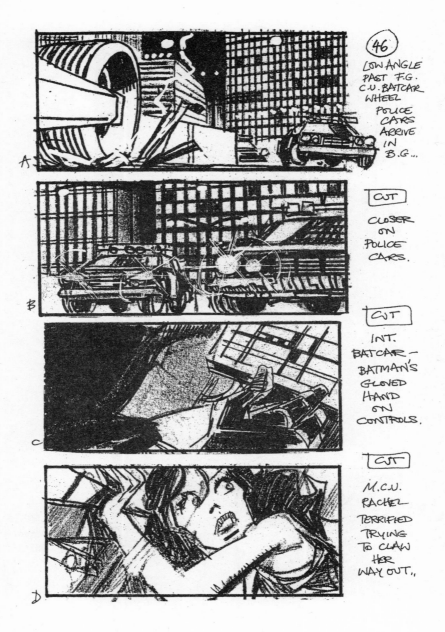

46

LOW ANGLE
PAST F.G.
C.U. BATCAR
WHEEL
POLICE
CARS
ARRIVE
IN
B.G...

CUT

CLOSER
ON
POLICE
CARS.

CUT

INT.
BATCAR —
BATMAN'S
GLOVED
HAND
ON
CONTROLS.

CUT

M.C.U.
RACHEL
TERRIFIED
TRYING
TO CLAW
HER
WAY OUT..

288

47

RACHEL
POV.
A DEMON

CUT

TWO
SHOT —
RACHEL
&
BATMAN

CUT

RACHEL'S
POV.
REVERTING
TO
BATMAN.

" TRUST
ME ! "

CUT

ANGLE
F.G.
CONTROLS
FOLDING
INTO
NEW
POSITION.

289

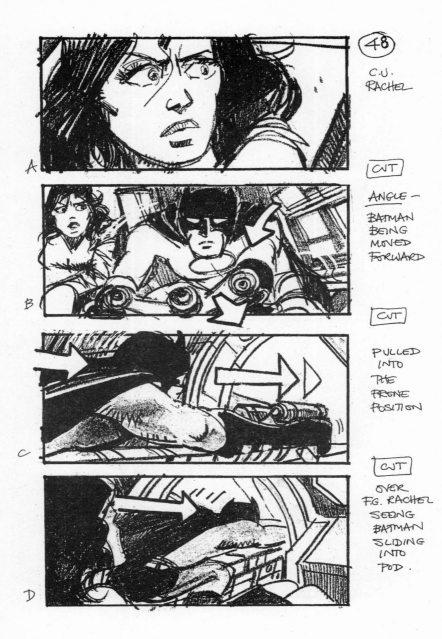

48

C.U.
RACHEL

CUT

ANGLE —

BATMAN
BEING
MOVED
FORWARD

CUT

PULLED
INTO
THE
PRONE
POSITION

CUT

OVER
F.G. RACHEL
SEEING
BATMAN
SLIDING
INTO
POD.

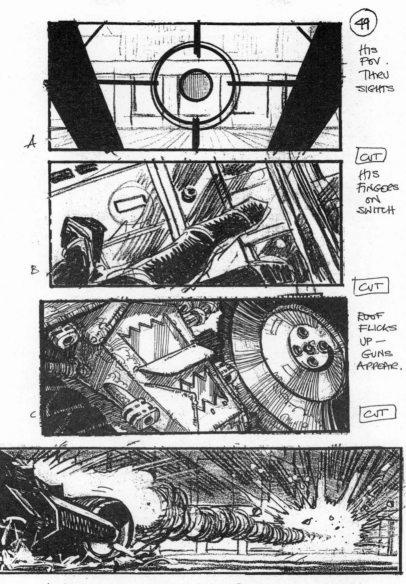

49

His
POV.
THRU
SIGHTS

A

CUT

His
FINGERS
ON
SWITCH

B

CUT

ROOF
FLICKS
UP —
GUNS
APPEAR.

C

CUT

D   ANGLE FROM F.G. BATCAR — WHIP PAN AS SHELLS
                        EXPLODE WALL
                             OF ROOF

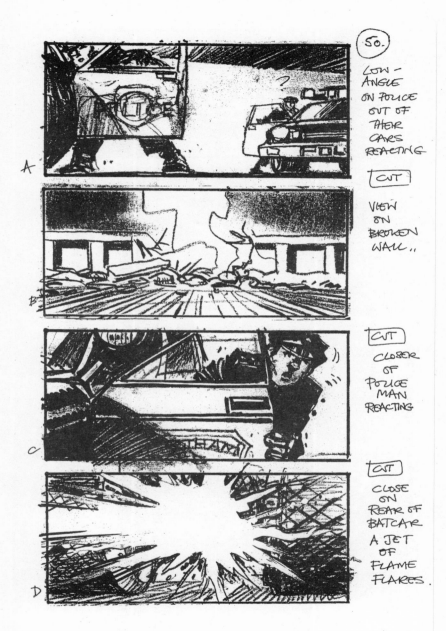

50.

LOW-
ANGLE
ON POLICE
OUT OF
THEIR
CARS
REACTING

CUT

VIEW
ON
BROKEN
WALL..

CUT

CLOSER
OF
POLICE
MAN
REACTING

CUT

CLOSE
ON
REAR OF
BATCAR
A JET
OF
FLAME
FLARES.

A

B

C

D

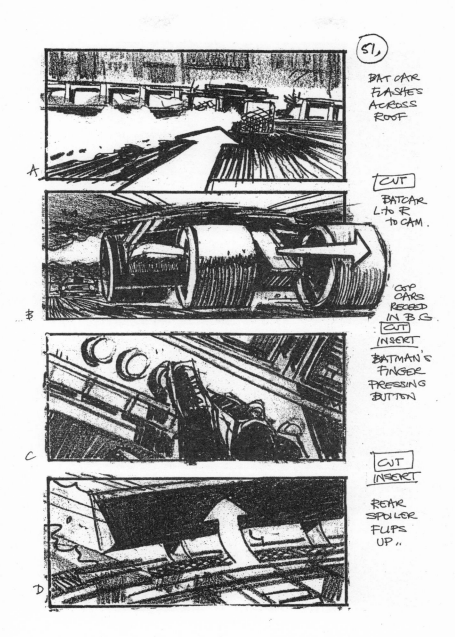

51.

BAT CAR
FLASHES
ACROSS
ROOF

A

CUT

BATCAR
L. to R
TO CAM.

COP
CARS
RECEED
IN B.G.

CUT

INSERT

BATMAN'S
FINGER
PRESSING
BUTTON

B

C

CUT

INSERT

REAR
SPOILER
FLIPS
UP.,

D

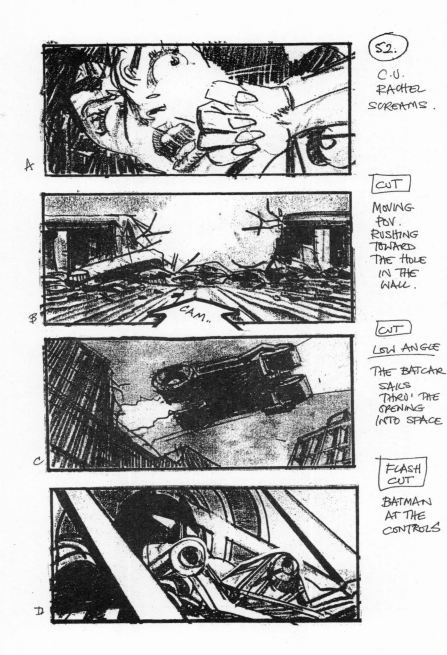

52.

C.U.
RACHEL
SCREAMS.

CUT

MOVING
POV.
RUSHING
TOWARD
THE HOLE
IN THE
WALL.

CUT

LOW ANGLE

THE BATCAR
SAILS
THRU' THE
OPENING
INTO SPACE

FLASH
CUT

BATMAN
AT THE
CONTROLS

A

B

CAM."

C

D

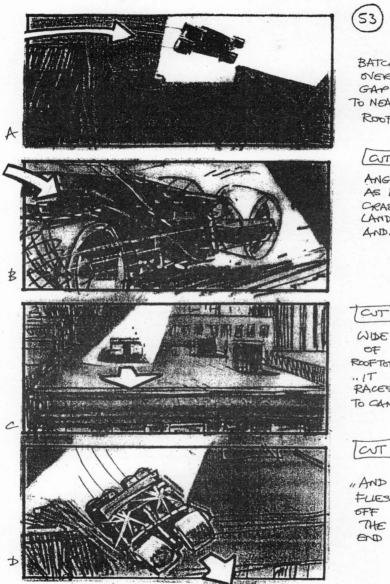

53

BATCAR
OVER
GAP
TO NEARBY
ROOF

CUT

ANGLE
AS IT
CRASH
LANDS
AND..

CUT

WIDE
OF
ROOFTOP
.. IT
RACES
TO CAM.

CUT

" AND
FLIES
OFF
THE
END

A

B

C

D

295

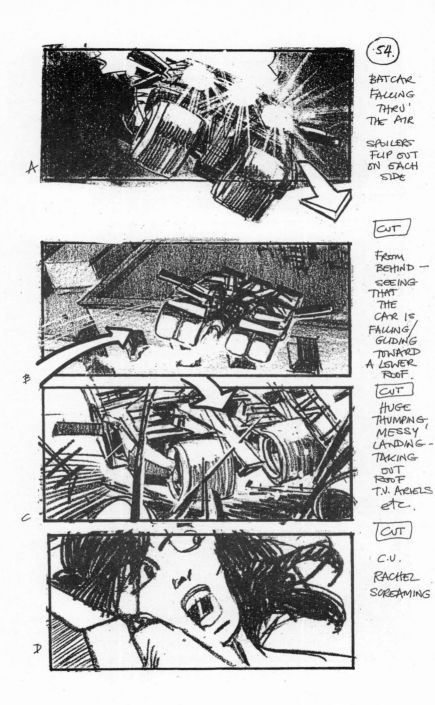

54.

BATCAR
FALLING
THRU'
THE AIR

SPOILERS
FLIP OUT
ON EACH
SIDE

CUT

FROM
BEHIND —
SEEING
THAT
THE
CAR IS
FALLING/
GLIDING
TOWARD
A LOWER
ROOF.

CUT

HUGE
THUMPING,
MESSY,
LANDING —
TAKING
OUT
ROOF
T.V. AERIELS
etc.

CUT

C.U.
RACHEL
SCREAMING

A

B

C

D

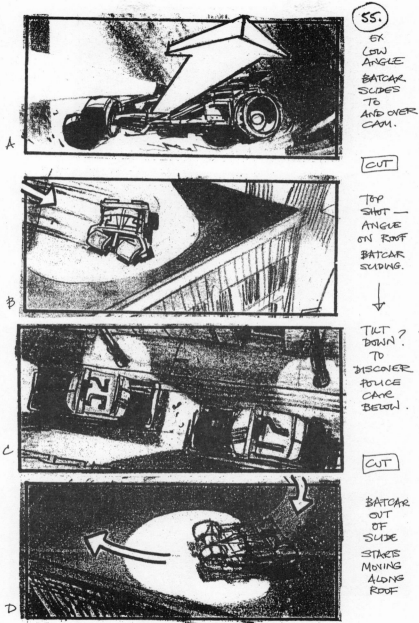

55.
EX
LOW
ANGLE
BATCAR
SLIDES
TO
AND OVER
CAM.

CUT

TOP
SHOT —
ANGLE
ON ROOF
BATCAR
SLIDING.

↓

TILT
DOWN?
TO
DISCOVER
POLICE
CAR
BELOW.

CUT

BATCAR
OUT
OF
SLIDE
STARTS
MOVING
ALONG
ROOF

A

B

C

D

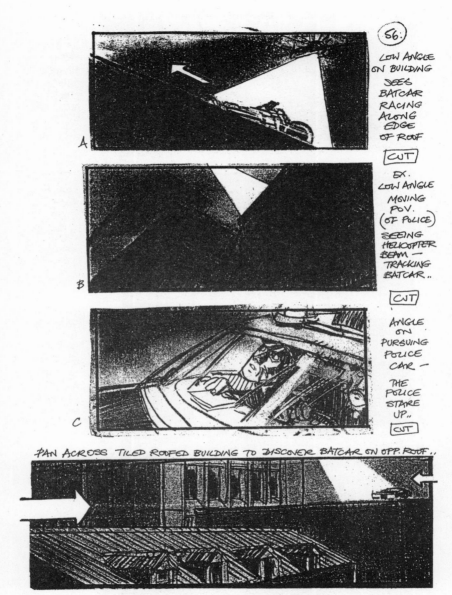

56:

LOW ANGLE
ON BUILDING
SEES
BATCAR
RACING
ALONG
EDGE
OF ROOF

CUT

EX.
LOW ANGLE
MOVING
P.O.V.
(OF POLICE)
SEEING
HELICOPTER
BEAM —
TRACKING
BATCAR ..

CUT

ANGLE
ON
PURSUING
POLICE
CAR —

THE
POLICE
STARE
UP ..

CUT

PAN ACROSS TILED ROOFED BUILDING TO DISCOVER BATCAR ON OPP. ROOF..

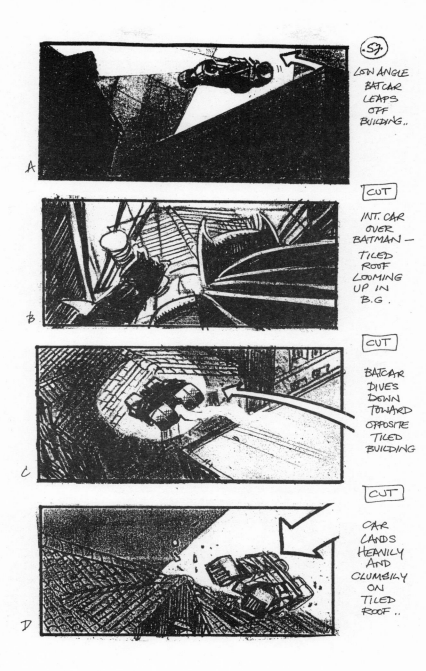

.57

LOW ANGLE
BATCAR
LEAPS
OFF
BUILDING..

A

CUT

INT. CAR
OVER
BATMAN —
TILED
ROOF
LOOMING
UP IN
B.G.

B

CUT

BATCAR
DIVES
DOWN
TOWARD
OPPOSITE
TILED
BUILDING

C

CUT

CAR
LANDS
HEAVILY
AND
CLUMSILY
ON
TILED
ROOF..

D

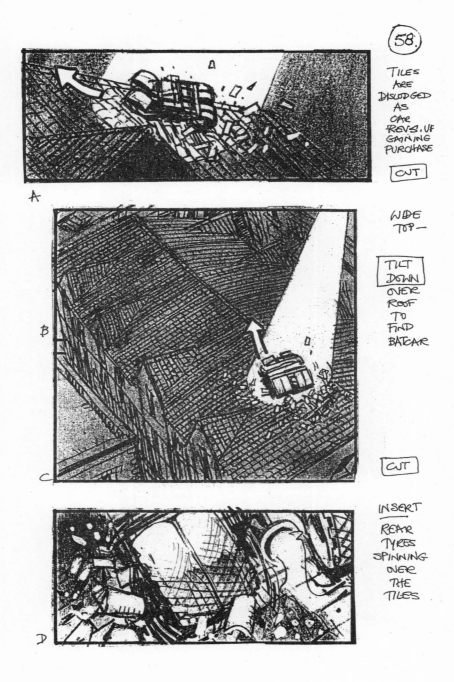

58.

TILES
ARE
DISLODGED
AS
CAR
REVS. UP
GAINING
PURCHASE

CUT

A

WIDE
TOP—

TILT
DOWN
OVER
ROOF
TO
FIND
BATCAR

B

C

CUT

INSERT

REAR
TYRES
SPINNING
OVER
THE
TILES

D

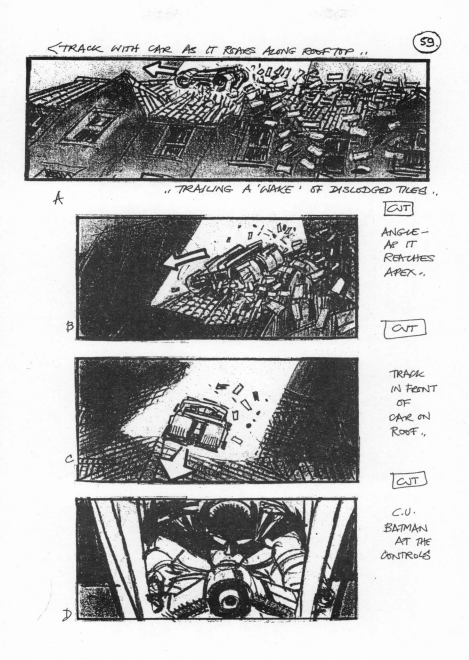

<TRACK WITH CAR AS IT ROARS ALONG ROOF TOP ..

A

.. "TRAILING A 'WAKE' OF DISLODGED TILES ..

CUT

ANGLE —
AS IT
REACHES
APEX ..

B

CUT

TRACK
IN FRONT
OF
CAR ON
ROOF ..

C

CUT

C.U.
BATMAN
AT THE
CONTROLS

D

301

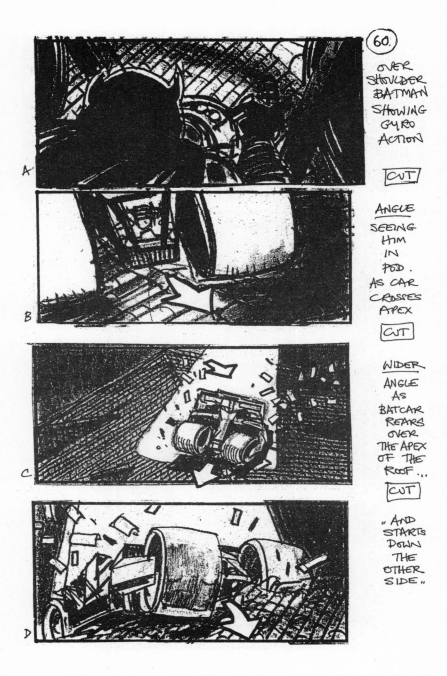

60.

OVER
SHOULDER
BATMAN
SHOWING
GYRO
ACTION

CUT

A

ANGLE
SEEING
HIM
IN
POD.
AS CAR
CROSSES
APEX

CUT

B

WIDER
ANGLE
AS
BATCAR
REARS
OVER
THE APEX
OF THE
ROOF...

CUT

C

"AND
STARTS
DOWN
THE
OTHER
SIDE"

D

ROOFTOP TO FREEWAY 'JUMP'

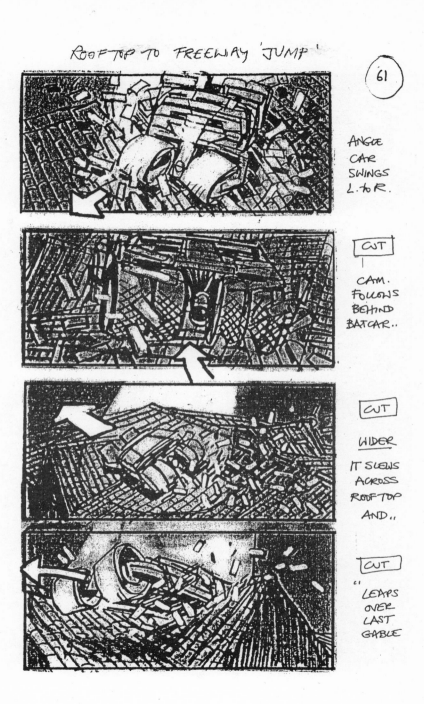

ANGLE
CAR
SWINGS
L. to R.

CUT

CAM.
FOLLOWS
BEHIND
BATCAR..

CUT

WIDER

IT SLEWS
ACROSS
ROOF TOP
AND..

CUT

" LEAPS
OVER
LAST
GABLE

303

FREEWAY 'JUMP'

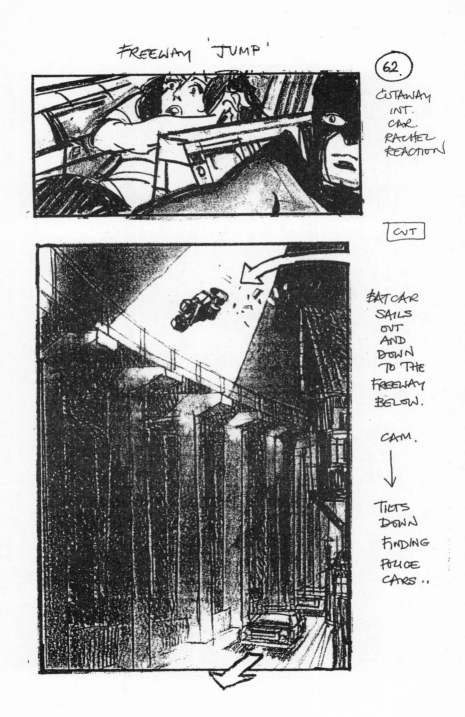

62.

CUTAWAY
INT.
CAR.
RACHEL
REACTION

CUT

BATCAR
SAILS
OUT
AND
DOWN
TO THE
FREEWAY
BELOW.

CAM.

↓

TILTS
DOWN
FINDING
POLICE
CARS ..

FREEWAY 'JUMP'

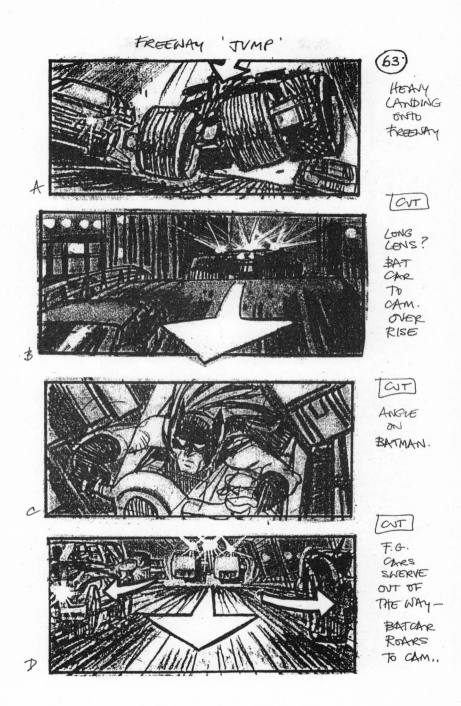

A

B

C

D

63·

HEAVY
LANDING
ONTO
FREEWAY

CUT

LONG
LENS?
BAT
CAR
TO
CAM.
OVER
RISE

CUT

ANGLE
ON
BATMAN.

CUT

F.G.
CARS
SWERVE
OUT OF
THE WAY —

BATCAR
ROARS
TO CAM..

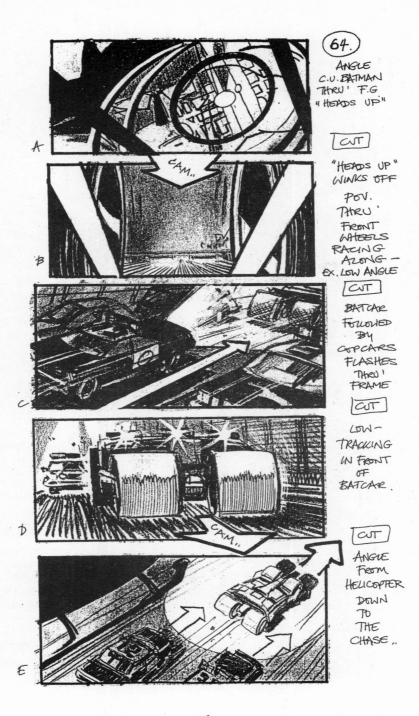

64.

ANGLE
C.U. BATMAN
THRU' F.G
"HEADS UP"

A

CUT

"HEADS UP"
WINKS OFF

POV.
THRU'
FRONT
WHEELS
RACING
ALONG —
EX. LOW ANGLE

B

CAM..

CUT

BATCAR
FOLLOWED
BY
COPCARS
FLASHES
THRU'
FRAME

C

CUT

LOW —
TRACKING
IN FRONT
OF
BATCAR.

D

CAM..

CUT

ANGLE
FROM
HELICOPTER
DOWN
TO
THE
CHASE..

E

306

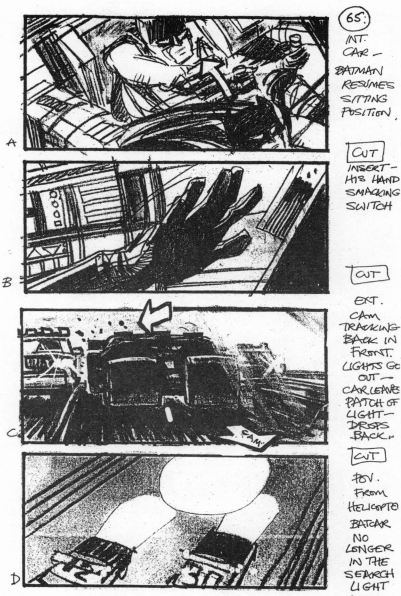

65:
INT.
CAR —
BATMAN
RESUMES
SITTING
POSITION.

CUT
INSERT —
HIS HAND
SMACKING
SWITCH

CUT
EXT.
CAM
TRACKING
BACK IN
FRONT.
LIGHTS GO
OUT —
CAR LEAVE
PATCH OF
LIGHT —
DROPS
BACK.

CUT
P.O.V.
FROM
HELICOPTER
BATCAR
NO
LONGER
IN THE
SEARCH
LIGHT
BEAM.

A

B

C

CAM.

D

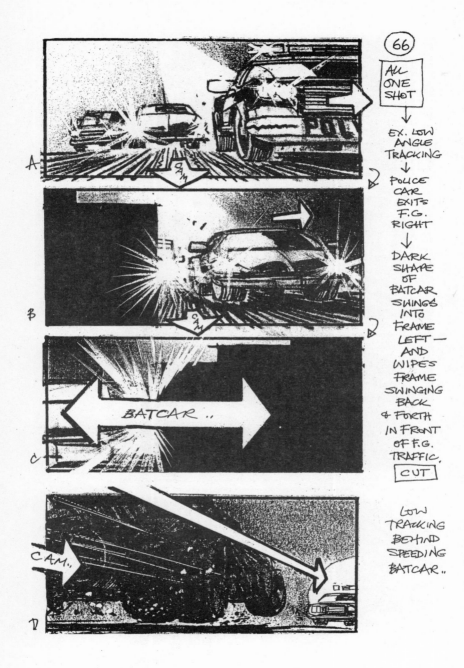

66

ALL
ONE
SHOT

EX. LOW
ANGLE
TRACKING
↓
POLICE
CAR
EXITS
F.G.
RIGHT
↓
DARK
SHAPE
OF
BATCAR
SWINGS
INTO
FRAME
LEFT —
AND
WIPES
FRAME
SWINGING
BACK
& FORTH
IN FRONT
OF F.G.
TRAFFIC.

CUT

LOW
TRACKING
BEHIND
SPEEDING
BATCAR..

A

B

BATCAR ..

C

CAM..

D

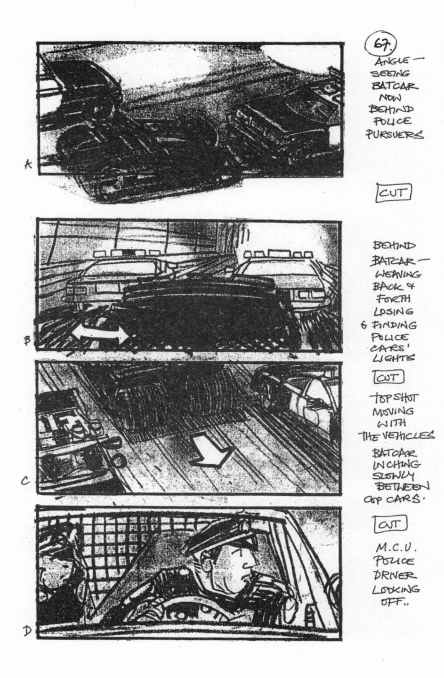

67.
ANGLE —
SEEING
BATCAR
NOW
BEHIND
POLICE
PURSUERS

CUT

BEHIND
BATCAR —
WEAVING
BACK &
FORTH
LOSING
& FINDING
POLICE
CARS'
LIGHTS

CUT

TOP SHOT
MOVING
WITH
THE VEHICLES
BATCAR
INCHING
SLOWLY
BETWEEN
COP CARS.

CUT

M.C.U.
POLICE
DRIVER
LOOKING
OFF..

68

HIS
MOVING
POV.
THE DARK
SHAPE OF
THE BATCAR
INCHING
BETWEEN
THEM.

CUT

POLICE
REACTION

CUT

WIDER
SUDDENLY
THE
HELICOPTER
BEAM
BLAZES
DOWN
AGAIN

CUT

POV.
FROM
CHOPPER.

A

B

C

D

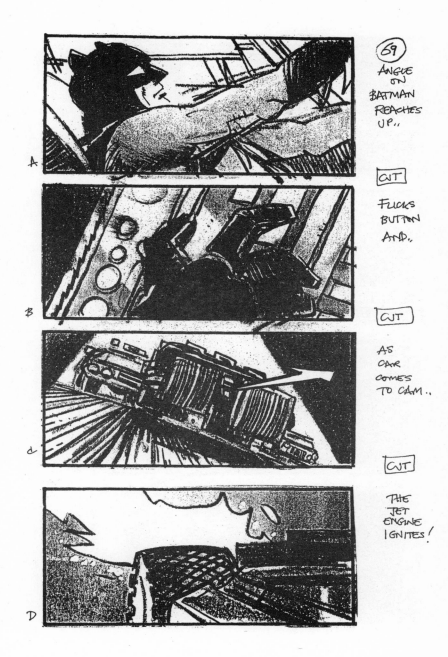

69
ANGLE
ON
BATMAN
REACHES
UP..

CUT

FLICKS
BUTTON
AND..

CUT

AS
CAR
COMES
TO CAM..

CUT

THE
JET
ENGINE
IGNITES!

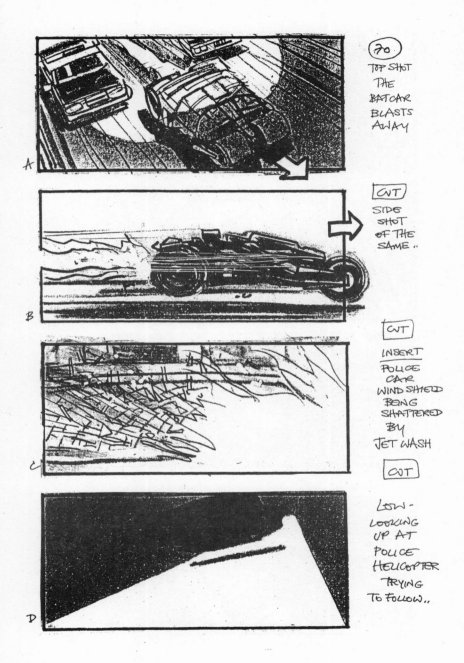

70 TOP SHOT THE BATCAR BLASTS AWAY

A

CUT SIDE SHOT OF THE SAME..

B

CUT INSERT POLICE CAR WINDSHIELD BEING SHATTERED BY JET WASH

C

CUT LOW - LOOKING UP AT POLICE HELICOPTER TRYING TO FOLLOW..

D

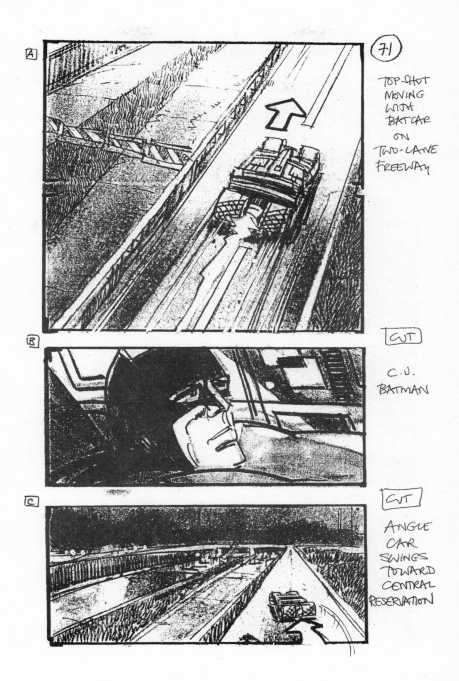

A

71

TOP-SHOT
MOVING
WITH
BATCAR
ON
TWO-LANE
FREEWAY

B

CUT

C.U.
BATMAN

C

CUT

ANGLE
CAR
SWINGS
TOWARD
CENTRAL
RESERVATION

313

FREEWAY TO WOODS

A

.72:

MOVING
P.O.V.
TOWARD
CRASH
BARRIER

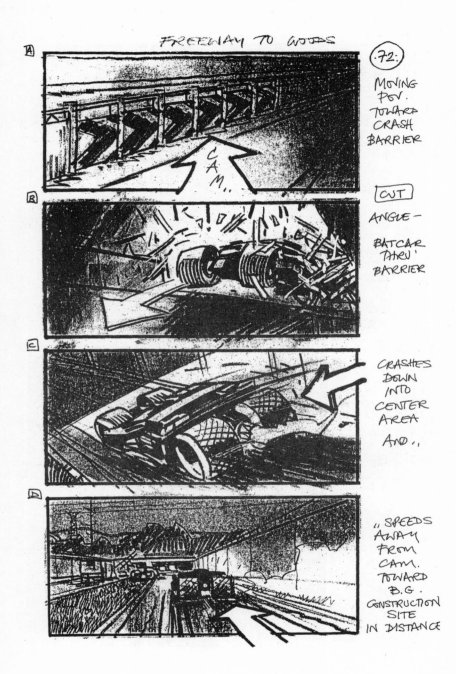

B

CUT

ANGLE —

BATCAR
THRU'
BARRIER

C

CRASHES
DOWN
INTO
CENTER
AREA

AND..

D

"SPEEDS
AWAY
FROM
CAM.
TOWARD
B.G.
CONSTRUCTION
SITE
IN DISTANCE

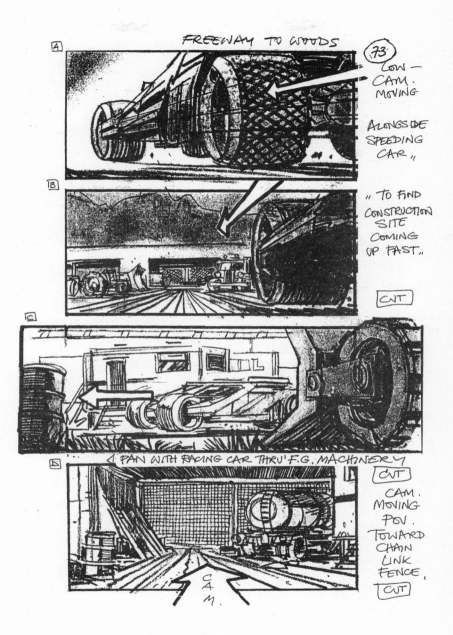

FREEWAY TO WOODS

73

LOW — CAM. MOVING

ALONGSIDE SPEEDING CAR "

" TO FIND CONSTRUCTION SITE COMING UP FAST "

CNT

PAN WITH RACING CAR THRU' F.G. MACHINERY

CNT

CAM. MOVING POV. TOWARD CHAIN LINK FENCE.

CUT

CAM.

315

FREEWAY TO WOODS

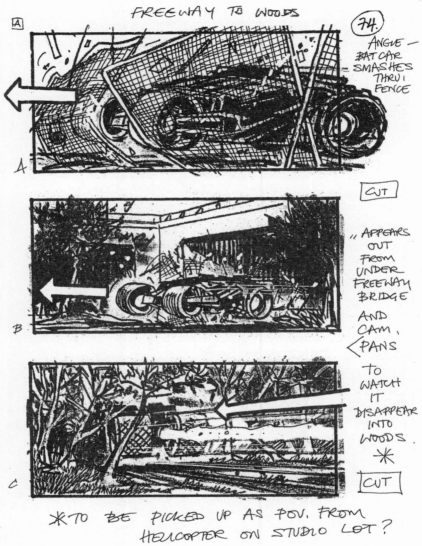

A ⟶ (74.) ANGLE — BAT CAR SMASHES THRU FENCE

A

CUT

" APPEARS OUT FROM UNDER FREEWAY BRIDGE

B

AND CAM. PANS

TO WATCH IT DISAPPEAR INTO WOODS.

※

C

CUT

※ TO BE PICKED UP AS P.O.V. FROM HELICOPTER ON STUDIO LOT?

75.

E.C.U.
RACHEL'S
EYES
WIDEN
AS SHE
SEES,,

CUT

MOVING
P.O.V.

CANOPY
OF TREES
WHIPPING
OVERHEAD.

CUT

MOVING
P.O.V.
CAM.
HURTLING
DOWN
COUNTRY
ROAD,

CAM"

A

B

C

317

76

CUT

C.U.
BATMAN:
"Rachel!"

CUT

WIDE —
BATCAR
SPEEDS
IN
RUN·BY

CUT

TWO
SHOT —
FAVORING
RACHEL —

SHE
DOESN'T
RESPOND

A

B

C

77 POV.
APPROACHING
BEND —

B.G. CHASM
WITH
TUMBLING
WATERFALL.

CUT

WITHOUT
HESITATION
THE
BATCAR
BARRELS
OUT INTO
SPACE

CUT

LOW
ANGLE —
OF THE
SAME ..

CUT

WIDE

SEE THE
CAR
SOAR
OUT
ACROSS
THE CHASM ..
TOWARD
WATERFALL.

A

B

C

D

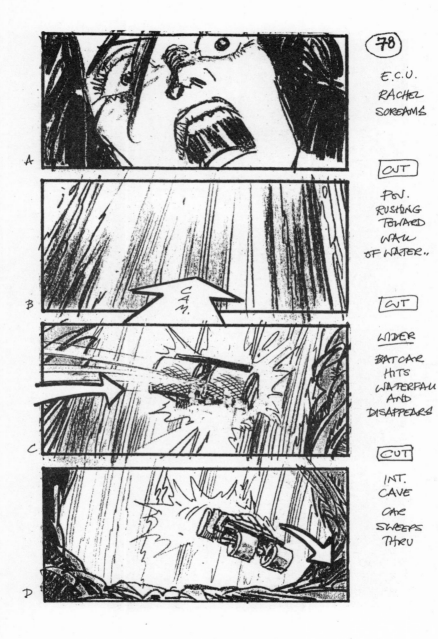

78

E.C.U.
RACHEL
SCREAMS

CUT

P.O.V.
RUSHING
TOWARD
WALL
OF WATER..

CUT

WIDER

BATCAR
HITS
WATERFALL
AND
DISAPPEARS

CUT

INT.
CAVE

CAR
SWEEPS
THRU

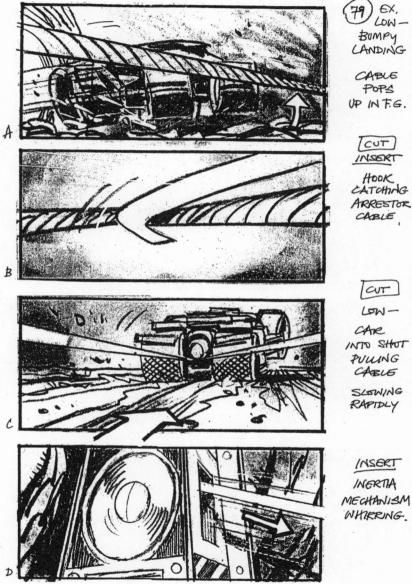

79 EX.
LOW —
BUMPY
LANDING

CABLE
POPS
UP IN F.G.

CUT
INSERT

HOOK
CATCHING
ARRESTOR
CABLE.

CUT
LOW —
CAR
INTO SHOT
PULLING
CABLE

SLOWING
RAPIDLY

INSERT
INERTIA
MECHANISM
WHIRRING.

A

B

C

D

80.

TOP SHOT CAVE—

THE BATCAR STOPS.

CUT

ALL ONE SHOT

CLOSE ON STATIONARY CAR

CAM. RISES TO,,

↓

,, FIND THE BLACK WIND SCREENS

CUT

INT. BATMAN LOOKS ACROSS TO F.G. RACHEL

SHE IS UNCONSCIOU:

CUT

END of SEQUENCE.

HOW IT ENDS

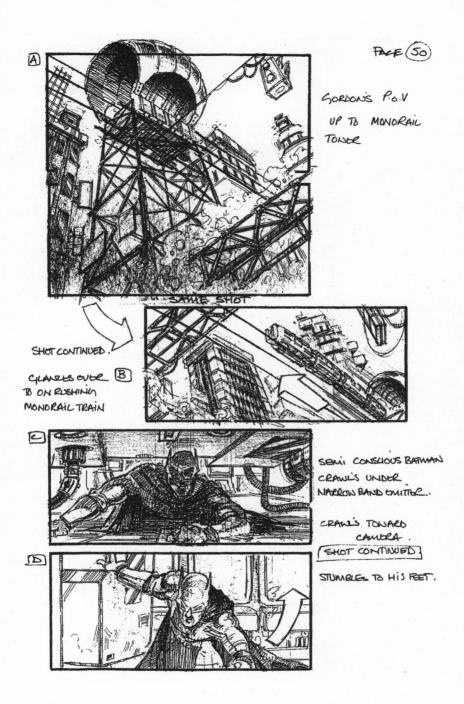

A

GORDON'S P.O.V
UP TO MONORAIL
TOWER

"SAME SHOT"

SHOT CONTINUED.

GLANCES OVER B
TO ON RUSHING
MONORAIL TRAIN

C

SEMI CONSCIOUS BATMAN
CRAWLS UNDER
NARROW BAND EMITTER.

CRAWLS TOWARD
CAMERA.

SHOT CONTINUED

D

STUMBLES TO HIS FEET.

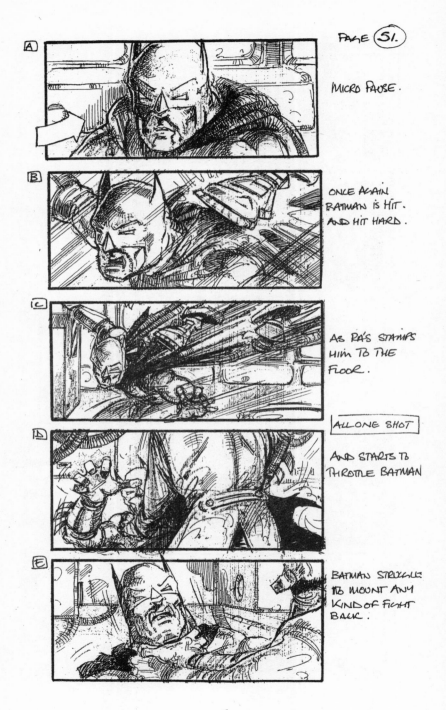

A — MICRO PAUSE.

B — ONCE AGAIN BATMAN IS HIT. AND HIT HARD.

C — AS RA'S STAMPS HIM TO THE FLOOR.

ALL ONE SHOT

D — AND STARTS TO THROTTLE BATMAN

E — BATMAN STRUGGLES TO MOUNT ANY KIND OF FIGHT BACK.

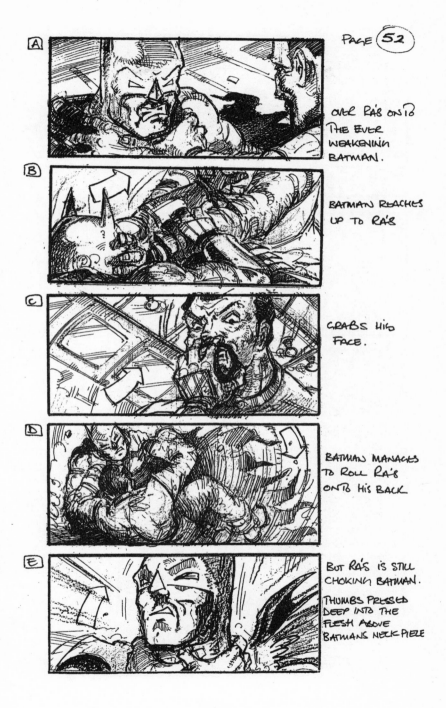

A — PAGE ⑤2

OVER RA'S ONTO
THE EVER
WEAKENING
BATMAN.

B

BATMAN REACHES
UP TO RA'S

C

GRABS HIS
FACE.

D

BATMAN MANAGES
TO ROLL RA'S
ONTO HIS BACK

E

BUT RA'S IS STILL
CHOKING BATMAN.

THUMBS PRESSED
DEEP INTO THE
FLESH ABOVE
BATMANS NECK-PIECE

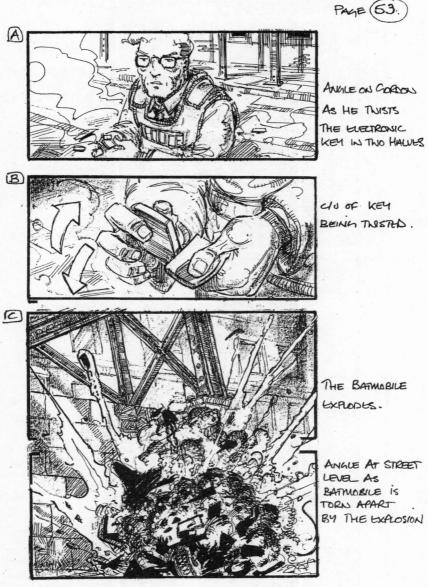

A ANGLE ON GORDON AS HE TWISTS THE ELECTRONIC KEY IN TWO HALVES

B C/U OF KEY BEING TWISTED.

C THE BATMOBILE EXPLODES.

ANGLE AT STREET LEVEL AS BATMOBILE IS TORN APART BY THE EXPLOSION

A CAMERA.

EXPLOSION STARTS TO TEAR THE MONORAIL SUPPORT APART.

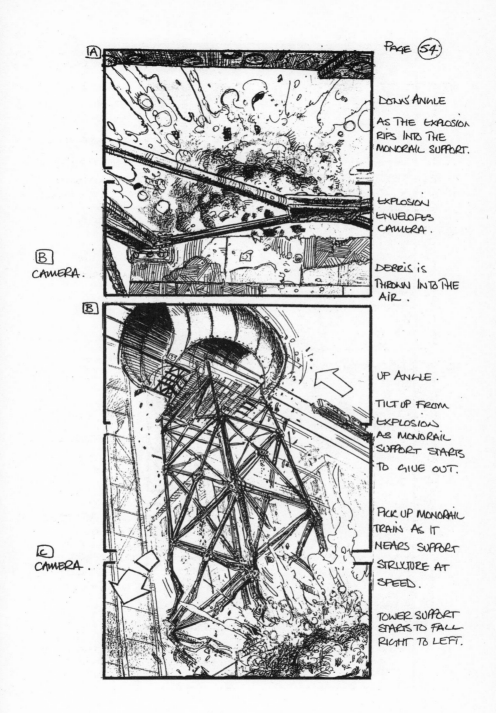

PAGE (54)

DOWN ANGLE

AS THE EXPLOSION
RIPS INTO THE
MONORAIL SUPPORT.

EXPLOSION
ENVELOPES
CAMERA.

DEBRIS IS
THROWN INTO THE
AIR.

UP ANGLE.

TILT UP FROM
EXPLOSION
AS MONORAIL
SUPPORT STARTS
TO GIVE OUT.

PICK UP MONORAIL
TRAIN AS IT
NEARS SUPPORT
STRUCTURE AT
SPEED.

TOWER SUPPORT
STARTS TO FALL
RIGHT TO LEFT.

329

A - BATMAN STRUGGLES USELESSLY AGAINST RA'S AL GHUL'S IRON GRIP.

B - SINGLE. ON RAS AL GHUL

"YOU HAVE FAILED".

BATMAN HAS STOPPED PUSHING AGAINST RA'S.

C - UP ANGLE ON TO BATMAN.

"OR PERHAPS YOU'll NEVER LEARN!"

D - SAME SHOT

PAN FROM BATMAN AS ARMS MOVE TOWARD CLOAK.

E - SAME SHOT

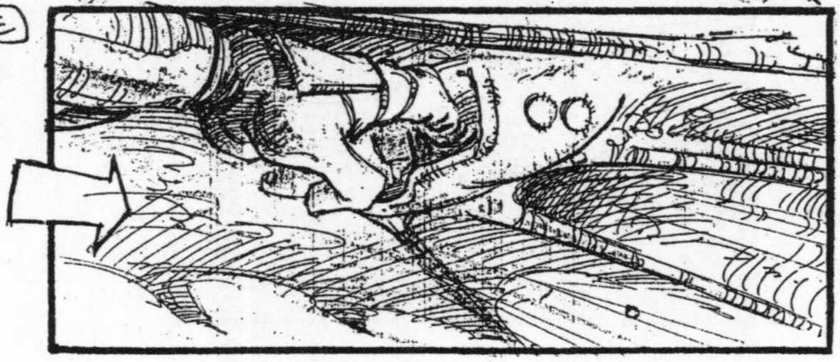

HANDS MOVE TOWARD THE CLOAKS ACTIVATION POCKETS.

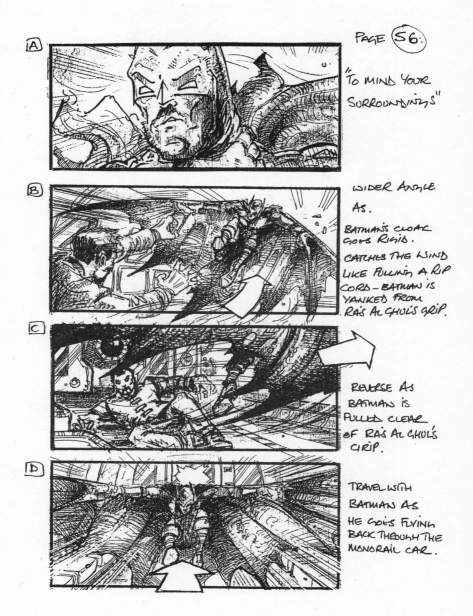

A — "TO MIND YOUR SURROUNDINGS"

B — WIDER ANGLE AS. BATMAN'S CLOAK GOES RIGID. CATCHES THE WIND LIKE PULLING A RIP CORD — BATMAN IS YANKED FROM RA'S AL GHUL'S GRIP.

C — REVERSE AS BATMAN IS PULLED CLEAR OF RA'S AL GHUL'S GRIP.

D — TRAVEL WITH BATMAN AS HE GOES FLYING BACK THROUGH THE MONORAIL CAR.

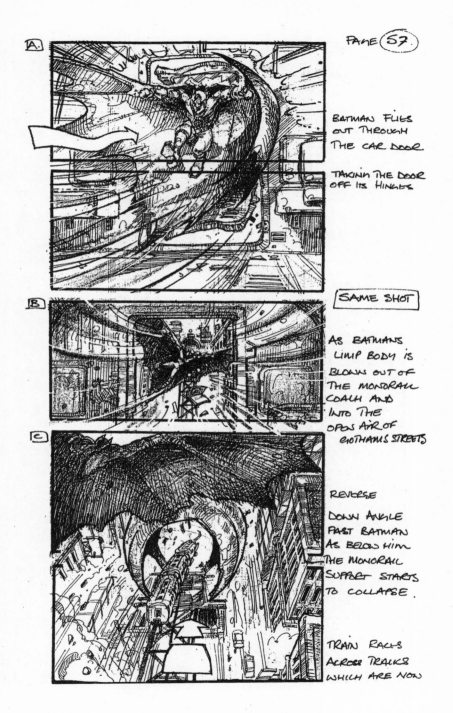

A.

BATMAN FLIES
OUT THROUGH
THE CAR DOOR

TAKING THE DOOR
OFF ITS HINGES

B.

SAME SHOT

AS BATMANS
LIMP BODY IS
BLOWN OUT OF
THE MONORAIL
COACH AND
INTO THE
OPEN AIR OF
GOTHAMS STREETS

C.

REVERSE

DOWN ANGLE
PAST BATMAN
AS BELOW HIM
THE MONORAIL
SUPPORT STARTS
TO COLLAPSE.

TRAIN RACES
ACROSS TRACKS
WHICH ARE NOW

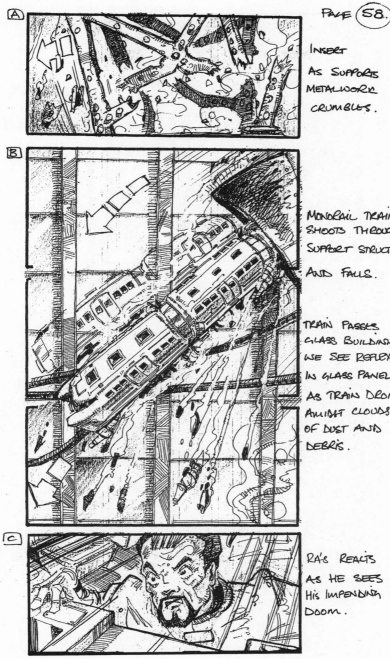

PAGE 58.

A — INSERT
AS SUPPORTS
METALWORK
CRUMBLES.

B — MONORAIL TRAIN
SHOOTS THROUGH
SUPPORT STRUCTURE
AND FALLS.

TRAIN PASSES
GLASS BUILDING.
WE SEE REFLEXTION
IN GLASS PANELS
AS TRAIN DROPS
AMIDST CLOUDS
OF DUST AND
DEBRIS.

C — RA'S REACTS
AS HE SEES
HIS IMPENDING
DOOM.

333

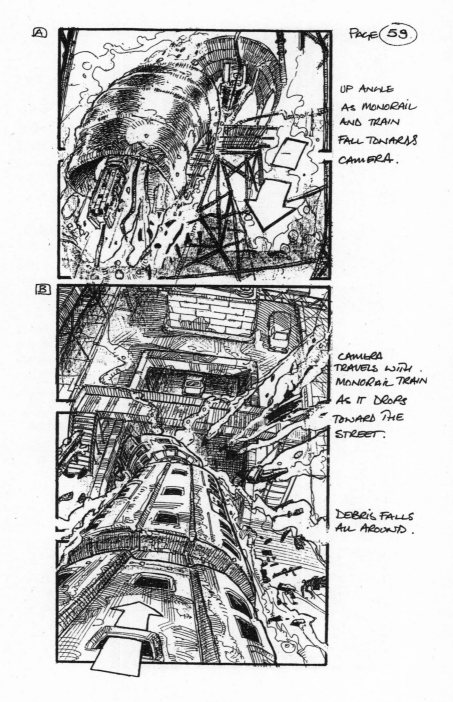

A

UP ANGLE
AS MONORAIL
AND TRAIN
FALL TOWARDS
CAMERA.

B

CAMERA
TRAVELS WITH
MONORAIL TRAIN
AS IT DROPS
TOWARD THE
STREET.

DEBRIS FALLS
ALL AROUND.

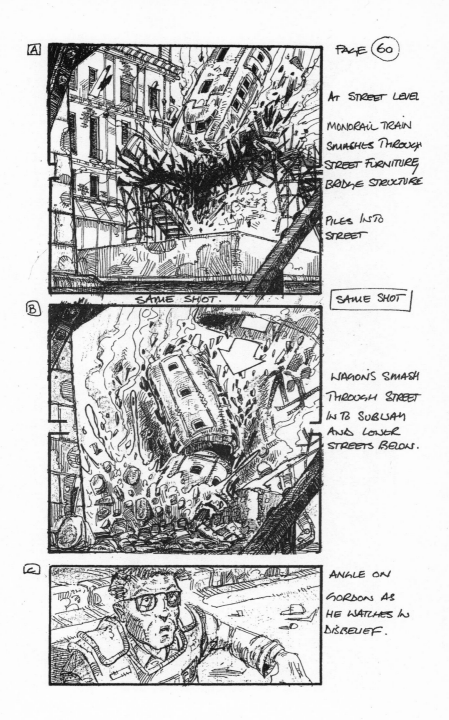

A

AT STREET LEVEL

MONORAIL TRAIN
SMASHES THROUGH
STREET FURNITURE,
BRIDGE STRUCTURE

PILES INTO
STREET

SAME SHOT.

SAME SHOT

B

WAGONS SMASH
THROUGH STREET
INTO SUBWAY
AND LOWER
STREETS BELOW.

C

ANGLE ON
GORDON AS
HE WATCHES IN
DISBELIEF.

335

A

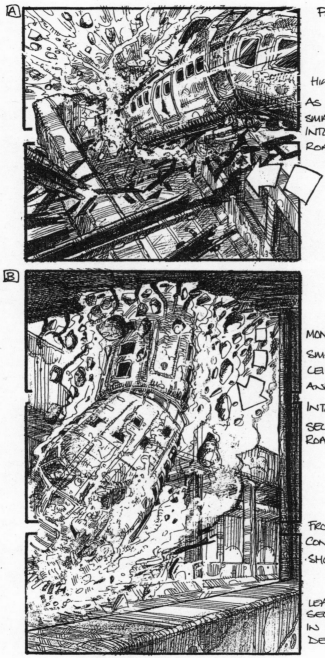

B

PAGE ⑥①

HIGH ANGLE.

AS MONORAIL
SMASHES DOWN
INTO LOWER
ROAD SECTION.

MONORAIL TRAIN
SMASHES THROUGH
CEILING STRUCTURE
AND THUNDERS
INTO UNDERGROUND
SECTION OF
ROADWAY.

FRONT SECTION
CONTINUES OUT OF
SHOT — LEFT.

LEAVING END
SECTION LODGED
IN AMONGST
DEBRIS.

336

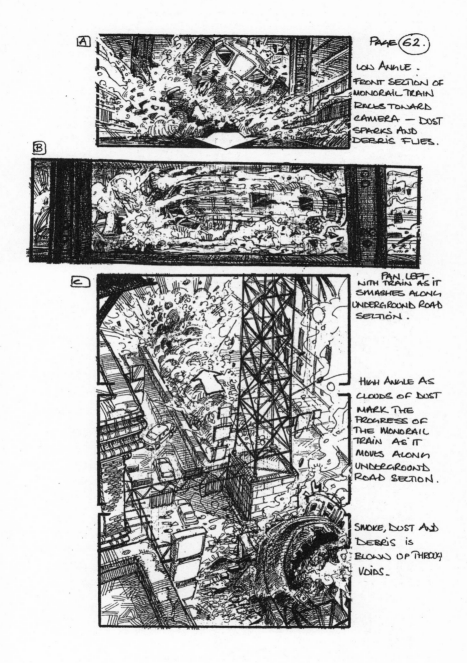

Ⓐ

Page ⓺2.

LOW ANGLE.
FRONT SECTION OF
MONORAIL TRAIN
RACES TOWARD
CAMERA — DUST
SPARKS AND
DEBRIS FLIES.

Ⓑ

Ⓒ

PAN LEFT
WITH TRAIN AS IT
SMASHES ALONG
UNDERGROUND ROAD
SECTION.

HIGH ANGLE AS
CLOUDS OF DUST
MARK THE
PROGRESS OF
THE MONORAIL
TRAIN AS IT
MOVES ALONG
UNDERGROUND
ROAD SECTION.

SMOKE, DUST AND
DEBRIS is
BLOWN UP THROUGH
VOIDS.

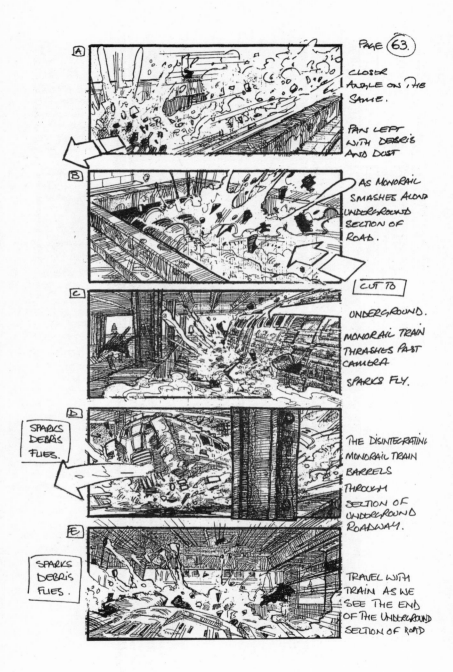

A

CLOSER
ANGLE ON THE
SAME.

PAN LEFT
WITH DEBRIS
AND DUST

B

AS MONORAIL
SMASHES ALONG
UNDERGROUND
SECTION OF
ROAD.

CUT TO

C

UNDERGROUND.

MONORAIL TRAIN
THRASHES PAST
CAMERA
SPARKS FLY.

D

SPARKS
DEBRIS
FLIES.

THE DISINTEGRATING
MONORAIL TRAIN
BARRELS
THROUGH
SECTION OF
UNDERGROUND
ROADWAY.

E

SPARKS
DEBRIS
FLIES.

TRAVEL WITH
TRAIN AS WE
SEE THE END
OF THE UNDERGROUND
SECTION OF ROAD

338

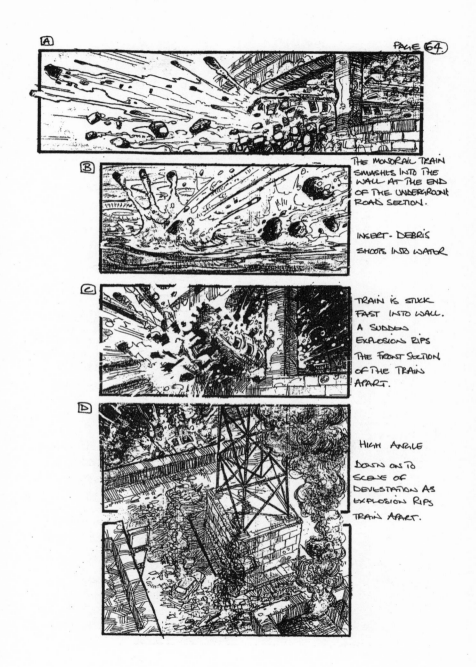

A

B

THE MONORAIL TRAIN
SMASHES INTO THE
WALL AT THE END
OF THE UNDERGROUND
ROAD SECTION.

INSERT - DEBRIS
SHOOTS INTO WATER

C

TRAIN IS STUCK
FAST INTO WALL.
A SUDDEN
EXPLOSION RIPS
THE FRONT SECTION
OF THE TRAIN
APART.

D

HIGH ANGLE
DOWN ONTO
SCENE OF
DEVESTATION AS
EXPLOSION RIPS
TRAIN APART.

Ⓐ

TILT UP
FROM WRECK
OF TRAIN TO REVEAL
HIGH ABOVE, THE
FORM OF BATMAN

Ⓑ

CLOSER ON
BATMAN
HE LOOKS DOWN
SURVEYING
RA'S AL GHUL'S
FUNERAL PYRE.

Ⓒ

HE TURNS.
BANKS AND
DRIFTS AWAY
LEFT OUT OF
SHOT.